LONGMAN STUDY GUIDES: A-LEVEL ENGLISH

A-LEVEL
AND AS-LEVEL

ENGLISH

Stuart Sillars

 LONGMAN

Addison Wesley Longman Limited,
Edinburgh Gate, Harlow,
Essex CM20 2JE, England
and Associated Companies throughout the world.

First published 1990
Updated edition 1997
Third impression 1998

British Library Cataloguing in Publication Data

Sillars, Stuart, 1951–
    English.– (Longman A Level revise guides).
    1. England. Secondary schools. Curriculum subjects.
    English language. G.C.E. (A level) examinations
    I. Title
    420'.76
    ISBN 0-582-31656-1

Set in 10/12pt Century Old Style

Produced by Addison Wesley Longman Singapore Pte Ltd
Printed in Singapore.

EDITORS' PREFACE

Longman A Level Study Guides, written by experienced examiners and teachers, aim to give you the best possible foundation for success in your course. Each book in the series encourages thorough study and a full understanding of the concepts involved, and is designed as a subject companion and study aid to be used throughout the course.

Many candidates at A Level fail to achieve the grades which their ability deserves, owing to such problems as the lack of a structured revision strategy, or unsound examination technique. This series aims to remedy such deficiencies, by encouraging a realistic and disciplined approach in preparing for and taking exams.

The largely self-contained nature of the chapters gives the book a flexibility which you can use to your advantage. After starting with the background to the A, AS Level and Scottish Higher courses and details of the syllabus coverage, you can read all other chapters selectively, in any order appropriate to the stage you have reached in your course.

Geoff Black and Stuart Wall

ACKNOWLEDGEMENTS

The author and publisher would like to thank the following for permission to reproduce material: Ms Frances Browne for the essay reproduced in chapter 2; the editors of *Critical Quarterly* for the article reproduced in part in chapter 2; Faber and Faber Ltd, for 'The Jaguar' which is taken from the book *The Hawk In The Rain* by Ted Hughes; Jonquil Publishing Ltd for the page from *Grammar Rules OK!* by Stuart Sillars; Robin Maunsell Esq, for 'Two Views'; Ms Jenny Ruddock for the essay reproduced in chapter 17; University of London Secondary Examinations Board for English Language questions in chapter 16. Every effort has been made to trace copyright holders of other material used in this book, from whom the publishers will be pleased to hear if material has inadvertently been reproduced without permission.

Any publication of this kind is inevitably the product of many minds, and the author would like to thank all those who have contributed to its writing and production. Stuart Wall's energy and enthusiasm was a great source of encouragement in the writing, and the insights of Michael Jones added greatly to the book's depth while wisely eradicating moments of pomposity. Finally, I should like to thank D & S Plumbing and Heating of March, Cambridgeshire, for promptly and efficiently repairing a burst water pipe and so allowing the book to be completed in relative tranquillity and complete dryness. And speaking of dryness: the book itself and any errors or omissions which remain are the result of the author's own unaided perversity.

I would also like to thank Trevor Gamson for his assistance in compiling the syllabus chart in Chapter 1.

Stuart Sillars

CONTENTS

NAMES AND ADDRESSES OF THE EXAM BOARDS

Associated Examining Board (AEB)
Stag Hill House
Guildford
Surrey GU2 5XJ

University of Cambridge Local Examinations Syndicate (UCLES)
Syndicate Buildings
1 Hill Road
Cambridge CB1 2EU

Northern Examinations and Assessment Board (NEAB)
Devas St
Manchester M15 6EX

Edexcel Foundation (London) (ULEAC)
Stewart House
32 Russell Square
London WC1B 5DN

Northern Ireland Council for Curriculum, Examinations and Assessment (NICCEA)
29 Clarendon Road
Belfast
BT1 3BG

Oxford and Cambridge Schools Examinations Board (OCSEB)
Purbeck House
Purbeck Road
Cambridge CB2 2PU

The Oxford Delegacy is also administered
from this address.

Scottish Examinations Board (SEB)
Ironmills Road
Dalkeith
Midlothian EH22 1LE

Welsh Joint Education Committee (WJEC)
245 Western Avenue
Cardiff CF5 2YX

EXAM SYLLABUSES AND STUDY TECHNIQUES

GETTING STARTED

English Literature, like no other A-level, is a subject in which using your knowledge and applying your skills are far more important than presenting information which has simply been learnt. You have to know your set texts – poems, plays, novels and other prose works – but you also have to *apply* this knowledge to comments that are made about them as the basis of questions in the exam. Above all, you have to be able not only to put across your capacity to read and understand, with sympathy and sensitivity, what's happening in a text but also to show that you appreciate *how* the writer uses the skills of his or her craft to bring it all to life.

For this reason, no single book can give you all the answers that you'll need when tackling an A-level literature paper. Only *you* can take your knowledge and apply it to the individual questions. And, because the number of texts that are set for A-level each year is vast, and is always changing and growing, no single book can cover *all* the topics, themes or even techniques you need to know about and use in each text that you're studying.

So instead of trying to achieve the impossible, this book aims for practical goals. It concentrates on the most important *techniques* and *skills* that you'll need when you are working for your A-level, AS-level or Scottish Higher exam. It tells you:

- how to read a text and what to look for in it;
- how to apply that knowledge to a question;
- how to understand and write about a poem or other piece of writing that you haven't seen before;
- how to cope with coursework;
- how to tackle questions on the texts you've studied;
- how to plan and pace your reading and revision.

The main emphasis, then, is on techniques and approaches. But the book does also give you some help with the texts that are more commonly set at A-level, to help you bring into sharper focus the work you've already been doing when studying them. The chapters on poetry, prose and drama, along with those on Chaucer and Shakespeare, do discuss some of the most common texts, give examples of likely questions and suggest how they should be answered. More advice about approaching the study of individual texts is given in Chapter 2, which discusses the critical essay and the best ways to approach it.

As well as preparation for the A-level exams in England, Wales and Northern Ireland, this book will help you master the basic techniques for the Scottish Higher Grade in English. If you are studying English or English Literature at Advanced Supplementary (AS) level, too, you'll find that it covers many of the basic skills and approaches that you need.

ESSENTIAL PRINCIPLES

SYLLABUSES AND EXAMS

" What's relevant to your board? "

Because the range of topics and texts set in the exam is so great, you need to know which parts of the book are relevant to the syllabus you're studying. Most chapters are relevant to all the boards' syllabuses, but some are rather more specialised – you can check with Table 1.1. If in doubt you can contact your Examining Board. The addresses are provided at the front of the book. Remember, too, that syllabuses are regularly revised; this table is a guide only.

	Relevant chapters																
A-level and AS-level English and English Literature Syllabuses	1	2	3	4	5	6	7	8	9	10	11	12	13	14	15	16	17
AEB English Literature A 0660	√	√		√	√	√	√	√	√	√	√	√	√	√	√		√
English A 0623	√	√		√	√	√	√	√	√	√	√	√	√	√	√	√	
English Language A 0659	√	√														√	√
English Literature S 0660S	√	√		√	√	√	√					√	√	√	√	√	
English S 0623S	√	√		√	√	√	√					√	√	√	√	√	
English Language AS 0985	√	√														√	√
English Literature AS 0986	√	√		√	√	√	√	√	√	√	√	√	√	√	√		√
CAMBRIDGE English Literature A 9000	√	√	√	√	√	√	√	√	√	√	√	√	√	√	√		√
English Literature Modular A 8570	√	√	√	√	√	√	√	√	√	√	√	√	√	√	√		√
English Literature Modular AS 8570	√	√	√	√	√	√	√	√	√	√	√	√	√	√	√		√
English Literature Modular A 9505	√	√	√	√	√	√	√	√	√	√	√	√	√	√	√		√
English Literature Modular AS 9505	√	√	√	√	√	√	√	√	√	√	√	√	√	√			√
NEAB English Language AS	√	√														√	√
English Language A	√	√														√	√
English Literature AS	√	√		√	√	√	√	√	√	√	√	√	√	√	√		√
English Literature A	√	√		√	√	√	√	√	√	√	√	√	√	√	√		√
English Language and Literature A	√	√		√	√	√	√	√	√	√	√	√	√	√	√	√	√
Special Paper	√	√		√	√	√	√	√					√	√	√		
Optional Test in Creative Writing	√																√
LONDON English Language A 9174	√	√														√	
English Literature A 9171	√	√		√	√	√	√	√	√	√	√	√	√	√	√		√
English Literature AS 8171	√	√		√	√	√	√	√	√	√	√	√	√	√	√		√
English AS 8177	√	√										√	√	√	√	√	√
NICCEA English Literature Syllabus A A	√	√		√	√	√	√	√	√	√	√	√	√	√	√		√
English Literature Syllabus A AS	√	√		√	√	√	√	√	√	√	√	√	√	√	√		
English Literature Syllabus B A	√	√		√	√	√	√	√	√	√	√	√	√	√	√		√
English Literature Syllabus B AS	√	√		√	√	√	√	√	√	√	√	√	√	√	√		√
OXFORD English Literature A 9903	√	√		√	√	√	√	√	√	√	√	√	√	√	√		√
English Literature AS 9903	√	√		√	√	√	√	√	√	√	√	√	√	√	√		√
English Language and Literature A 9905	√	√		√	√	√	√	√	√	√	√	√	√	√	√	√	√
English Language and Literature AS 9905	√	√		√	√	√	√	√	√	√	√	√	√	√	√	√	√
O & C English Literature A 9620	√	√		√	√	√	√	√	√	√	√	√	√	√	√		√
English Literature AS 8395	√	√		√	√	√	√	√	√	√	√	√	√	√	√		√
English Language and Literature A 9621	√	√		√	√	√	√	√	√	√	√	√	√	√	√	√	√
English Language and Literature AS 8396	√	√		√	√	√	√	√	√	√	√	√	√	√	√	√	√
SEB Higher Grade English	√	√		√	√	√	√		√	√	√	√	√	√	√		√
Certificate of Sixth Year Studies, English	√	√		√	√	√	√	√	√	√	√	√	√	√	√		√
WJEC English Literature A	√	√		√	√	√	√	√	√	√	√	√	√	√	√		√
English Literature AS	√	√		√	√	√	√	√	√	√	√	√	√	√	√	√	
Special Paper	√	√		√	√	√	√	√	√	√	√	√	√	√	√		

Table 1.1 Syllabus coverage chart

ENGLISH LANGUAGE SYLLABUSES

Several A-level English syllabuses incorporate some English language elements, or are wholly concerned with language rather than literature. Chapter 16 of this book looks at the main provisions of these syllabuses and gives you practice in answering some of the questions from their exams.

COURSEWORK

If your syllabus contains a coursework element, you'll find Chapter 17 helpful in suggesting ways to approach and organise this part of your studies.

READING AND WRITING

> Detailed critical reading is the basis of success.

Whatever syllabus you are studying, your work will be based on key skills of reading and writing. Knowing *how to read* literary works of all kinds – poetry, prose and drama of all periods and styles – is the basic skill of literary work. You will find advice on reading texts in Chapters 4, 5, 9 and 13. Although these are mainly concerned with written exercises in critical appreciation of passages you haven't seen before, the advice they contain about reading and interpreting should help you in *all* your literary studies.

Don't overlook the importance of talking, either. Studying a text is much easier when you can do it with other people, because then you can discuss your ideas, sharing points until you reach a clear conclusion. This can be very valuable, since you can try out ideas without the finality of writing them down – so do make use of every chance you get to discuss and argue about the books you're studying.

KNOWING YOUR SYLLABUS

Whatever work you do, you need to know exactly what is required of you. You can find this out by obtaining a copy of the syllabus produced by your Examining Board. At the same time, you should be able to buy copies of past examination papers, which will give you an idea of what the questions will be like and give you practice in answering them.

To obtain a syllabus, you should write to the Publications Department of the Examining Board with which you're entered – your teacher will be able to tell you which one this is. The addresses can be found at the front of the book.

STUDY SKILLS

GETTING ORGANISED

All the investigations into how the process of study works conclude that you take in more and understand better if you work according to a *regular study timetable*. This is true not only of revising just before your exam, but of the whole process of taking in new ideas and information. Even at the very start of your course you should try to get yourself organised.

So just what is it that you need to organise?

Organise your space

You need somewhere to work – ideally, a separate room or part of a room that you can set aside for work. You need:

- *A desk or table*. Don't think you can work in an easy chair, or out in the country or on the beach – forget it. The only place for serious study is sitting with books and notes in front of you;

> A special shelf for your texts will help.

- *Shelves for books*. Keep your texts in order, so that you can consult them whenever you need them – which will be very frequently;
- *Files for notes*. It's worth spending a little money on card folders, loose-leaf files and file paper, so that you have plenty of resources for making notes. Try to use paper that's of good quality and will last the two or so years you'll be studying.

Organise your time

If you're studying at school or college, much of this will be done for you, with your day being split up into classes on the subjects you're following. But there will be time that *isn't* organised. So get into the habit, right from the start, of deciding what to do with this time, and sticking to a firm timetable. You need time off, certainly – but you can fit this in at times when the work has been done!

- If you have free time at school or college, decide how to use it. Divide it between the subjects you're studying. Set aside times for working in a library or study area, and always have an idea of what you're going to *do* during this time – this will be covered in more detail later on.
- Organise your time in the evenings and at weekends. Give yourself one evening a week off, and some free time at weekends. The rest of the time needs to be devoted to study.

Organise your notes

Over the time that you're studying, you will amass a large volume of notes. Keep them clear and well organised.

- If you make quick notes in classes, write them up clearly afterwards.
- Put the points in the best order, use headings, sub-headings and numbered points.
- As your notes increase, keep those for each text in a separate folder, or separate part of a loose-leaf binder.
- Make an index of your notes, so that you know where your notes on each topic are. If you have a lot of notes, make a separate card-index, with a summary of topics on each card.

> Use wall space for charts and diagrams.

Keeping your notes organised right from the start will save you a lot of time searching for the right piece of paper when it comes to revising. And writing them out clearly and precisely will help you remember the ideas – so it will make revising a lot easier because the ideas will be that much fresher in your mind.

USING TEXTS

When you're studying literature, everything depends on the *text*. If you have an edition that's old, in small print, difficult to read and generally unattractive, the process of studying will be unpleasant and you'll get little pleasure or help from it.

Always make a point of getting the best text you can. Often your school or college will provide a text for you. If it's a 'school' edition, find out whether there's another version which is better. Many schools use old-fashioned editions of Shakespeare, for example. If you get hold of a first-rate modern edition – such as the *New Arden Shakespeare*, published by Methuen – you'll have a great advantage, because a modern edition will give you a great deal of essential information and help you in your studies.

A good text should have these features:

> A good text will give you a lot of material for your studies.

- the words of the play, novel or poems edited from the original manuscripts or other reliable sources, presented with the original punctuation or edited to make clear for the modern reader the writer's original intentions. It must be accurate and rest on the latest academic research;
- full notes to explain difficult words or ideas in the text, and which let you make up your own mind about alternative interpretations;
- an introduction which will cover the themes and ideas of the text, summarise critical views and in general give you the information you need in order to study, understand, appreciate and interpret the text.

Close critical reading

This is really the essence of literary study at all levels. What you need to do when reading critically is to work through the text, using all the features of your critical edition to make sure that you grasp fully what the writer is saying. When you are involved in close textual study of this sort, you should follow this procedure:

1 Choose a part of the text you are studying – a scene in a play, a chapter of a novel, or a poem. Read it carefully and, at the same time, ask yourself questions about it. The kind of things to look for are dealt with in detail in Chapters 4 and 5 for poetry, Chapter 9 for drama and Chapter 13 for prose.
2 Look up difficult words in a glossary or dictionary.
3 Consult the notes of your edition.
4 Think about the important features of expression the passage uses, and consider whether or not these are representative of the whole work.
5 Think about the ways in which the passage contributes to the themes or ideas of the text as a whole.
6 Make brief notes to record these themes and features, either on paper or in the book itself (see Fig. 1.1).
7 Think about brief passages (no more than a line or two) which you might like to learn, and so be able to use in the exam to demonstrate key aspects of the text.
8 Read again the passage of the text you've been working on; this will help in bringing together the work you have done on it and in remembering it as a complete unit.

BOOK THREE

nature, instead of forming originals from the confused heap of matter in their own brains; is not such a book as that which records the achievements of the renowed Don Quixotte more worthy the name of a history than even Mariana's;[129] for whereas the latter is confined to a particular period of time, and to a particular nation; the former is the history of the world in general, at least that part which is polished by laws, arts and sciences; and of that from the time it was first polished to this day; nay and forwards, as long as it shall so remain.

I shall now proceed to apply these observations to the work before us; for indeed I have set them down principally to obviate some constructions, which the good-nature of mankind, who are always forward to see their friends virtues recorded, may put to particular parts. I question not but several of my readers will know the lawyer in the stage-coach, the moment they hear his voice. It is likewise odds, but the wit and the prude meet with some of their acquaintance, as well as all the rest of my characters. To prevent therefore any such malicious applications, I declare here once for all, I describe not men, but manners; not an individual, but a species. Perhaps it will be answered, Are not the characters then taken from life? To which I answer in the affirmative; nay, I believe I might aver, that I have writ little more than I have seen. The lawyer is not only alive, but hath been so these 4000 years, and I hope G..... will indulge his life as many yet to come. He hath not indeed confined himself to one profession, one religion, or one country; but when the first mean selfish creature appeared on the human stage, who made self the centre of the whole creation; would give himself no pain, incur no danger, advance no money to assist, or preserve his fellow-creatures; then was our lawyer born; and whilst such a person as I have described, exists on earth, so long shall he remain upon it. It is therefore doing him little honour, to imagine he endeavours to mimick some little obscure fellow, because he happens to resemble him in one particular feature, or perhaps in his profession; whereas his appearance in the world is calculated for much more general and noble purposes; not to expose one pitiful wretch, to the small and contemptible circle of his acquaintance; but to hold the glass to thousands in their closets, that they may contemplate their deformity, and endeavour to reduce it, and thus by suffering private mortification may avoid public shame. This places the boundary between, and distinguishes the satirist from

Handwritten margin notes:

(left) cf Lawyer in Book 1 ch 12.

(left) 'Prude' in (18) is woman who only pretends to be v. modest, but is really corrupt.

(right) v. imp. general statement of author's aim

(right) shows moral purpose of novel: to correct people, not ridicule them

Fig 1.1 Making notes in a text. Points on the left draw links with other parts of the text or comment on key words. Points on the right comment on themes. Notice the use of underlining and lines in the margin. The three lines at the top right show this is an important page when you've going quickly through the book

9   Think about how the individual section contributes to the work as a whole; this will help you to make the transition between reading a short passage in detail and knowing the whole of the text in the depth you'll need for the exam.

You will need to undertake close critical reading throughout your period of study, for a range of reasons – to prepare for an essay and to revise, as well as to get to know the text thoroughly. If you are working through a novel or play, it will also help to begin your session of critical reading by quickly going through the passage you read the *day before*, just to revise the points you noted about it and to put the passage you're reading today in context.

Reading in this way may be strange and unfamiliar at first – most of us are used to reading things quickly, and not to looking at words in such depth. But with a little practice you'll soon find that the process comes almost naturally. Doing it *regularly* will help you to read critically with both accuracy and speed.

> " Get into the habit of studying like this – after a while you'll do it automatically. "

READING CRITICAL TEXTS

You may find it helpful to read what *other people* have to say about the texts you are studying. Certainly, there is no shortage of critical writing about most of the texts set at A-level. But be careful:

■   reading a critical text can be confusing, especially if you choose something that goes too deeply into an aspect of the text you're studying;

- make sure that you don't accept the writer's interpretation at face value; he or she may take one particular view of the many that are usually possible, so don't end up with a limited or one-sided stance to the text;

- don't assume that critics impress examiners – they don't. Clear, well-thought-out and relevant points of your own will be worth far more in an exam than impressive-sounding references to critics, or restatements of half-digested critical views which have nothing to do with the question;

- *above all* don't assume that you can read a critical text or set of notes *instead of* the text if you want to do well. Remember that a knowledge of the texts themselves, your ability to understand the question and to apply your knowledge of the texts to the question set, are all that's needed in the exam. Careful knowledge and intelligent application are far more important than some pseudo-sophisticated name-dropping.

> **Critical reading expands your study of the text – it DOESN'T replace it!**

To sum up: if it stimulates your own thoughts and you can read critically, by all means read what others have to say. But if you're unsure about major points, go back to the text or get help from your teacher. And *never* put reading a critical essay or guide before reading and thinking about the text itself.

USING CLASS TIME

If you're following a course, you'll spend quite a lot of your time going to *classes*. In them, you'll be reading through your set texts, discussing their authors' ideas and your responses to them, looking at the techniques the writers use, and generally getting to know these texts. In addition, you'll be writing essays based on the texts. So you might think that you're already doing all that you need in order to cover the ground thoroughly.

Certainly all this will give you a basic knowledge of your texts, but the process shouldn't stop there. As well as going along to classes, you should set aside a time *every day* to go through the work you've covered in your class earlier that day.

In this time, you should:

- copy out the notes that you've taken, making sure that you have all the points in the best order, and that all your points are clear – both in terms of their meaning and in the way that you write them down. Write legibly – remember that you may have to revise from these notes over a year away;

- read the passages of the text you've covered during the day, using the critical reading procedure outlined in the last section;

- if time permits, read *ahead* to cover that part of the text you'll study in your next class.

This whole process shouldn't take longer than forty-five minutes. And if you do it every day, you'll end up with a full set of notes which record your work on each text you're studying. You can then use these notes as the basis for essays as well as for revision when the exam is near. Fig. 1.2 sets out in rather more detail how you can make the best use of your class time.

As well as this, of course, you'll need to gather material for the essays which will form an important ingredient in your course. Preparing for essays is covered in Chapter 2. Don't forget, too, that you will have your essays returned by your teacher or lecturer with comments about what went well, and which areas need more attention. When you get an essay back, don't just look at the grade and hide it in your file. Instead:

> **USE the essays you write – they're a valuable part of your study.**

- read the comments, and think carefully about them;

- make notes on points which your teacher suggest you've neglected;

- find quotations or other evidence to support the points you've made, if the comments suggest that these are needed.

In this way you'll capitalise on the work you did for the essay and be able to incorporate it into your other work – such as the notes on the text you made in class, and those that you took yourself as part of the critical reading process.

Another part of your study regime will involve the process of bringing together the work you have done on a text – the kind of continuous revision which stops you from ever really losing touch with the work you have done in the past. This will be covered in more detail in the next section of this chapter – but remember that there are really three key elements to

A BEFORE THE SESSION

1 Make sure you have enough paper, 2 pens, and perhaps carbon paper (in case a friend's away)
2 Know the context of the class – discussion or formal lecture.

B DURING THE SESSION

1 Don't write all the time: listen for the complete point before writing.
2 Listen carefully, questioning what you hear.
3 Try to distinguish between new points and enlargements of old ones.
4 Be selective with examples – go for main points first.
5 Use digressions/questions/anecdotes to get points down.

C THE SPEAKER

1 Get to know how the speaker works. Does he/she:
   • list main points at start of class;
   • allow points to emerge during class;
   • pause regularly to sum up or draw points together;
   • give final summaries;
   • give references for the points made.

2 Vary your note-making technique according to the speaker's approach.

D LAYOUT

1 Note time, date, speaker and subject.
2 Leave plenty of space when writing. This allows for later additions.
3 Use any abbreviations & codes you can.
4 Use main headings, sub-headings & numbered points as far as possible.
5 Alternatively, use 'pattern' or 'spidergram' notes.
6 Note questions, uncertainties and points for checking as you go.
7 Put names and unfamiliar terms in capitals.
8 If speaker permits, ask about unfamiliar terms.

E AFTER THE SESSION

1 Re-write using clear layout at first opportunity.
2 Check names, dates, spellings and other uncertainties with reference books and re-write.
3 Ask speaker if unsure of anything.
4 Add points and comments of your own, making sure they're separated from speaker's points.
5 Compare notes with friends if subject is difficult.

Fig. 1.2 Taking notes in class

a study session. Not each session will necessarily contain all three, but you need to be aware that all are just as important.

1 Close critical reading.
2 Work preparing an essay, or extending an essay already written, in the light of your teacher's comments.
3 Revising and bringing together your work so that you have a clearer view of the whole text.

REVISING FOR THE EXAM

CONTINUOUS REVISION

Most people think about revising as something that they should do only in the period just before the exam. It's true that you should concentrate your revision in the six weeks or so before the exam; but it's also true that careful organisation of your work throughout your studies will make the process much easier and far more effective.

As you progress through your course, you should always be revising the work that you have done so far. In practice, this means going over the work you've done each day, as I suggested in the last section. More particularly, it means pulling together the work you've done on each text as you complete it and before you go on to another one. Do this in the following way:

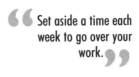

Set aside a time each week to go over your work.

1 **Get your notes in order.** Your notes will be of various kinds:
   - *notes on specific sections of the text*. Taken together, these will form a continuous commentary. Make sure they are clear, legible and complete. Get them in order and copy out pages if necessary. File them and keep them safe.
   - *notes on particular themes and topics*. These may be notes that you've made in preparation for class discussion, or the outline plans for essays (see Chapter 2). You'll probably have eight or ten sheets of these, each covering a separate aspect of a text. Again, be sure that they're clear, legible and well-titled so that you can recognise straightaway what they are about.
   - *notes from critical texts and commentaries which you've read*. You may or may not have these; it depends on how you approach your work. If you *do*, then make sure that they are kept safe and ready for easy reference.

2 **Index your notes.** Make sure that you know where each sheet is and what it covers. You can do this in a small notebook, under the subject they cover, or as a card index. If you use a card index, you can briefly summarise the contents of each sheet of notes.

3 **Read your notes through.** Preferably in a single sitting, to refresh your memory of the work you've done. If there's anything you don't understand, check it with the text and put it right NOW. If it's not clear when you've just worked on the text, imagine how confusing it will be some months in the future when you need to revise for the exam. This process will often suggest questions which you can discuss with your teacher or lecturer.

4 **Read the text through again quickly.** This will bring together your work on it, in the same way as reading through a passage will crystallise the work you do in each study session.

Following these procedures will ensure that you make the best use of the work you've done, by keeping the ideas clear in your mind and the notes safe and in order for when you need them again.

After you've finished your work on a text, try not to forget it completely. Every so often, try to fix a time to look at the notes on a text you studied a few months ago, to make sure that you still remember its main features. If you made a card index, look quickly at the cards and try to recall the main points they contain.

Make a big wall chart from your card index notes.

These procedures will help to ensure that you never entirely lose contact with a text or forget about its main points, even while you're working on something different. It won't make revision nearer the exam unnecessary – but it will make it easier, because you'll be able to recall earlier material much more readily.

SORTING OUT THE DETAILS

Between eight and six weeks before the exam, you need to start thinking seriously about your preparations. Before you do any final revision, you need to sort out several basic points.

1 Check the syllabus

I have already mentioned the need for you to know the full details of the course you're following as they are laid out in the syllabus. As the exam comes closer, have another look at it. Make sure you know:

- which texts are on which papers;
- if there are any choices between texts;
- whether you'll have short answer questions on passages (see Chapter 3) or essay questions on each text.

Know which texts come in what papers, and avoid unpleasant surprises.

This will help you in planning and carrying out your revision. If you *do* have any choices between texts, think very seriously before deciding *not* to revise some of them at all. In the exam you may find that the question on the other text is something you haven't covered, and so are unable to answer properly. It's always best to be as fully prepared as you can, and dropping a text is a very considerable risk to take – so think very carefully before you make a decision like this, and only do so under extreme circumstances.

2   Look at past papers

However detailed the syllabus, it's only past question papers which tell you exactly what the questions look like and the kind of topics that come up. Look at:

- *the layout of the paper.* If there are alternative sections, make sure you know which you are preparing for. In the exam it's easy to get a little flustered and to mis-read the instructions, so keep the chance of a mistake to a minimum by knowing what you're expected to do in advance.

- *the number of questions and the time allowed.* This will help you to revise by allowing you to write answers in the time you'll have in the exam – generally it works out at between 30 and 45 minutes for each question, but there are exceptions.

- *the nature of the questions.* Find out whether you're more likely to be given an excerpt from a text as the basis of a question, or a quotation for discussion. Don't waste time trying to 'spot' questions and predict what's going to come up and base your revision on that: there's little chance that you'll be right. Instead, get a general idea of the topics and the wording used.

3   Look at an examiners' report

Examiners' reports will help you avoid common mistakes.

Most Examining Boards publish reports which say how candidates actually approached the exam in that year. These can be very useful, as they point out frequent errors and can suggest ways in which answers are more likely to gain good grades.

PLANNING YOUR REVISION

At this stage, it's a good idea to do a dummy run of the exam. Try a few past questions and see how much you remember. Look especially at the texts you studied first – you covered them some time ago and were just learning the skills of the subject at the time, so you may need to do more work on them. When you've written the essays, look at your notes to see what you could and should have said. You might find it helpful to work with a classmate on this, to comment on each other's strong and not-so-strong points – but be gentle about it!

When you've done this, you'll know which texts need to be covered in more detail. Don't leave the ones you dislike to the last – tackle them first of all, so that you can remedy deficiencies in your knowledge and build your confidence, instead of having to tackle them just before the exam when you're tired and probably fed up with the whole thing. Nothing gives confidence so much as really knowing your material, so work here will be doubly helpful in the exam.

Make a diary or wallchart to show your revision timetable.

Make a detailed timetable showing what texts you're going to revise and when. It should cover the four or six weeks before the exam, and set out clearly what texts you will cover on particular days and times. Divide it up into periods like those you are used to at school or college, to give you a set rhythm of work. Don't expect too much, though: starting at eight in the morning and ending at ten at night solidly for four weeks may sound possible, but you won't be able to keep it up – and even if you were to, you'd find that you wouldn't take in a great deal after the first few hours of each day.

REVISING

What do you actually *do* when you revise? There are several approaches which help to bring your work together and prepare you for the exam.

1   Read the text

This is the fundamental process of all revision. However good your notes, you will still need to have a detailed, first-hand knowledge of the books themselves – so a significant part of the revision must be devoted to this. At first, read through the text quickly. Most novels can be read quickly in a day if you have read them already, and most plays in an evening.

> *Try working in a different place for a change – a local library, perhaps.*

Try to vary the approach here. Get together in groups and read through a play with each of you taking a different role – and, if you like, stopping at the end of each scene to discuss it. Read poems aloud, thinking about how they work by using language imaginatively to make their point. If you find that going to a performance of a play helps and you can find one locally, go along – but be careful not to accept it as the *only* way of performing it, and ask yourself how *you* would have directed it if given the chance.

But however you do it, remember that a *knowledge of the text* is the basis of all the questions – so anything you can do to increase that knowledge is going to be valuable at this stage.

2   Make 'maps'

> *Maps are useful – but no substitute for the text itself.*

These are *outlines* of the events of a novel, play or long poem. This won't be a substitute for reading the book itself, but it will help you to find particular passages quickly and to clarify the growth of themes and ideas. You could draw a diagram to 'map' a novel, showing its main concerns in a visually striking way.

Another kind of 'map' can be made by listing the chapters and their contents or striking features, like this example:

TOM JONES – section 1, Books 1–V1

Book 1	Notes
1 Fielding as omniscient, self-conscious narrator: Human nature as theme; stress on practical philosophy	
2 Allworthy's pragmatic goodness; Bridget's sourness	
3 Tom's appearance; Deborah's pretence and suggested rejection contrasted with Allworthy's delight	
4/5 B approves; angry only with T's mother	

Notice that each chapter is summarised in terms of content or themes in a very few words, with the 'Notes' column free for critical points or references to other notes you may have on particular aspects. Going through a text and *preparing* such a map is a valuable exercise in itself. It will also provide a useful *reference* when it's finished, since it gives you a detailed and fairly rapid overview of the text, which is exactly what you need if you are to answer questions accurately and fully.

3   List key aspects

Structure your revision by making a list of eight or ten *key aspects* which you regard as essential for a knowledge of the text. Some of these may have been covered by essays that you've written; others by notes; and some will be quite new.

4   Make single-page plans

For each of these aspects or topics, make a *single-page plan* which shows anything between six and a dozen key points to make about them (see Figs. 1.3 and 1.4 below). Each point should be supported by a quotation – followed by a page, chapter and line number, or act, scene and line number for easy identification. Add these to your notes on topics in the texts, and to your plans for essays. Eventually you should have a collection of single-sheet accounts of key areas of the text. If you like, arrange to share the work on these with a friend, dividing topics among you – but don't rely too much on other people's work. It can be an excellent way to lose a friend.

5   Meet to swap ideas

As well as for reading plays, getting together can be a useful way of getting new ideas and approaches to texts. Such meetings can be especially useful if you ask each person to prepare a little talk on one aspect of the text, or to write a single-page account of a theme. If you can, photocopy these so that everyone has a copy. Just getting together to share ideas can be very helpful and reassuring – but make sure that you pool your expertise rather than share your ignorance!

6 List passages

Making a list of short passages and quotations sounds a rather cold-blooded approach, and it's important to remember that you'll get no credit for just putting down lines from a text unless you use them appropriately to answer the question. Nevertheless, bringing together the passages you have cited in your single-page accounts can be a useful exercise, and it's much easier to learn lines if you have them on a single sheet of paper.

7 Read critical interpretations

> Read other works by the same author – they can shed light on the one you're studying.

If you're happy with your knowledge of the text, you could extend your knowledge by reading critical essays about it; BUT don't do this unless you're sure you'll understand what they say, and won't take everything they say as the *only* reading. You need to be selective when reading critics, and in absorbing what they say into your own reading of the text, as stressed earlier. It may help your revision to read something new at this stage – but it may also confuse you, so be careful.

8 Answer questions in measured time

One of the best forms of revision is *active* revision – actually doing the task for which you're preparing. In this case, simply sitting down and answering a question in measured time is both necessary and reassuring. Set aside the correct amount of time for the question, and work under strict exam conditions, without access to the text – unless it's an 'open book' examination – or to your notes. If you can, get someone else to set you a question which you won't see until you have to answer it, as this will test the depth and breadth of your revision to the full. Use an alarm clock to tell you when the time's up, and stick rigidly to the limit.

> A five-minute essay plan can be just as useful as writing a full essay in getting your ideas flowing.

Afterwards, get someone to read through your answer. If you have a teacher to do this, that's obviously best, but a classmate can help too, by pointing out ways in which your answer might be clearer, fuller, or better supported with evidence from the text. Once again, getting together can help a lot here, if it's done carefully and with tact.

9 Read the text

Again. And again. It's the only basis for thorough and complete answers in the exam, so make sure that you know the books thoroughly.

10 Take care of yourself

Revising for an exam is a worrying time, and you can do without health problems. So:

- get regular, balanced meals;
- take regular breaks. You won't be able to concentrate for hours on end – five minutes off in each hour is a good rule;
- don't stay up all night – if you plan your revision you shouldn't need to, and you won't perform well in the exam if you're worn out;
- don't go to bed straight after you finish revising. Try to get half an hour off, to go for a walk, read a magazine, listen to some music, or do anything else that helps you relax;
- get plenty of exercise. It'll help you sleep and take your mind off things;
- keep things in proportion. The exam's important, certainly – but it's only an exam, after all.

> If you fail it isn't a total disaster . . .

THE EXAM

The best way to gain confidence for the exam is to have a thorough *knowledge of the texts* and of the *techniques* you will need in order to write about the texts. Knowledge of the texts is something which you can acquire by careful and sustained study along the lines suggested above; the techniques of answering questions in an exam are the subject of this part of the chapter.

> 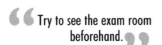 Try to see the exam room beforehand.

HOW TO START

First of all, have a quick look at the paper. Make sure that it *is* in the format you'd expected – the same number of parts, with alternative sections or questions. In almost all cases it will be as you expected, but just occasionally it will be slightly different, perhaps because it is the first year of a new format or – in exceptional circumstances – because there has been an error in production.

If you find that something is wrong with the paper, keep calm. Go on and read through the rest of the paper quickly, and then go back. It's easy to mis-read things in moments of stress, so check that what you thought was an error is really there. If it is, raise your hand and tell the invigilator. It's important to do this as soon as possible, because someone will have to call the Examining Board and get guidance on what to do. If it isn't a mistake, no harm will have been caused – it's far better to speak up and be proved wrong than not to say anything and have the wrong paper or some other mistake to contend with.

But it's very unlikely that this will happen. You'll probably be faced with a paper that is exactly what you thought. In your first quick reading of the paper, you should:

- look at the sections which you are doing, getting a quick idea of the topics on which the questions are based;

- look at all the paper – make sure that there isn't another question on the back page which you don't notice until you're running out of time;

- think in general terms about which of the later questions you'll do, but don't make any firm decisions yet.

If your revision has gone well, you should at this stage be feeling comfortably reassured and confident that, though it won't be easy, you'll be able to write something on all of the questions you are required to answer. It's worth looking at the whole paper for this reason, as well as to check that it's what you'd expected in format, as the reassurance is worth a good deal when you come to start writing.

DIVIDE THE TIME

Once you've read the paper, work out how much time you have for each question. Make sure that your watch is right, or that you can see the clock in the exam room. Now divide up the time fairly between the questions, remembering that 'fairly' doesn't mean 'evenly': you'll probably want to give slightly less time to the short-answer question, if there is one, than to the essay questions. If, as you should, you know the length and format of the paper, dividing the time should be straightforward. Before the exam, you will have worked out the timings of the questions with a calculation like this, leaving ten minutes at the end for a final check:

START 9.00 am	(3 hour exam: 1 passage and 4 essays)
Question 1	30 mins
Other four questions	35 mins each = 140 mins
Checking time	10 mins
Total	180 mins = 3 hours

> Don't forget to go by the exam room clock – check your watch against it.

Once you've looked at the paper, write down the times on some spare paper that you can keep in front of you. Give a starting and finishing time for each question, so that you are constantly aware of how many minutes you have left for the question you're working on.

Question	1	2	3	4	5	Checking
START	9.00	9.30	10.05	10.40	11.15	11.50
FINISH	9.30	10.05	10.40	11.15	11.50	12.00

This may take a moment or two, but it will achieve a lot in organising the time you have available, especially if the times do not fall conveniently on hours and half-hours, as is the case here.

Remember that two brilliant answers and one that isn't started will not do as well as three competent ones – so don't get carried away with writing at excessive length. The answer is to stick to the time-plan as rigidly as you can while you are working through the paper. Look upon the final ten minutes checking time as a 'crumple-zone' – it can go if you get held up in one of the questions, but it's useful to plan for it as it will give you time for a last-minute check and can be used as writing time if you need it.

SHORT-ANSWER QUESTIONS

If the paper has a *short-answer question,* in which you are asked several questions on a given passage, it makes sense to do this first. It gets your concentration working, as it makes you think about small, significant details in a passage and their relation to the whole. It also means that you can get something *done* fairly quickly at the start: even if it's only a question which earns you two or three marks, it is still an achievement, and this will build your confidence and get you into your stride for the more arduous questions to follow.

> See Chapter 3 for more on short-answer questions on passages.

Chapter 3 has more to say on the techniques to use for short-answer questions on passages.

READING ESSAY QUESTIONS

The first thing to do when approaching an *essay question* is to *read* it carefully and thoroughly. If you mis-read it the first time you look at it, the likelihood is that you'll continue to mis-read it – so make sure that you get it right.

Different kinds of essays, and the responses they require, can often be identified by the VERB which gives the instructions. Those which ask you simply to 'list' for example would be fairly straightforward, but it's unlikely that you'll see any as simple as that on an English paper. Instead, you'll probably be asked to analyse, discuss or explain, generally with reference to an idea stated in the question.

Often you'll encounter questions which are quotations or statements about the text. You may be asked 'How far do you agree?' or 'To what extent is this true?', for example. In almost all cases, these demand what is often called a 'Yes, but . . .' answer. They are true up to a point, but need to be limited and qualified.

Be aware, too, of what the question does *not* say. Look at this question:

'The main significance of *The Rainbow* is in its picture of North-country working life.' How far is this true?

You could answer this by giving a long account of how the novel treats working life. But this wouldn't be a full answer. To answer completely, you'd have to think of other significances of the novel – as an exploration of human relationships, for example, or as a study of the relationship between humankind and nature. You'd then need to evaluate the statement, to say whether or not this really was the main significance, and, if it was not, which of the others was the major theme of the novel.

> Answer what the question asks, not what you THINK it asks.

You should also be sure not to confuse what the question says with what you think it says. It is easy, for example, to think that this question

Discuss Wordsworth's concept of nature in *The Prelude* Books 1 and 2

means simply

Discuss nature in *The Prelude* Books 1 and 2.

The former is concerned with philosophical attitudes; the latter simply with a catalogue of geographical features.

Remember, then, that reading the question is of the utmost importance; a few seconds spent concentrating hard on working out what the question really means here can be immensely valuable in ensuring the relevance of your answer.

PLANNING, WRITING AND CHECKING

An exam essay, like any other piece of writing, consists of three stages – planning, writing and checking. Of these the most important is probably the first since, if you don't have the ideas clearly formed and well ordered before you start, you run the risk of omitting key points or including irrelevant ones. Try to divide the time available for each essay so that you have time for all three activities, and try to keep calm and give yourself enough time to plan – it pays dividends in the long run.

Planning an essay

The process of essay planning is described in depth in Chapter 3: in an exam, you simply go through it a little more quickly, using your memory as the source of information rather than a detailed reading of the text. You may feel tempted to go straight into an essay, as the time is very limited. But resist the temptation for just a few minutes and make a clear, detailed plan which you can follow when you write the essay. This has many advantages:

- it lets you sort out all the points first without the added task of having to write clearly about them;
- you can put them down in any order, and then change it to the most suitable one, before you write;
- you can cross out irrelevant points without wasting time;
- once you've got a plan to follow, you can relax and concentrate only on writing the essay;
- if you make mistakes here, you can change things quickly; if you make a mistake in an essay, you will have lost time and it may be difficult to get back on target and finish the paper.

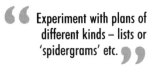

> Experiment with plans of different kinds – lists or 'spidergrams' etc.

Your plan should include the main points together with brief details of quotations and other references to make in the essay, as shown in the illustration (see Fig 1.4). In this way, *before* you start writing, you will be able to work out a clear, reasoned argument, to check the relevance of your points and to list quotations, all in a matter of moments, leaving yourself free to write the essay and to concentrate on expressing yourself clearly.

The importance of relevance

What you *say* in your plan will of course depend on the question, but it's vital that you remember one thing: relevance is all. The aim of the examiner is to get you to show your knowledge of the text by applying it to the issues raised in the question. If all goes well, you should;

a) know the text;
b) understand the question;
c) use your knowledge in order to answer the question.

The whole process, then, is one of *application* of knowledge to the given topic or statement. If you do *not* make your answer relevant, however much you know the text, you will not do well. As a result, you should *avoid* the following:

1   'Introductions' which give the story of a novel;
2   Worse still, lengthy biographies of the writer or accounts of how the text came to be written;
3   Summaries of critical interpretations of the text which are not related to the question;
4   Lists of quotations which are not used to make a point.

Your essay should instead be structured around eight or ten key points, each supported by a quotation or close reference to the text. Do not go through the text in chronological order, telling the story as you make points about it. You can safely assume that the examiner knows the story; instead, organise your answer around ideas – make the point first, and then give the evidence to support it.

Writing the essay

The process of writing is really the process of fleshing out the plan into a finished piece of prose. Try to follow this advice:

- write in a clear, straightforward style;
- make frequent reference to the text, either by quoting it or by referring to episodes within it;
- use the words of the question frequently to show that you are really engaging with the issues it raises.

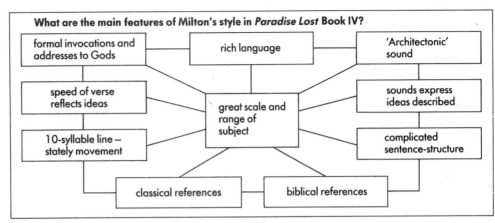

What are the main features of Milton's style in *Paradise Lost* Book IV?

formal invocations and addresses to Gods

rich language

'Architectonic' sound

speed of verse reflects ideas

great scale and range of subject

sounds express ideas described

10-syllable line – stately movement

complicated sentence-structure

classical references

biblical references

Fig. 1.3 A 'spidergram' set of notes on a topic or aspect

"The sad elegiac note is seldom absent from Tennyson's poetry." Discuss.

Often present – not always a note, sometimes entire subject matter.

1. Elegiac 'note'
    i) 'Rizpah' a note: narrative poetry
    ii) 'Passing of Arthur' – lamentation of Author's death. 'From the great deep to the great deep he goes': only 'note': obedience contemplation and action.
    iii) 'Lotos Eaters': lamentation of war's existence in 'confusion worse than death'.
        note: Richness, languidity, sweet exoticness. Contemplation worse than death.

2. In some, more than just a 'note'
    i) In Memoriam: entire poem an elegy
    ii) 'Garden of Swanston' – entirely concerned with the 'three men have I loved'.

3. Absence of elegiac note: 'Ulysses' – more concern, dissatisfaction, yearning "I cannot rest from travel'.

Conclusion:

'Sad elegiac note' sometimes present – often though more than a note – not present at all in 'Ulysses'.

Fig. 1.4 A student outline plan for an exam question

As you have already established the points you are going to make in the plan, in the essay you can write a very brief outline of your approach in the first paragraph. This will give the examiner an indication of your main ideas, and also show that you have considered the points carefully. In addition, should you be unable to finish the essay you will gain some credit for stating these ideas at the outset. Similarly, the final paragraph should summarise the points you have made or reach a clear conclusion in direct response to the question. Other points about essay-writing are made in Chapter 2; they are all of importance in an exam.

Checking your essay

Always try to read through an essay after you have finished to check for errors. You may, for example, have inadvertently used one character's name instead of another's, or made a statement which you thought was clear but, on second reading, is really rather ambiguous.

There will not be much time for this, however, and you may prefer to go on and write the second essay before going back to check the first. This has several advantages:

- it gives you time to move away from the essay before checking it – if you were to read it immediately after finishing it, you would probably read what you *thought* you said, rather than what is actually there;
- it provides a short break from writing roughly in the middle of the exam – a very welcome breather before the final onslaught on the remaining questions.

OPEN-BOOK EXAMINATIONS

Some boards give you the chance to take the texts into the exam room with you. In some ways this may seem to make the exam easier, but in practice it makes little difference. In general, you will be asked to write in detail about one passage of the text – a chapter from a novel, or a scene from a play, say. You will probably be asked to say how the passage is typical of a particular aspect of the writer's style, or how it contributes to a particular theme or concept.

> **Find out well in advance what kind of text you can use.**

The point to remember here is that while you need to refer closely to this passage and to other parts of the book to show how the two are related, you should *not* spend a great deal of time looking through the text to find examples. It is very easy to lose a great deal of time in this way – so make sure that you *know* the text thoroughly and can find examples you need without spending a lot of time looking for them in your text.

Remember, too, that the text will have to be 'clean' – without any notes or comments which you have added during the year. If you have a heavily-annotated edition, you may well be refused permission to take the exam – so do make absolutely sure of your Examining Board's policy by checking the syllabus well in advance and, if necessary, buying another, plain copy of the text to use in the exam.

CONCLUSION

If you follow these principles and, above all, if you know your texts thoroughly, you should be able to answer all of the questions in the time allotted.

With carefully-planned study and revision, you should be able to approach the exam without too much terror. Once you have started to write, try to relax – remember, you have been working for this for several months, so you might as well enjoy it!

GETTING STARTED

In Chapter 1, the process of critical reading was described as the essence of all literary study. That's true; but unless you're able to express what you've gained from that critical reading, you won't do very well in your studies. Putting together the information and ideas you've gained from a critical reading is the second vital component for success in literary studies, and this is almost always done in one way: *writing a critical essay*. In this sense, of course, the word 'critical' doesn't mean making a condemnation of what you've read; it means approaching with a sense of detached, objective analysis to make clear its ideas and themes and the ways in which the writer has chosen to express them. Not always objective, though: your own response to the text is important, too.

The critical essay is likely to form the backbone of your written work, in which you express your own ideas and responses to the texts you're studying. You will come across it in two, or perhaps three, ways:

1 Essays you write on your texts as part of your course, which will be read and assessed by your teacher or lecturer;
2 Essays you write on the texts in answer to exam questions, which will be read and assessed by the examiner;

and, in some cases

3 Longer essays which you will write during your course of studies, which will be graded by your teacher and then moderated by an examiner as a 'coursework' component of the examination.

The special nature of coursework essays will be discussed in Chapter 17, and Chapter 1 has already made some points about exam essays. But although you have far less time for exam essays than those you write while studying, there are still so many similarities between the two that the basic techniques hold good for them both. This chapter looks at the process involved in writing a critical essay, and suggests how you can do it more effectively both during your course and in the exam.

CHAPTER

THE CRITICAL ESSAY

DEFINING YOUR TITLE

DEFINING YOUR TASK

DOING THE RESEARCH

MAKING A PLAN

DRAFTING

CHECKING AND EDITING

THE FINAL VERSION

ESSENTIAL PRINCIPLES

Writing an essay isn't just a matter of sitting down, starting at page one and going on until you get to the end. Doing it properly involves several separate *stages*, each of which needs to be completed with care and using a number of special skills. It's worth looking at the whole process before taking each stage in turn:

> If you follow this method while studying, you'll have a firm pattern to follow while writing exam essays.

1   Defining your title
2   Defining your task
3   Doing the research
4   Brainstorming
5   Making a plan
6   Drafting
7   Checking and editing
8   The final version

Looked at in this way, the essay seems quite a task – and it's certainly not easy. Perhaps you need to look at the task rather as a science student would look at the process of conducting an experiment, with all the stages of designing and setting up the apparatus, observing the results, checking and analysing them, drawing diagrams, checking with other research, and then writing up the results. In your course, you'll probably be given several days in which to write an essay; when you realise what's involved, you'll understand why.

DEFINING YOUR TITLE

> Care in defining question and task can save a lot of wasted energy and time.

Unless you know *what* you are expected to write about, you'll be unable to do it. That doesn't just mean that you'll get a poor grade for the essay – it means that there'll be a gap in your notes and study material which you'll notice when you come to revise. This might mean that you're not fully prepared on the particular text and so are unable to answer a key question in the exam. Overall, then, knowing what the title *means* is an essential foundation for your larger success.

- Look at the *verb* to see what you're requested to do – discuss, analyse or compare, for example;
- study the *key words* of the question, to see what aspect of a text you're asked to approach – as discussed in Chapter 1.

DEFINING YOUR TASK

Once you know what the question is about, you need to decide what work is necessary for you to undertake in order to write it. This may include:

- deciding whether you need to read the whole text, or part of it – all of an anthology, for example, or just those poems on a particular theme;
- deciding what you need to consult amongst the notes you already have. These might include notes made in class or in your detailed textual readings;
- deciding what new notes you need to make. This might mean going through all or part of the text, looking for examples of a particular theme or for characteristic features of expression – and, in most cases, this is what the essay will involve;
- thinking about whether you may need to consult anything *other than* the text – a critical study, for example – and to take notes from it on the subject of the essay.

Taking a few moments to identify the nature and extent of your task will help you a great deal in completing it. It will also help you to decide how much time the various stages of the essay are going to take, and so prevent your running out of time at the last minute.

DOING THE RESEARCH

This is the stage which will probably take the longest. The most important task will be going through all or part of the text to find *evidence* of the way in which the writer covers the topic mentioned in the essay.

a) Using the text

The text should be your first and most important source for every critical essay. Go

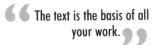

> The text is the basis of all your work.

through it, constantly asking yourself what is relevant to the topic, and making *quick* notes of passages which are important, and why. Using the following layout may help:

Discuss the treatment of _____	
Page/Chapter/Act.scene.line	Nature of treatment

At the end of your critical reading, you will have a large number of references to the theme or topic under discussion. But don't imagine that you can use them as they stand; you'll need to edit and select from them, to arrange them in the best order, and perhaps to group them under related headings in order to make the series of points which are the basis of your essay. This happens at the planning stage of the essay.

b) Using your notes

Go through your *notes* to the text. They may point out things that you've missed while reading through the text and looking for relevant pasages. Look, too, at any notes you've taken from class sessions – they may include relevant points, or spark off important ideas which you can develop in the essay.

c) Using critical texts

The advantages and disadvantages of using critical writings have already been discussed; remember, they need to be approached with caution, and it's always better to think for yourself about a text than to accept someone else's view without question. If you *do* decide to read a critical text, though, do so with care.

- If you're reading a critical article, make sure that it's relevant to the topic by 'scanning' through it quickly, perhaps looking at the first and last paragraphs to get an idea of its subject.
- If you're reading a book, don't start at the beginning and go all the way through. Instead:
  – use the contents page to pick out the chapter or chapters which look the most relevant to your needs;
  – use the index to look up words which are related to your topic of interest. This can often take you to the heart of the discussion and allow you to find quickly points which are relevant to your essay.
- Once you've found the relevant parts, read the whole section through without notes – just *concentrate* on what's being said.
- When you've done that, take notes, recording the relevant points. Follow the technique described in Fig. 2.1 (p. 20) and use its layout - clear headings, sub-headings and numbered points, so that you can come back to the notes several months later and still understand them.
- Only record what the writer says – or, if you add points of your own, make sure that you separate them. Put them in [square brackets], or put your initials after them, to show that they're your points, not the writer's.
- If the critic says something briefly which you can't express better yourself, then write it down in quotation marks. But don't copy out whole paragraphs, either in your notes or in the essay. This will only show that you haven't understood the ideas fully enough to absorb them into your own writing.

> Not all critical texts are worth taking notes from.

TAKE A BREAK

At this stage, you have finished the research and have a sizeable body of notes and ideas. It's best now to have a day away from the essay, so that the ideas can sort themselves out in your mind and you can come back to them afresh. Careful planning and a little experience will soon allow you to do this – if you're studying two or three subjects you'll probably have no shortage of other work to be doing, and a day or two away from the essay will allow you to keep up-to-date with that.

> Let the ideas marinate.

A   READING
1   Read the whole passage through without taking any notes.
2   Divide it into short sections

B   FIRST DRAFT
1   Select the main points by:
    (a)   deciding whether each point is relevant and including only those which are;
    (b)   looking at beginning and ends of paragraphs for key points.
2   Use your own words as far as possible, BUT quote short phrases which you can't put better yourself.
3   Use sub-headings, number each point and start new points on a fresh line.

C   CHECK
1   Check your draft against the original for:
    (a)   inclusion of all relevant points;
    (b)   accuracy of all points recorded.

D   FINAL VERSION
1   Rearrange the order of the points if you think it could be clearer.
2   Present the points as clearly as possible.
3   Make sure that abbreviations are clear.

E   REFERENCE
1   Give author, title, date and place of publication, page numbers of source.

Fig. 2.1 Taking notes from critical texts

Before you go on to *write* the essay, though, there are several more stages to go through. You need to go back to the notes, and to read them through carefully. Most essays contain between six and twelve key points, each supported by quotations or close references to the text. You need to begin thinking about what these points are, and how the material you've collected makes and supports them. While reading through your notes, you need also to be on the lookout for anything that isn't relevant to the essay title. These two processes will help enormously when you start planning.

BRAINSTORMING

Don't write full sentences – sometimes a single word is enough.

This is the process in which you take the essay title, sit down and just write down any points at all which you think are relevant to it. This *doesn't* mean writing a full essay. Instead, you should:

- write each point as briefly as you can, but clearly enough to express the idea;
- write each on a separate line, or in a different part of the page;
- leave plenty of space around each point – later you can go back and add related points to clarify it;
- don't worry yet about textual evidence – you can add that later.

Like most notes, you can produce 'brainstorms' in two ways – *linear* (a list of points) or as a pattern or *spidergram* (Fig. 2.2).

Your first brainstorm may include a lot of ideas that aren't relevant or are inaccurate. It doesn't matter – you can always cross them out later. The important thing here is to get all your ideas down quickly, to give you a working basis to build on later.

MAKING A PLAN

The plan is really the most important part of the essay. It will state in note form:

- each of the key points you intend to make;
- textual evidence for each one – not in full, but with line or chapter numbers.

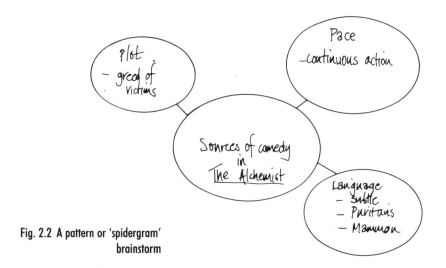

Fig. 2.2 A pattern or 'spidergram' brainstorm

> You can add numbers to a pattern plan once you've found the best order for your points

In short, it will be a complete, note-form answer to the question, and will look rather like the examples shown in Figs. 2.3 and 2.4. Don't expect to get the plan right first time – it may need several drafts which are halfway between a brainstorming session and a final plan. The plan shown in Fig. 2.4, for example, was arrived at only *after* the rough plan shown in Fig. 2.3.

Study the plan in Fig. 2.4 and notice:

- the way the introduction states the main ideas briefly and clearly;

- the organisation into three main sections in answer to the question;

- the way in which *points* are made *first*, and then supported by quotations or references to the text;

- that the plan is complete in its own right – it conveys all the ideas needed to answer the question fully, on a single sheet of file paper.

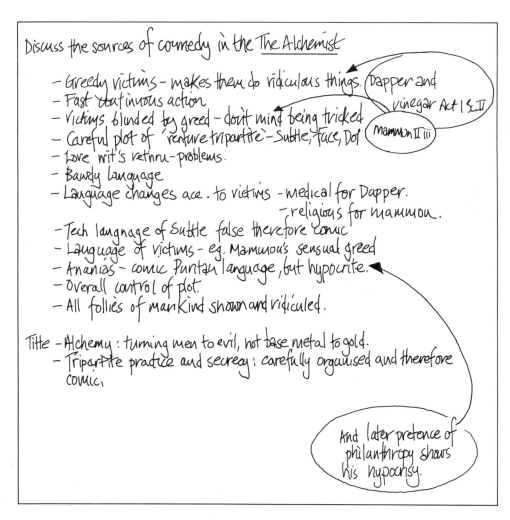

Fig. 2.3 A rough plan or brainstorm

The Sources of Comedy in The Alchemist.

Plan
            Main sources are:
    1) Pace - continuous action.
    2) Plot - control and organization
    3) Language - reveals follies of victims
In play - follies of mankind shown and ridiculed. What is comic and why is it comic?

Plot
    1) Victims' greed makes them perform ridiculous tasks eg. Dapper and
        Vinegar Act I scene ii
    2) Victims blinded by greed therefore willingly gulled. eg. Mammon.
        Act ii scene iii
    3) Tripartite practice: chivalry under pressure of secrecy and time.
    4) Return of Lovewit causes chaos in tripartites carefully laid plans

Language
            Bawdy and scurrilous crossfire comic because wits matched Act I
        scene i (add pace and vitality).
    1) Changing language of Subtle; medical terms for Dapper; religious
        language for Mammon (change comic)
    2) Overblown language of Mammon - reveals sensual greed.
        Later change to philanthropic attitude reveals his pretence
        (change comic)
    3) Puritan Language of Ananias comic because of his hypocritical
        motive
    4) Highflown technical language of Subtle comic because of spurious
        logic

Subject of plot

        Alchemy usually metal - gold. here bad - to worse in men

Fig. 2.4 Final plan for the rough
plan in Fig. 2.3

Plans of this sort are essential to good essay writing. They:

- allow you to arrange your material clearly and precisely;
- give you the chance to cross out irrelevant or inaccurate material *before* you've got half-way through a complete essay;
- give you the essence of the essay in a single sheet, which is much easier to revise from than an essay of several pages.

" Sometimes it's worth making a fair copy of your plan to keep for revision. "

For all these reasons, then, you should always make a plan of this kind when writing an essay. Many teachers will accept full plans of this kind instead of essays – not always, but perhaps on one occasion out of four. And remember that they will be of much more use than full essays when revising – it's much easier to take in ideas from a single sheet than from a full essay.

The way that the essay plan is organised is so important that it can't be stressed too often. It's organised around *ideas*, not around the chronological order of the play or novel you're writing about. You'll have to go through the work chronologically when researching for the essay: but you then need to change that, at the planning stage, into a sequence of points in a carefully grouped and logically arranged order. Only if you do this will you write a clear, logical and relevant essay.

DRAFTING

This is the process of actually writing the essay. Now that you know what you're going to say, it should be straightforward: all you have to do is to find the best words to use to say it.

- Write in a simple, clear and direct style, aiming to make your points directly.

- Follow the order of your plan – avoid 'introductions' which tell the story of the play or novel, or which give biographical information about the writer. If you have an introduction at all, it should summarise your main points very briefly, as suggested in the last section of Chapter 1.

- Each paragraph should have one major point as its basis.
  - first, use a 'topic sentence' to make the main point simply and clearly;
  - next, support it with a quotation or reference to the text to establish where this is shown;
  - then conclude with a brief reference to how the point is demonstrated elsewhere in the text.

- If you can, use the words of the question quite often. This shows that you are really engaging with its ideas, and it will stop you straying off the point into irrelevance.

- At the end of the essay, summarise *briefly* what you have said so far, and draw a conclusion which:
  - draws together your points;
  - relates them to the question;
  - rests firmly on a close reading of the text.

> When you get more proficient, you can start bending these rules – but they help to get you started and are useful in exams.

When you use quotations, follow the advice given in Fig. 2.5, which reproduces part of a critical article. If you quote from a critic, do so briefly or, better still, express his or her

---

1   In many ways 'Strange Meeting' is a poignant and confused completion of
2 'Hyperion', the fourth and final book Keats himself never wrote. In simplified terms, the major theme of Hyperion is the process of evolutionary change through successive generations, exemplified in the ousting of the Titanic Gods by the Olympian to produce a finer race of deities, a new loveliness at the expense of the power, beauty and strength of that preceding. The Keatsian themes of beauty and the vale of soul-making
1 are strongly present in 'Strange Meeting' – the war is even referred to as 'Titanic' – and it is in the way in which they contribute to the notion of rebirth through sacrifice and death that the poem is most profoundly effective. A Keatsian hope for beauty and its intrinsic sadness is immanent in Owen's idea and expression:

3   I went hunting wild
    After the wildest beauty in the world,
    Which lies not calm in eyes, or braided hair,
    But mocks the steady running of the hour,
    And if it greives, grieves richlier than here.

Yet there is little hope that a better race will emerge from the loss of this beauty. There
2 is some, certainly, in the line 'Now men will go content with what they spoiled'. But the notion of future content seems short-lived, and in any case refers to a renewal of the existing pattern which has been destroyed by war – perhaps the Arcadian England once again – rather than to a better state made possible by its sacrifice. And the inevitability of a future and communal failure is made clear in the lines which follow it:

    Or, discontent, boil bloody and be spilled.
3   They will be swift, with swiftness of the tigress
    None will break ranks, though nations trek from progress.

Here the move towards barbarity – the trek from progress – is national, and unbroken by personal advance or feeling.
2   In this light, the final 'Let us sleep now' connotes nothing more than resignation, and the whole poem is poignant because of its despair in the face not only of universal slaughter and the destruction of the hope of beauty, but also in the total absence of any movement towards anything finer and better, as in the case with the Hyperion poems.
1 For, despite its sadness, 'Hyperion' is ultimately a hopeful poem, and the apparent hopelessness in Owen is all the more shocking in comparison.
    Yet despite this, the poem is hopeful.

---

1 Title of poem is given in single inverted commas. Underline titles of novels, plays or other long works.

2 Short quotations – anything from a single word to two lines – can be given in the text, as part of the syntax of the sentence involved.

3 Longer quotations (three lines or more) are indented, and presented in their original layout. The text of the essay is not interrupted by such quotations – that is, they come at the end of a sentence.

By the way, avoid substantial omissions from passages quoted, but where a word or two are omitted, use three dots (. . .) to show this.

Fig. 2.5 Using quotations

idea in your own words, but acknowledge it by saying 'as Christopher Ricks has pointed out' or using a similar phrase. *Never* copy out whole sentences or paragraphs from critics and pass them off as your own work: apart from the moral implications of this, it just won't work in practice, as the difference in style will be obvious to a practised reader. You'll lose marks and, most important, you won't have fully absorbed the ideas into your own writing.

CHECKING AND EDITING

At this stage, you need to go through and check your writing. Check for:

- *accuracy of expression*. Do you say what you meant to, or is the expression ambiguous?
- *accuracy of spelling*. Make sure that spelling is correct – especially that of the names of characters, as teachers and examiners get annoyed if it isn't!
- *clarity of expression*. Make sure that you *don't* use long, winding sentences which get lost in the middle, or have sentences without main verbs. Also avoid using syntax that's awkward and confusing to the reader.

> Try to get a short break between writing and checking.

When you've had a little practice at this kind of checking, you'll find that any changes can usually be made on your draft version. Cross out the incorrect expression and write the replacement clearly next to it. Don't bother with correction fluid – most exam boards won't allow its use, and it wastes time.

THE FINAL VERSION

If your draft version is so covered in corrections that it's hard to read, you may need to write it out again as a fair copy. But after a little practice you should be able to make most corrections to the draft so that the final version is legible and accurate.

Now you can give it in and wait for the comments. But, of course, it doesn't end there – read the comments carefully when you get the essay back, if necessary adding points to the plan so that you have a full coverage of the topic that you can then use for revision.

The Process in practice

You might feel that the process outlined above is lengthy, complicated and time-consuming. It is – especially at first, when you're not used to working in such detail. But with practice, you'll find that you'll be able to produce essays much more quickly, but still following the same approach. Planning your time is one of the most important aspects – make sure that you work steadily on the essay through all the time available, building in a short break of a day or so in the middle between getting the information and starting the plan. In this way you'll produce something that is carefully thought out, rather than being hastily thrown together.

> Once you've learnt the process, you'll be able to use it quickly in the exam.

In an exam, you may feel there's no time for such an approach. Of course, you won't be able to consult the text or look at critical writings – but you will be able to consult your memory of the text, which by this time should be considerable. You'll also be able to go through the same stages, looking at the question, brainstorming, making a plan and then writing. All of this will take you probably five minutes at the start of the half-hour or 45 minutes you have for each question. A few moments at the end to check, as suggested in Chapter 1, will complete the process. All this will help you produce a far better essay than you would if you'd just sat down and started writing straightaway.

Following this procedure in the exam also has one further advantage. It gives you a clear scaffolding to cling to at a time when you might not be feeling too happy or secure about things. This helps you get over nerves, and makes it easier for you to concentrate and perform at your best.

The Essay in practice

This chapter ends by looking at a complete essay – the one which you saw in plan stages in Figs. 2.3 and 2.4. It's reproduced on the following pages together with detailed comments. Look at it closely – it's an example of the sort of work that you need to produce during your studies, and should give you some help in the process of writing. Don't worry if you don't know the text it's written about – in one way its better if you don't, since that will allow you to concentrate on *how* the essay makes its points, rather than the points themselves. There are good and not-so-good things here, as there are in any piece of writing – but work through it and through the examiner's comments, thinking carefully about how *you* can apply them to your own essays, both in your course and in the exam itself.

The numbers running alongside the student essay relate to the location of the specific examiner comments which follow the essay.

STUDENT ESSAY WITH EXAMINER COMMENTS

Question: Discuss the sources of Comedy in *The Alchemist*.

STUDENT ESSAY

1

2

In his play *The Alchemist*, Jonson satirizes the natural follies of all types of people during the London plague in the 17th century. The language, the fast pace and the control, organization and subject matter of the plot are the main sources of the play's comedy.

As the play is continuous (with no interruption for scene changes), the action in the play is fast-moving and this adds to the comedy. By skilful organization of the plot, each victim meets the alchemist at an appointed time and this allows particular follies to be satirized. This timing is vital to allow Subtle – the alchemist – Dol and Face – his partners – to change their roles in order to appear convincing to their various victims. At the end of the play the chaotic meeting of the victims is contrived to cause the discovery of the follies of the tricksters – Subtle, Dol and Face. This

3

control and organization of the plot is therefore an important element in the play's comedy.

4

Through the plot and language, we see that the victims of the Tripartite (Subtle, Dol and Face) are willing to be tricked because of their own greed and this makes the trickery work. We see an example of this in Act II scene III (these divisions have been added some time after the play was written) where the greed of Sir Epicure Mammon blinds him to the trickery of the Tripartite. As the cynical Surly warns –

5

'Be not gulled, Sir Mammon.'

6

As the blindness of Mammon is due to his greed, we see here that he deserves his fate.

Again through his own greed, Dapper the clerk is made to look ridiculous. In Act I scene II, to clear the way for another victim, Subtle instructs Dapper –

'Sir, against one o'clock prepare yourself

Till when you must be fasting; only take

Three drops of vinegar in, at your nose;

Three at your mouth, and one at either ear,'

Here we see the ridiculous tasks that Dapper is prepared to perform to help him satisfy his greed.

7

As we have shown, Subtle, Dol and Face have a Tripartite agreement to trick victims into parting with their money and their goods. Through the plot the fact that they have to work in secrecy and under the pressure of time is revealed, as the

8

house where they practise belongs to Lovewit, Face's master, who is out of town. In Act I scene I, Face says –

'Pray heaven

The master do not trouble us, this quarter.'

9

By placing the Tripartite's trickery under the pressure of time and secrecy, [Jonson makes] their dealings become more intricate and this adds to the comedy. The unexpected return of Lovewit at the end of the play causes confusion and this is

10

another element of the play's comedy.

The language is very important to the comedy of the plot. The play begins in the

11

middle of an argument and this sets a fast pace which continues throughout the play.

In scene I Act I, the vituperative cross-fire between Subtle and Face add pace, vitality and comedy to the opening scene.

Face – 'Sirrah, I'll strip you.

Subtle – What to do? Lick figs.

Face – Out of my ——

Subtle – Rogue, I'll rogue you out of your sleights.'

12

13

By alluding to excrement and animals, Face and Subtle denigrate each other. Both are quick-witted and well matched in the argument and this balance of wits adds to the comedy. In this scene the allusions to filth are comic due to the pace and balance of wits.

> Face — 'When you went pinned up in the several rags,
>   You raked, and picked from the dunghills, before days —' p33
> Subtle — 'Yes, in your master's house.
>   You, and the rats, here, kept possession.' p39

In this scene the comedy of the scurrilous language is heightened by the actions of Dol, who interposes between Subtle and Face in an attempt to calm them down. Ironically Dol resorts to violent action to produce the desired effect as she takes Face's sword and breaks Subtle's glass.

14

The language used by the characters of the Tripartite changes several times during the play to convince their victims of their pretended sincerity. This contrast in language is both for the purpose of the plot and also adds to the comedy of the play. When with Dapper, Subtle poses as a doctor and uses medical terms and in contrast with Mammon, while pretending religious devoutness, Subtle calls him 'my son'.

The language used by the victims of the Tripartite reveal their various follies and both their language and actions are a target for Jonson's satire.

The overblown language of Sir Epicure Mammon reveals his lust for sensual gratification —

> 'I will have my beds, blown up; not stuffed:
> Down is too hard . . . My mists
> I'll have of perfume, vapour 'bout the room,
> To loose ourselves in; and my baths, like pits
> To fall into:'

As in this scene Subtle pretends to be a devout person by using religious language, Mammon feigns a philanthropic attitude in order to be able to purchase Subtle's magic. Mammon says

> 'No, I assure you; in pious uses
> Founding in colleges and grammar schools
> Marrying young virgins, building hospitals
> And now, and then, a church.'

15

This philanthropic attitude of Mammon is obviously a pretence because of his evident sensual greed and here the folly of the victim is comic.

In Act II scene III, Ananias uses the specialist diction of a Puritan and in this context it is comical because the reason for his contact with Subtle is to buy the Philosopher's Stone to gain power with which he can win supporters for his religious sect. Here we see the language used by Ananius is an attempt to conceal his hypocrisy, and because this is obvious it is comic.

> Ananius —   'I have not edified more, truly, by man,
>   Nor, since the beautiful light first shone on me:
>   And I am sad, my zeal hath so offended.'

The specialist language of alchemy used by Subtle to blind his victims is comic as the logic he uses is often spurious. In an attempt to justify the validity of alchemy Subtle says —

> 'Why I think that the greater miracle
> No egg, but differs from the chicken, more,
> Than metals in themselves.'

16

17

The process of alchemy was for the purpose of changing base metals into gold — thus to heighten the quality of metals. It is ironic and comic that in the play *The Alchemist*, the alchemist, with his promise of riches, heightens the corruptive greed present in his victims.

18

19

Through the fast pace, variety of language and the organization of the plot, the follies of the victims are ridiculed in a comical manner which reveals the fact that greed, as Subtle says —

> 'Make — 'em haste towards their gulling more.'

EXAMINER COMMENTS

1   As was suggested by the final plan, the opening paragraph gives a clear, brief indication of the three main sources of comedy in the play. Notice that 'introductory' matter is kept to a minimum, with only a single sentence to describe the play in general terms. Notice, too, that the paragraph ends by using the words of the question – 'sources of comedy' – thus ensuring relevance right from the start.

2   The only weakness with this paragraph is the suggestion that the play satirises the follies of the people 'during the London plague in the 17th century'. '17th' should really be 'Seventeenth', but that's a minor point. What's important is that the statement is misleading. It suggests that only one historical period is being satirised, whereas it's clear that Jonson is satirising basic human behaviour regardless of time or place. In larger terms, this shows the importance of scrupulous accuracy, especially in the opening paragrah, when you have to win the confidence of the reader.

3   This is a very good paragraph. It starts with a direct statement of its ideas in simple terms, in a topic sentence which communicates the idea straightforwardly and directly. It again uses a key word from the title, so there's no question of irrelevance here.
      After the topic sentence come several pieces of carefully chosen supporting evidence, stated precisely and with just enough detail.
      The paragraph then concludes with a re-statement of its opening sentence, the addition of 'therefore' showing that it's a conclusion resting on sound evidence, and the use of 'comedy' again ensuring relevance.

4   A slight mistake here. It should be 'triumvirate' instead of 'tripartite', meaning a rule by three people, used comically to describe the three tricksters. The larger relevance of this is to show how important it is to get individual terms right – errors can suggest a lack of detailed knowledge, despite other evidence to the contrary.

5   Notice the careful use of quotation here, which is good for two reasons. First, only a few words are quoted, cutting out all but the essence of the point to be illustrated – a good purposeful approach. Secondly, it's laid out very clearly, on a line by itself, which makes it easier and more pleasing to read.

6   The important thing here is that, because the character deserves his fate, we can laugh at his being tricked with a clear conscience. Only half of this point is made in the essay. Again there's a general lesson: always make your points as clearly and precisely as possible, however obvious you feel they might be – otherwise there's no proof on paper that you actually know them.

7   Another half-made point. To make absolutely sure, this one needs to be related to the question. This can be done very simply, by adding another sentence at the end of the paragraph, such as: 'This is a further source of comedy in the play.'

8   The expression of this paragraph lacks the clarity of the rest of the essay. Clear expression is important, so it's worth re-writing paragraphs of this kind when they occur (as they do for us all, I assure you.). I'd suggest something like this:
      As the plot develops, it becomes clear that Subtle and Face are using the house of Face's employer, Lovewit, as their headquarters while Lovewit is away. In Act 1 scene 1, Face says . . .

9   There's a slight error of expression here. A participle ('placing') is used instead of a main verb, so that we don't know who's doing the placing. I'd add the main verb 'Jonson makes' after the comma before 'their dealings', to make things quite clear.

10   This is another direct statement in the question's own words. 'Element' isn't exactly the same as 'source', I know, but I think it's a justifiable alteration, to avoid using the same words over and over again.

11   A model topic sentence to introduce a major new section of the essay which deals with a new source of comedy.

12   Like the concluding sentence at 3, the sentence here brings the paragraph together by making a general statement which is clearly related to the question.

13   It's a good idea to include *exact* references for quotations, although act, scene and line numbers would be better here. References of this kind do save time when revising, and are thus a sound practice to follow. The only pity here is that it hasn't been done with the earlier quotations.

14   This paragraph begins with a slight variation of the topic sentence. It uses two sentences, the first to state the idea or subject under discussion, the second to relate it to the essay question. This is quite a useful technique for dealing with more complex ideas, presenting them more clearly by using two sentences instead of one very long one.

15   A good section, which goes through different kinds of language and analyses each in turn. It's the sort of paragraph you need to write quite often, especially in essays of the 'discuss' and 'analyse' kind which demand close treatment of a number of related but slightly different points.

16   This concludes the discussion of kinds of comic language begun at 14. As it's such an important section, it would have been a good idea to end it with a brief paragraph simply saying that the use of different kinds of language, by different characters and in different situations, is another source of comedy in the play. This would make clear to the reader that you were finishing off a section of the essay, and would also explicitly relate your points to the title once again.

17   A simple and direct point, which explains the last point of the plan.

18   A good conclusion, drawing together the three main aspects of the essay and relating them again to the title. In a way this does what the first paragraph did, but it does so with the added strength of the detailed analysis and evidence that the main body of the essay has provided.

19   It's often a nice idea, if you can, to end in a memorable way. You can afford to be a little more concerned with style at the end, making an effective conclusion either by a carefully-turned sentence or, as here, a well-chosen quotation.

Overall comment

Overall this is an essay which is carefully planned and well written. It shows a good knowledge of the text and careful selection of examples to support its points – and it avoids the error of going chronologically through a text, which so many essays fall into. In places it could be clearer in expression or deeper in analysis, but in general it's a solid example of the sort of essay produced during a course of study by a conscientious and capable student.

GETTING STARTED

Some papers start with a compulsory section which is a series of *short questions on a passage* from the text you have studied. This is most common in papers on Shakespeare or Chaucer, although it can appear on other papers – check your syllabus and past papers carefully. This type of question should not be confused with the type of essay question which gives you a passage to discuss as typical of the work as a whole, or a poem to discuss as typical of a selection you have studied.

The short questions on a passage come in various types. They may ask for:

- comments on the meaning or effect of *individual words*;
- comments on the meaning or effect of *phrases*;
- analyses of *particular kinds of language* – chains of images or metaphors, for example – which are found in the passage (see Chapter 4);
- an explanation of the *place of this passage in the text as a whole*;
- comments on the *main themes or issues* the passage discusses;
- discussion of the *dramatic effect* of the passage.

You may be asked three or four questions of one or more of these types, or two questions about themes, language, character or the function of the passage which will require longer answers.

The essential way to prepare for such questions is by knowing the text thoroughly by repeated reading and analysis.

QUESTIONS ON PASSAGES

WHAT THE QUESTION LOOKS LIKE

ANSWERING THE QUESTIONS

TYPES OF QUESTION

PRACTICE QUESTIONS

CONCLUSION

ESSENTIAL PRINCIPLES

WHAT THE
QUESTION LOOKS
LIKE

If you go into the exam room unprepared, you might find a question of this kind rather complicated. So the first thing to do is to make sure that you know *what it looks like* and *how it works*. Here is an example of this kind of question:

> *Falstaff.*
> If I be not ashamed of my soldiers, I am a soused gurnet. I have misused the
> King's press damnably. I have got, in exchange of a hundred and fifty soldiers,
> three hundred and odd pounds. I press me none but good householders,
> yeomen's sons, inquire me out contracted bachelors, such as had been asked
> twice on the banns such a commodity of warm slaves as had as lief hear the   5
> devil as a drum, such as fear the report of a caliver worse than a struck fowl or
> a hurt wild duck. I pressed me none but such toasts-and-butter, with hearts in
> their bellies no bigger than pins' heads, and they have bought out their
> services; and now my whole charge consists of ancients, corporals, lieuten-
> ants, gentlemen of companies — slaves as ragged as Lazarus in the painted   10
> cloth, where the glutton's dogs licked his sores; and such as indeed were never
> soldiers, but discarded unjust serving-men, younger sons to younger broth-
> ers, revolted tapsters, and ostlers trade-fall'n, the cankers of a calm world and
> a long peace; ten times more dishonourable-ragged than an old fazed ancient;
> and such have I to fill up the rooms of them as have bought out their services   15
> that you would think that I had a hundred and fifty tattered prodigals lately
> come from swine-keeping, from eating draff and husks.
>
> i)   Explain 'a soused gurnet' (l. 1), and 'Lazarus in the painted cloth' (l. 10).   (3)
> ii) Comment on the images of animals in lines 6–8.   (3)
> iii) Why does Falstaff want soldiers?   ($1\frac{1}{2}$)
> iv) Comment briefly on the statement that, in this passage, Falstaff is
>   no longer a comic character.   (5)

We shall return to this passage and the questions set on it at various points during this chapter.

ANSWERING THE
QUESTIONS

As well as simply getting to know what the question looks like you can also prepare by refining the actual *technique* of answering. Remember that many people fail not because they do not know the material, but because they do not *use* their knowledge to give direct, straightforward answers to the questions.

This chapter shows you how to read the passages thoroughly in preparation for the answers; how to identify exactly what it is that each question wants for an answer; how to write answers which are clear and precise; and how to avoid writing too much, or being irrelevant, and so wasting time and lessening your chances of success in later questions.

There are three important general points about which you must be sure before you can answer a question of this kind:

1   Whether you *have* to answer it, or whether it is optional – can you, for instance, choose between it and an essay?
2   Whether you have to do a question like this on TWO texts, or whether you can choose to do just ONE of them.
3   How it differs from an essay question which is based on a long extract from a text.

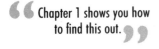

Chapter 1 shows you how
to find this out.

The answers to the first two points are simple. Make sure that you know whether you have to answer one or more questions of this type by studying your syllabus *and* the instructions at the start of the paper. It's best to find out points like this well in advance by asking your teacher or, to be really sure, by getting a copy of the syllabus and some past papers from your Examining Board. This way, there'll be no unpleasant surprises for you when you start to work on the exam.

The third point can be answered simply, too. An essay question based on a passage will be just ONE question of a few lines, usually printed *before* the passage itself. It will ask you to relate the passage to the work as a whole. Short answer questions of the kind we're discussing here usually have several separate parts and come *after* the passage, and they are more concerned with a close reading of the passage itself. In practice, it's usually easy to tell the difference, but people have got the two types confused, and have sometimes written a very short answer for a question which demands a full-length essay. Again, careful study of syllabus and paper should prevent this.

READING THE PASSAGE

Skim through the questions rapidly, too – it'll show you the main direction to think in.

The first thing to do when you see a question like this is to spend quite a lot of time *reading the passage*. Your first instinct will be to get something on paper as quickly as possibly, especially if – as is often the case – this question is the first one on the paper. Resist the temptation. Your answers will be superficial and limited, or even downright wrong, if they are based on a superficial reading of the passage. So, read the passage very carefully.

How long should you spend reading? It's not possible to give a hard and fast rule here, but if you have thirty minutes for this question you could well spend ten of them reading the passage *before* you tackle the questions.

How do I read? This question isn't as daft as it sounds – reading a passage like this in an exam isn't at all the same as reading a newspaper or a novel for recreation. Try to follow this approach:

a)   Read it through quickly just to get familiar with it.
b)   Read it again more slowly. While you do this, ask yourself questions to aid concentration and get the analytical process started. Here are some to try:

- Where does it come in the play or tale?
- How does it advance the development of particular themes?
- What does it *add* to the text as a whole – a key change in the plot, a theme treated in a new way, a character revealed, a new strand of imagery?
- What do individual words and images mean? What effect do they have on the passage?
- How does the writer use sound, rhythm, diction, tone and the other techniques to create different effects?

Look at Chapter 4 for more information on this.

c)   Read it again fairly quickly to pull together the ideas you've had when reading in more detail.

Don't be alarmed – this doesn't mean that you have to write a full-length critical analysis of the piece in your head. But it *does* mean that you should be alert to all these things while you're reading. Notice:

- why a particular word is used;
- whether it's part of a pattern of language;
- how everything comes together in this passage and how it, in turn, contributes to the progress of the text as a whole.

Just thinking like this will sharpen your critical faculties a good deal and prepare you for the sort of detailed work you'll be asked to do in the questions. It shouldn't take too long, either – in the concentrated atmosphere of an exam, you can get a lot done in ten minutes.

READING THE QUESTIONS

Once you have read the *passage* carefully, you need to read all of the *questions*. Don't start to answer the first one before you have read them *all*. You need to read them all for these reasons:

a)   to work out what each one wants by way of answer;
b)   to make sure that you don't answer two questions in one answer – something that is easily done. For example, if the third or fourth question asks you what the passage contributes to the imagery of the whole play, don't explain this in an earlier question which asks you just to explain the function of ONE image in this passage;
c)   to be sure that you know how important each question is, by looking at the number of marks it has next to it. Questions which have only one or two marks will need only a sentence or even a word or two for a satisfactory answer; those which have five, eight or ten marks will need a short paragraph.

Again, don't be alarmed. You can do this in a matter of seconds in an exam, and just knowing what kind of things are required will save you wasted effort, repeated material and the possible loss of nerve that this might bring on at the start of your paper.

QUESTIONS ON WORDS AND PHRASES

TYPES OF QUESTION

These can ask you to do various things. The simplest are those which ask you to 'explain' or 'translate', but these are getting less likely. For such questions you should simply say what the phrases mean. Consider the first part of question (i) on the passage quoted earlier for example:

> *Q:* Explain 'a soused gurnet' (line 1).
> *A:* A soused gurnet is a pickled fish.

More complicated questions can ask about the *effect* of a particular phrase in its context. These need slightly longer answers, to make quite clear how the phrases work. Take the following example:

> *Q:* What is the effect of 'a soused gurnet' (line 1)?
> *A:* A gurnet was a fish with a big head and small body which when soused or pickled was a great delicacy. It is ridiculous to think of Falstaff like this, and so it makes the idea that he is ashamed of his soldiers quite absurd.

> **This idea can also link with his 'force' – he is the vast 'head' of a very small 'body'.**

This is a longer answer, but is still only a single paragraph of a few lines, and it gets across both the meaning of the phrase and its effect in its context.

QUESTIONS ON IMAGERY

You might be asked about one particular image, or about a chain of images or metaphors which occurs in a passage. In the earlier passage, for example, you were asked, in question ii);

> *Q:* Comment on the images of animals in lines 6–8.

> **Keep a special pen or highlighter to pick out related images in a text.**

First you need to *find* the animal images here. If you've read the passage carefully in the way suggested above, you should already have noticed them, so it's only a matter of going through and finding them.

But just finding the images isn't enough. You need to say what they *do* – what particular shade of meaning or effect they add to the main point of the passage. Here, what's happening is that Falstaff is talking about his soldiers in terms of animals – a struck fowl and a hurt wild duck. These are animals which suggest fear and flight, rather than courage and fight, so the comparison makes the soldiers sound very weak.

A good answer to this question might go like this:

> *A:* Falstaff says he has chosen only people who fear a 'caliver' or musket as much as would a 'struck fowl' or 'hurt wild duck'. This makes clear that they are weak, cowardly people, who willingly 'bought out their services' – paid to be released from fighting.

This answer does three things:

> **Make sure your answers always have these three elements.**

- it *identifies* the images;
- it *explains* the way they colour the impression we get of the objects they are used to describe – here, the soldiers;
- it *puts them in context* by showing how they contribute to the larger meaning and progression of the passage.

An answer like this would get full marks; one which did only the first two would probably get two-thirds; one which simply identified the images would get only a third of the marks, or perhaps less.

QUESTIONS ON THE PASSAGE'S PLACE IN THE WHOLE TEXT

You *won't* usually be asked to give a detailed explanation of where a passage comes in a play, although you might have to say briefly what happens just before it and what comes immediately afterwards. But you might well be asked to explain the importance of the passage in the text as a whole – say how it contributes to themes and ideas, or develops a pattern of language, for example.

To do this, you have to know where it comes in the whole play or tale. But you do not need to say this *unless* it is essential in making clear the importance of the passage.

Always give the way in which the passage is important and *then* give your reason for saying this, if necessary showing where it comes in the play. That way, you'll keep the priorities right – the idea first, then the evidence for it. For example:

> A: This passage is important in showing Falstaff as the comic figure he is throughout the play. His language is comic in its references to animals, and his references to the kind of people he presses introduce the familiar element of comic trickery and dishonour.

Keep your answers SHORT – don't go into long, complicated explanations or give long narratives of the story. Usually all the questions on a passage together will be worth half the marks of an essay question, so they should be less than half the length of an essay. For most people, that means about a side and a half of A4 paper at the very most, and often half a page per question will be enough if you make your points clearly.

- First, make a rough *list of reasons* why you think it is important or what it adds to the play. This can be done in single words – comedy; irony; character extension; suspense – which will be enough to establish the point.

- Secondly, find some *evidence* to support each point – a line which is funny, an ironic statement, a way in which a character is extended, an element of suspense. Here you may need to refer to earlier or later stages in the play – but be careful. Make sure that you really *use* the references and don't just tell the story.

- Thirdly, get the points in *order*. This may be no more than just scribbling a number next to each key word you wrote down, but it's worth doing as it makes sure that your points are connected and keep to the point of the question.

- Finally, you can *write* your answer, following the points clearly and stating the ideas first before supporting each one with evidence.

Here's an example, again based on the earlier passage:

> Q: How is this passage important in the play?
> A: The passage is important because it shows the character of Falstaff within the changing circumstances of the move towards war at the end of the play. Falstaff's character is still bluff, comic and self-interested, shown in his forthright delight in using his powers as a recruiter to his own advantage (ll. 1–2) and his images of animals (ll. 6-7) and food and drink (ll. 1, 7–8). The language is still that of the low life we have encountered in the Boar's Head Tavern where Hal visits Falstaff. Yet the audience knows that things have changed. In the scene immediately before this one, we have heard Vernon describe the army raised by Prince Hal as 'gorgeous as the sun at midsummer', suggesting that he is now too serious to take part in Falstaff's joking. The passage also adds suspense, in coming before the preparations for war in the rebel camp. In all these ways it is an important contribution to the play's dramatic movement.

QUESTIONS ON THEMES AND ISSUES DISCUSSED

You may be asked to say what *themes* and *issues* of the play are discussed in the passage you are given. Here again, you should make a list of them, or a set of pattern notes. Single words will usually be enough for each point; write them down with a reference to the evidence which supports them, get them in order and then write the answer.

Remember that there may be only one or two themes which a passage discusses or extends, so don't spend a lot of time looking for others once you've found a couple of strong, firm ideas. Here's an example based on our passage:

> Q: What themes of the play does the passage continue?
> A: The main theme is the discussion of the idea of honour. The soldiers Falstaff collected are very different from the courageous army of Prince Hal which Vernon has just described. This shows that Falstaff is more concerned with comfort than with fighting.

Notice that only one theme has been discussed here. That's fine; the passage is only concerned with one. Other passages may require longer answers; again, be guided by the number of marks available.

QUESTIONS ON DRAMATIC EFFECTIVENESS

You may be asked how the passage is *dramatically effective* – that is, how it succeeds in the theatre.

To answer this question, you need to think about how the scene would look on stage, and how the audience would respond. Spend a few minutes trying to picture the stage in your mind. Then jot down a few key words (Fig. 3.1), find some evidence to support each one, and get them in order.

> 66 Look closely at the pattern plan, to see how it's developed into the finished answer here. 99

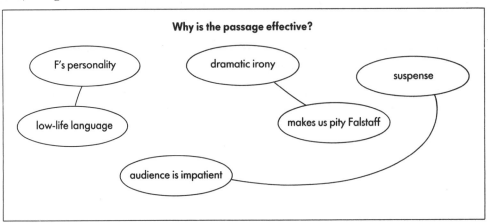

Why is the passage effective?

F's personality

dramatic irony

suspense

low-life language

makes us pity Falstaff

audience is impatient

Fig. 3.1 Draft pattern plan – before details of evidence have been added.

Now write your answer, like this:

Q: How is the passage effective on stage?

A: The passage is mainly effective because of the force of Falstaff's personality which comes across in this monologue. He has completely overturned the proper procedure for recruiting soldiers, and talks of them in the low-life language of the Boar's Head Tavern. Yet there is also dramatic irony in the passage's effect. The audience knows that Falstaff's behaviour is quite out of place in the coming fighting, and this makes us feel differently towards him – perhaps with pity or with impatience. A third way in which the passage is effective is in adding suspense to the play. We know that fighting is about to take place, but Falstaff's leisurely speech holds up the action and makes us want to know what will happen next.

Questions on a passage will normally come in a clear order, with the more straightforward first – those on single words or phrases – and the more complicated at the end. Go through them in the correct order, as this will help you to go from single details to a larger view of the passage. Questions about a single word or image should be answered first, as they help you to look at the passage in detail. Later ones will ask you to draw together readings of many such words – so it makes sense to get the sequence right.

This chapter has looked at most of the kinds of question which might arise, using the passage from *Henry IV* Part 1 as an example and inventing questions of the main types which will come up. In a real exam, you might have four questions, one of which might be of the more complex type we have outlined, demanding a side or so for a full answer. Alternatively, you might find a passage with just two questions, both of the longer sort, which will require answers of about a side and a half each, and so on.

> 66 Set an alarm clock to go off at the end of the time you'd get for the questions in an exam. 99

The best way of preparing for questions like this is to do as many of them as you can, if possible getting someone to comment on them when they are finished. Get hold of past papers and work through them; get your teacher to set questions for you; and set questions for yourself. When you've done them, talk over your answers with someone else – a teacher or fellow-student – to see what else you might have said to improve your answer.

This will not be of much help, though, unless you *know* the texts very thoroughly. So the ways of reading and revising suggested in Chapter 1 are very important here. So, too, are the reading techniques suggested in Chapters 4, 9 and 13 on critical appreciation. Such processes depend on detailed reading, and the more of this that you do the better your exam performance will be.

This chapter ends with some typical exam questions on passages. Try to answer them yourself before looking at the student answers and examiner comments.

Question 1

Hamlet.
O all you host of heaven! O earth! What else?
And shall I couple hell? O fie! Hold, hold, my heart,
And you, my sinews, grow not instant old,
But bear me stiffly up. Remember thee?
Ay, thou poor ghost, whiles memory holds a seat   5
In this distracted globe. Remember thee?
Yea, from the table of my memory
I'll wipe away all trivial fond records,
All saws of books, all forms, all pressures past
That youth and observation copied there,   10
And thy commandment all alone shall live
Within the book and volume of my brain,
Unmixed with baser matter. Yes, by heaven!
O most pernicious woman!
O villain, villain, smiling, damnèd villain!   15
My tables – meet it is I set it down
That one may smile, and smile, and be a villain.
At least I am sure it may be so in Denmark. [*Writes.*]
So, uncle, there you are. Now to my word:
It is "Adieu, adieu, remember me."   20
I have sworn't.

i) Explain briefly why Hamlet responds so passionately in this speech.   *(2)*
ii) Explain 'all pressures past/That youth and observation copied there' (lines 9–10).   *(2)*
iii) Explain what Hamlet is saying and to whom he is speaking in lines 2–6.   *(3)*
iv) How, in this passage, are Hamlet's feelings conveyed?   *(5½)*

Question 2

MARLOWE: *Doctor Faustus*

    Enter Dick.
Dick: What, Robin, you must come away and walk the horses.
Robin: I walk the horses! I scorn't, 'faith, I have other matters in hand; let the horses walk themselves and they will. *[Reading] A per se, a; t, h, e, the; o per se, o; deny orgon, gorgon.* Keep further from me, O thou illiterate and unlearned ostler.   5
Dick: 'Snails, what hast thou got there, a book? Why, thou canst not tell ne'er a word on't.
Robin: That thou shalt see presently. Keep out of the circle, I say, lest I send you into the hostry with a vengeance.
Dick: That's like, 'faith! You had best leave your foolery, for an my master   10
come he'll conjure you, 'faith.
Robin: My master conjure me! I'll tell thee what, an my master come here, I'll clap as fair a pair of horns on's head as e'er thou sawest in thy life.
Dick: Thou needest not do that, for my mistress hath done it.
Robin: Ay, there be of us here that have waded as deep into matters as other   15
men, if they were disposed to talk.
Dick: A plague take you! I thought you did not sneak up and down after her for nothing. But I prithee tell me in good sadness, Robin, is that a conjuring book?
Robin: Do but speak what thou'lt have me to do, and I'll do't. If thou'lt dance   20
naked, put off thy clothes, and I'll conjure thee about presently. Or if thou'lt go but to the tavern with me, I'll give thee white wine, red wine, claret wine, sack, muscadine, malmsey, and whippincrust, hold-belly-hold, and we'll not pay one penny for it.

> *Dick*:   O brave! prithee let's to it presently, for I am as dry as a dog.   25
> *Robin*:   Come, then, let's away.   *Exeunt.*

i) Comment on the language and humour of this passage and on the dramatic effectiveness of the scene within the play as a whole.   (12)

ii) What important concerns of the play are touched on here?   (8)

STUDENT ANSWERS WITH EXAMINER COMMENTS

STUDENT ANSWER TO QUESTION 1

> i) Hamlet responds so passionately because the ghost of his father has just told him that he was murdered by Claudius. In addition, the ghost has said that Gertrude, Claudius' mother, has committed adultery with Claudius.

EXAMINER COMMENT

Note that the answer combines points about the place where the passage comes in the play with the reasons for Hamlet's passion. Notice that TWO points are made – the murder and Gertrude's adultery: giving only one of these would result only in half marks.

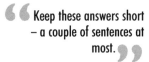
Keep these answers short – a couple of sentences at most.

STUDENT ANSWER

> ii) Here Hamlet is talking of the impressions ('pressures') which he has in his mind from what he has seen in his earlier life.

EXAMINER COMMENT

Note that the answer talks only about the phrase given. It *doesn't* say that he'll erase all these things from his memory – there's no need. Keep to the exact limits of the phrase given unless it's essential to its understanding to give some other information.

STUDENT ANSWER

> iii) In these lines Hamlet is speaking to his own body, asking his heart to 'Hold' – keep beating despite the shock he has just had – and his 'sinews' or muscles to support him and not become 'instant old', or weary and ineffective because of the shock.

EXAMINER COMMENT

Here the need is to explain the *whole* passage, which contains the two points made here. Notice that the answer explains each part of the phrase in turn – a careful, methodical approach is needed to make sure that you miss nothing out.

STUDENT ANSWER

> iv) Hamlet's feelings are conveyed by the cosmic images of the speech. He refers to both 'heaven' and 'hell', showing the enormity of what he has heard. That he is deeply upset is shown by the repetition of key words such as 'villain' (1.15); it is as if he cannot believe what he has just heard. The syntax of Hamlet's expression is often broken, most particularly in the opening lines, which are a series of short exclamations, and this too shows his depth of feeling. The vocabulary echoes this – 'pernicious', and 'damned' show his feelings about Gertrude and Claudius.

" A longer answer – because the question's more complicated. "

EXAMINER COMMENT

This is a full answer which covers the ground well, making a series of points. Notice that the point is made first, and then it is supported by an example or reference to the text – at the start, the 'cosmic' imagery is mentioned and then examples are given. The answer is densely packed with information but not repetitive – the result of going through and listing the key points, giving an example of each, and then writing the answer in simple, clear language.

STUDENT ANSWER TO QUESTION 2

> i) The main source of comedy in this passage lies in the parallel between Robin's attempts at magic and the magical powers which Faustus has obtained through his bargain with Mephistopheles. The way in which his comic mis-reading of magical formulae in lines 3–4 parody Faustus' spells shows this clearly. His threat to clap horns on Faustus is made comic when Dick says 'my mistress hath done it' – Faustus already has horns, the horns of a cuckold or husband of an unfaithful wife. This is comic because it turns Robin's threat of magic into something which is down-to-earth and bawdy.
>
> The dramatic effectiveness of the scene is that it makes us realise how improper it is for Faustus to gain magical powers. Robin's wishes are comically ridiculous, but they remind us of Faustus' desires, and so make them seem ridiculous too. Robin will use his power to get different kinds of wine and play tricks on people, and this makes Faustus' more serious wishes seem ridiculous too. It is an example of how Marlowe interweaves the comic and serious parts of the play to make clear the essential theme – that it is improper for man to wish to go above his natural place by the use of magic.

" Look at the number of marks available. Here, the answer's longer as there are more marks. "

EXAMINER COMMENT

This covers the main ground well and makes good points about the passage and the play. It could be improved by a mention of Robin's reference to the circle – Faustus' magic circle drawn on the ground within which he is standing. This certainly adds to the dramatic effectiveness of the scene – how it works on stage.

Notice the last sentence. This could really be left out, as it covers the ground required in the second question. Overlaps like this will not usually lose you marks – as long as you make the points in BOTH answers and do not omit them in the second. But it is far better to make sure that they don't happen. Do this by reading the questions very carefully and deciding exactly what points each one asks you to make.

STUDENT ANSWER

> ii) The main concern touched on here is that of man's proper place and the sinfulness of trying to go above it. Faustus goes against God's will by seeking for hidden knowledge in his pact with the devil; this is parodied when Robin, a

servant, tries to go above his place by using magical tricks. For Robin it is comic, but the point is still strongly made.

Another concern is the idea of appetite. Faustus' appetites are for learning and sensual fulfilment; Robin's are for wine. Both are discussed by the play in the context of what is proper and improper for man to have.

The passage is a good example of Marlowe's ability to discuss a serious theme even in the comic parts of the play and so give it a considerable unity.

> " Concluding general point sums up and amplifies what's been said so far. "

EXAMINER COMMENT

This answer has three major points, each made in a separate paragraph. Clarity of organisation like this is important and can often earn an extra mark or two. The question asks you to relate the passage to the play's larger concerns – notice how this is done in fairly general terms: there is no detailed summary of *how* Faustus makes his pact with the devil.

CONCLUSION

You'll find more questions of this kind in Chapter 8, on Chaucer, and Chapter 12, on Shakespeare. Read them carefully even if you're not studying the texts that they refer to – they'll still suggest ways of answering questions which will be helpful in the questions on your own texts.

POETRY 1: CRITICAL APPRECIATION TECHNIQUES

GETTING STARTED

Critical appreciation is one of the essential skills of literary study. It is the ability to read a text and understand both what it says and the techniques the writer has used in order to say it.

You may be doing a separate paper on this subject – check with your teacher or your syllabus to make sure. If you are, you'll be given two or three passages – usually one of poetry, one of prose and one from a play. You'll then be asked to discuss them, showing what their main themes and ideas are, and what techniques the writer has used to put them across, perhaps giving your own feelings about them.

Even if you're *not* doing a critical appreciation paper, the skills of critical reading are still important. In fact, they are the basic equipment of literary study: knowing how to read and understand a passage is the essence of the whole subject. So whether or not you're doing a paper of this sort, you need to master these skills.

Looking at *poetry* in this way is particularly important. Poetry often uses language in a much more imaginative, inventive or unorthodox way than prose does. This means not only that the possibilities of the readers getting it wrong are greater – but also that there are more *clues* to what's going on: for example, why one word is used rather than another, why the order of words is reversed, or why a particular rhythm is there.

Many people worry about answering questions on poems they don't know. If you haven't *seen* the poem before, they say, how can you prepare for it? In one sense, of course, you can't – there's certainly no way of telling which poem is going to appear on the paper. But in other ways, you can prepare for the exam by developing certain *techniques* of reading.

You can learn how to:

- read a poem in detail;
- discover who is 'speaking', and what the situation is;
- work out its 'meaning';
- identify particular ways in which language is used – metaphor, simile, imagery;
- recognise how the sound of the words adds to the effect;
- recognise the role of rhythm in creating effect;
- see how the structure of a poem adds to the overall impact;
- think about your own response to the poem;

– and, as important as all of these

- write clearly, concisely and quickly to express all these points.

This chapter gives you help and guidance on these techniques so that you can read and respond to a poem. The next one shows you how to use these techniques in order to write an appreciation of the sort you'll need to produce in the exam. But remember that this is a process which takes time to develop: you need to get lots of practice in reading, discussing and thinking about poems, so make a point of testing and developing what you learn here by using your skills as often as you can.

ESSENTIAL PRINCIPLES

There are several features that you need to look for when you're reading a poem. Some will be more important than others according to the nature of the poem. The features given here obviously won't all appear in every poem – and they certainly aren't given in order of importance. In most poems, several of these features will work together to produce the effect, but, for ease of discussion, they need to be teased out so that you'll be able to recognise them when you see – and hear – them.

MEANING

Even though you may think that poetry works in a very imprecise way, and can be interpreted in different ways by different readers, for the great majority of poems one can still say that there is a clear meaning. Sorting out this meaning is a major priority when tackling appreciation exercises. Some poets will use words for their sounds, or rhythms, or for the general associations they create; but, in most poems, each word will have a *specific meaning* which you need to identify. This *doesn't* mean that you have to write a prose translation of the poem; but it *does* mean that you need to have a very clear idea of the meanings of the words used in the poem before you can begin to write sensibly and clearly about it.

Words can have difficult meanings, for several reasons.

> *Try exploring the history of words with a good dictionary.*

- A poet may deliberately use an unfamiliar word to make the reader think hard.
- A word which is familiar now could have had a quite different meaning in the time when the poet was writing. 'Punk' is an interesting example: to the Elizabethans it meant 'prostitute'; in America earlier this century it was a term of abuse, rather like 'heel'; today it refers to a particular style of dress and type of social attitude amongst teenagers.
- A poem may contain a word which you haven't encountered before.
- A poet may use a word which has a very specific meaning in order to convey a particular area of experience – the tools of a particular trade, for example, or a word in the dialect of a particular region.

Knowing how to deal with such words does not depend on a standard routine, but it is certainly not always easy. Here are some suggestions:

- Do all you can to develop your own vocabulary. Read as widely as you can, and use a dictionary – not a pocket or compact one, but the full Oxford English Dictionary. This will give you a whole range of different meanings for a word, and show you how they have changed down the years.

> *Don't assume that words always only mean what a dictionary says they do.*

- Try to tease out a meaning by its *context*. You may not be able to get it completely right, but you can probably have a good stab at it. Think, for example, about the last word in the first line of this passage:

> Turning and turning in the widening gyre
> The falcon cannot hear the falconer

There is no reason why you should know the word 'gyre', which Yeats uses to mean a whirling circular motion; but you could perhaps work out that it means motion of some sort and, if you've ever seen a falconer control a falcon, might know that the bird often flies in a circle around its master.

In most cases this mixture of research and intuition will be successful. In an exam it's very unlikely that you'll be able to use a dictionary. A very difficult or uncommon word may be explained in a footnote – so make sure that you look to see if there *are* any notes of this kind. If there aren't, do the best you can from the context, using your common sense to tell you whether your reading is roughly accurate.

ALLUSION

Some unfamiliar words occur because the poet is making an *allusion* – a reference to someone or something which brings in a series of associations which extend the meaning of the poem and enrich its significance.

> Apollo hunted Daphne so,
> Only that she might laurel grow;
> And Pan did after Syrinx speed,
> Not as a nymph, but for a reed.

Some poets make a lot of allusions, others none at all.

These lines, from 'The Garden' by Andrew Marvell, refer to two pursuits from classical mythology. Apollo 'hunted Daphne' who, to avoid being raped, turned into a laurel; Syrinx, when pursued by Pan, was changed to a reed. These are allusions which someone with a classical education – like that which Marvell's original readers would have had – would recognise.

What is more important, though, is what the allusions *achieve*: why does Marvell use them? Here, the answer is to make a witty comment on the attractiveness of the garden. The Greek gods pursued the nymphs not for sexual gratification, Marvell suggests, but simply so that they would turn into plants. The pleasure of a garden, then, is wittily said to be greater than that of love, and Marvell has used the allusion to a strikingly original comic end.

In an exam, it's unlikely that you'd be given a poem to write about which has allusions as complex as these. If you are given such a poem, the allusions will probably be identified in a note. What matters, though, is not simply *identifying* the allusions – rather, as with changes of grammar and syntax, you must *say what they are used for*, and what they *contribute* to the poem as a whole.

The best way to prepare for allusions and references is to read as widely as you can, trying to extend your knowledge into all kinds of areas. Don't worry if you come across something that you don't recognise in the exam: think hard, and try to find an explanation which fits with the context and tone of the rest of the poem.

DICTION AND TONE

Try rewriting poems in different kinds of diction.

'Diction' refers simply to the *kind of language* that a poem uses. Many modern poems, for example, use words which you would overhear in everyday conversation. Those from an earlier period might be much more formal; a sixteenth-century poem might use language influenced by a translation of the Bible into English; whereas an eighteenth-century one might use a diction full of references to Classical gods and heroes. Some poems might use a *specialist diction*, perhaps referring to a particular trade or way of life, to the language spoken in one part of the country, or in order to capture the character of a speaker through the words he or she uses. Being aware of a poem's diction plays an important part in deriving a full appreciation, because it tells you about the poet's attitude to the subject.

Related to this is the question of *tone*. This really means the tone of *voice* in which the poem is written. Is it, for example, tender, gentle, angry, vigorous, comic, self-mocking, or none of these? The best way to approach tone is to read the poem carefully and try to *hear* it. Then try to think of a way to describe it. There will be no single 'right answer' for this, so it's up to you to choose an adjective which fits the tone well. Be aware, too, that the tone of a poem might change quite a lot during its course, just as there may be two or more 'speakers'. Thomas Hardy's 'The Ruined Maid', for example, is a dialogue between two women; Edward Thomas' 'As the team's head brass', a conversation between an observer and a farmer.

Don't assume that the poet is always speaking.

SITUATION AND SPEAKER

Many poems take place within a particular *situation*. Although you should not spend a long time exploring this – you will end up giving a paraphrase of the poem – you should try to understand what the situation is and be able to express it briefly in your answer.

Sometimes you will be able to do this from an early line or lines, as in this poem by Hardy:

> I leant upon a coppice gate
> When frost was spectre-grey

where we learn straight away that the speaker is talking about an occasion in winter where he is leaning against the gate of a small clearing in a wood.

In other poems, you will need to piece together the situation by looking closely at details. Look closely for signs which will tell you:

- who is speaking;
- who is being spoken to;

- how many people are speaking – the poem may well be a conversation between two or more 'voices', which you can tell apart because they use different diction and tone;
- where and when this is happening;
- any information about what has happened before which we need to know.

Of course, not all poems contain a situation of this sort. Many are more meditative, the poet thinking aloud about ideas or feelings;

> Even such is Time, that takes in trust
> Our youth, our joys, our all we have,
> And pays us but with earth and dust

or

> Well then; I now do plainly see,
> This busy world and I shall ne'er agree;

GRAMMAR AND SYNTAX

> If you're uncertain about grammar, it might be worthwhile reading a book about it.

Grammar and syntax are rules of writing – the first is about parts of speech, using the right form of a verb, and other 'rules' of language; the second is about getting words in the right order. You might think that these two rules have nothing to do with the freer elements of writing that you associate with poetry. In a way you'd be right – poets and other writers often break the rules to create a particular effect. But the rules are important when you come to read a poem – because they help you to work out exactly what the poem is saying.

When you're reading a poem for the first time, it helps to make sure that you know what each word is doing, and you can do this by thinking about its *grammatical role*. Is it a verb, a noun or an adjective? Is it the subject or object of the sentence? These are questions which can be very useful in sorting out what's going on in a poem at a very basic level, especially when you're just finding your way around it.

Sometimes this can work at a straightforward level.

> The sparrow's chirrup on the roof
> The slow clock ticking, and the sound
> Which to the wooing wind aloof
> The poplar made, did all confound
> Her sense;

Here the poet is using several different effects of sound, rhythm and imaginative language; but we will not get far in grasping any of them until we know how the lines work in a simple grammatical way. Looking at it *grammatically*, we can separate the elements like this;

The sparrow's chirrup on the roof	*Subject 1*
The slow clock ticking, and the sound	*Subject 2*
Which to the wooing wind aloof	*Subject 3*
The poplar made, did all confound	*Verb*
Her sense;	*Object*

We know, then, that these three sounds all worked to 'confound her sense'. Now that we know this, we can think about how they did it, what sort of sounds they were, and how the poet uses them to create atmosphere and other effects as part of the whole poem from which this excerpt comes. But unless we appreciate this simple structural form, a deeper reading is very difficult.

In this example, the poet has used a conventional order of words – subject, verb, object. But sometimes a poet can change the order and, unless you can work this out quickly, you can get the meaning quite wrong.

Here's an example.

> A cold coming we had of it,
> Just the worst time of the year
> For a journey, and such a journey

> Meanings change if you read the grammar wrongly.

At first reading this can be confusing, but thinking about grammar helps us to disentangle the first line:

- 'We' is the subject;
- 'had' is the verb;
- 'a cold coming' is the object

– so, in everyday language, what the poem is saying is 'We had a cold coming – it was cold when we came'.

This sorts out the meaning of the first line, but it doesn't tell you much more. You need to ask *why* the poet has written it in such a way – why has he turned round, or inverted, the usual word order or syntax? The answer is simple – to make 'cold' the most striking word in the line by putting it at the start.

Changing the order of words, so that more emphasis is given to a word which is particularly important, is a technique which poets can use to create an effect. It's not something that happens all the time, of course, and it's not the only way to give emphasis – but it's one of several techniques which are available for a poet to use. A knowledge of syntax and grammar will therefore help you to recognise this, when you see it.

Notice that it is important not only to explain the effect of a particular technique: but also to explain *why* it is used. This is a key principle in critical appreciation: don't just write about what the poet has done, but go on to say *why*, and *what it adds to the poem's effect*.

So: a knowledge of the basic principles of syntax and grammar will help you to sort out the basic meaning of a poem, and can sometimes allow you to recognise a particular effect and understand why it is being used.

FIGURATIVE LANGUAGE

> Figurative language is often more straightforward than you think.

This is the term used for language which describes one thing in terms of another – the kind of comparison which is frequent in poetry of all kinds. As with the other features we've discussed so far, your aim should be:

- first, to identify such use of language;
- then to say what it achieves – how it adds to the poem as a whole.

Figurative language can be divided into various kinds.

Simile

Similes are the simplest kind, because the comparison is made quite openly. The poet will say, for example

> My love is like a red, red rose

This establishes the likeness in a very straightforward manner, and it's hard to miss something like this in a poem. But you still need to point out the effect of the *comparison*. *Why* is she like a rose? Because she is red-faced and has a thorny disposition? Presumably it is something more positive than that; but unless you make clear wherein the similarity lies, the examiner will not be sure that you have grasped the full effect of the language.

Metaphor

This is a comparison which is stated *by implication* – there is no particular word of comparison – 'like' or 'as' for example – to reveal a metaphor. Here, for example, is John Donne using the idea of a woman as the true Church – Christ's 'Spouse' or bride:

> Show me, dear Christ, thy Spouse, so bright and clear.
> What! Is it She, which on the other shore
> Goes richly painted? or which rob'd and tore
> Laments and mourns in Germany and here?

> First identify; then explain.

Here, Donne is asking whether the true church is the Catholic church of Rome – 'which on the other shore [continental Europe] Goes richly painted', a reference to the richly coloured statues of saints used by the Catholic Church. Or is the true church the 'rob'd and tore' figure lamenting in Germany and Britain – the Protestant church with its much starker rituals?

Once again, identifying the metaphor is not enough; you have to explain the effect. In Donne's poem, the metaphor is very striking because it makes the Church like a person, and helps Donne attach to a religious poem something of the passion of a love poem – a drawing together of different areas of experience which is very powerful.

The best metaphors work in exactly this way. They link things together which most people would never think of linking, and so offer us a startling new insight. Your writing about metaphor should always aim to make clear *what* this insight is, and the impact it makes on you, the reader.

Image

This is a word which is often used to describe an especially complex metaphor, one which may well involve comparison of the thing being described to a whole series of related other things. Most particularly, image can be used to refer to a whole series of metaphors which describe one thing repeatedly in terms of another. In such a sense, critics often talk of 'chains of imagery' or 'recurrent images'. Here, for example, is the opening of a Shakespeare sonnet which uses an image of this sort:

> That time of year thou mayst in me behold
> When yellow leaves, or none, or few, do hang
> Upon those boughs which shake against the cold,
> Bare ruin'd choirs, where once the sweet birds sang.

> 66 Don't confuse 'image' with 'imagination'. 99

Here, the speaker is bringing together a whole series of parallels to the 'time of year' he is going through – his age. He mentions tree boughs almost devoid of leaves, those few that remain being yellow with age, and the boughs shaking in winter's cold. He then moves on to refer to ruined 'choirs', parts of a church or abbey, which continue the idea of age and desolation.

As before, you need both to *identify* the way an image works – by saying what it is that the writer is comparing the subject with – and to *comment on its effect*. Here, for instance, the effect is greatly to reinforce the idea of age by the stress on exposure and ruin: this is no rich old age, but rather a time of bleakness.

Personification

This is a very particular kind of metaphor in which an object, most frequently a part of the natural world, is addressed as a person. Philip Sidney, for example, begins a sonnet with these lines:

> With how sad steps, O moon, thou climbst the skies
> How silently, and with how wan a face.

> 66 WHY is it important? 99

As before, you need to say what the effect of such a technique is. You will usually need to read the whole of a poem before you can do this. In Sidney's poem, for example, the use of the technique – to ask if the moon is in love, because she moves slowly and looks sad and pale – only becomes apparent later on. It's a witty and unusual use of the technique of personification which, in less able hands, can become conventional and rather dull.

Symbol

This is rather like a metaphor for which we can't easily find an exact meaning. For example, when W. B. Yeats writes

> Surely thine hour has come, thy great wind blows,
> Far off, most secret, and inviolate Rose,

we cannot identify exactly what it is that he is discussing. In a similar way, the symbols used by William Blake in his poems generally defy complete explanation, although they are very precise in their context. The symbols of 'the invisible worm' and the rose in the poem 'The Sick Rose', for instance, stand for corruption and purity, experience and innocence, evil and good – large, general qualities which cannot be precisely 'translated', but which are clear enough to *feel* on reading the poem.

> 66 Often the most effective symbols are those you can't fully explain . . . 99

If you are confronted by a poem which seems to use language in this way, you should be aware of the *range* of possible meanings, and also of the fact that the symbol cannot be expressed fully in any other way. A sentence like this would be an acceptable response:

> Although the exact significance of 'Rose' cannot be made clear, it seems that Yeats here is referring to a time of great beauty and spiritual perfection which he hopes is about to dawn.

SOUND

Language doesn't only communicate through meaning: it conveys a lot of things through *sound*. Try reading these lines aloud:

> The moan of doves in immemorial elms
> And murmuring of innumerable bees

> Only the stuttering rifles' rapid rattle
> Can patter out their hasty orisons
>
> How a lush-kept, plush-capped sloe
> Will, mouthed to flesh-burst,
> Gush!

The first sounds like the slow, drowsy moaning and humming of bees and doves which it speaks of; the second captures the staccato rattle of gunfire in its harsh 't' sound; the third conveys a sense of great richness in the 'sh' sounds, to give an impression of great sensuality.

All of these are achieved by using the sounds of words to reinforce their meanings. Not all poems will use this technique; many make no effort to recreate sound in this way. But you should be alive to the possibility that a poem will work in this way; when it does you should note the fact and explain the effect of the sound when you write about it.

Rhythm

Rhythm – the alternation of quick and slow sounds or 'beats' in a line – can be just as important as sound in conveying an impression or meaning. But there's no point in just going through and marking stresses on some syllables, or talking about lines in terms of 'feet' of 'spondees', 'dactyls' and so on – so if you haven't heard of these terms, don't worry at all about them! Here are some examples of *how* rhythm is used in poetry to create effect.

> “ Rhythm often works with sound, meaning and association to create an effect. ”

> Stitch – stitch – stitch,
>   In poverty, hunger, and dirt
> Sewing at once, with a double thread,
>   A Shroud as well as a Shirt
>
> The plunging limbers over the shattered track
> Racketed with their rusty freight
>
> Listen! You hear the grating roar
> Of pebbles which the waves draw back, and fling,
> At their return, up the high strand,
> Begin, and cease, and then again begin,
> With tremulous cadence slow

The first of these examples stresses in its rhythm the repetitive and exhausting nature of the work of a seamstress sewing a shirt; the second presents the uncontrolled lunging of a wagon on uneven ground; the third recreates very subtly the rhythmic patterns of waves moving forward and back on a shore.

As is the case with sounds, rhythms are not always used in a poem to suggest or recreate a mood or movement, but they are another technique which you should be aware of. You can then both identify the rhythms and write about their effect and contribution to the poem, if you are working on a poem in which they are important.

Rhyme

> “ Don't spend long describing rhyme schemes. Explain their effect. ”

People often think that *rhyme* is much more important than it is. Many examiners are frustrated to find long explanations of a poem's rhyme scheme which have nothing to say about what the rhyme adds to a poem's overall effect. There is no point in simply saying 'This poem rhymes abab cfcd efef gg'.

The only time when you need to talk about rhyme is when it contributes to what a poem is saying in some way. This may be:

- to give formality to a structure – in the 'Shirt' poem quoted above, for instance, where it adds to the monotonous regularity of the action;
- to draw together words which we would not usually think of as being related, by rhyming one with another to make a point of this sort.

If a poem uses rhyme, but only as a structural principle, by all means mention this in your answer, but don't spend longer than a sentence or two on it: if, however, rhyme is really an important part of the poem's effect, then by all means spend longer in explaining just what it adds to the poem.

STRUCTURE

Look through an anthology to find examples of different uses of structures like these.

Many poems make their effects in part by their *structure*. This could be:

- by having a refrain or repeated line at the end of each stanza, in order to convey a sense of order;
- by subtly changing the refrain in the last stanza, to show a departure from a pattern;
- by having a pattern which in some way reinforces the meaning of the poem – perhaps changing from order to disorder to mirror such a change in a dramatic situation, for example, or changing in just the opposite way to show a sudden resolution.

Once again, you should look out for these things. They will not *always* be there but, when they are, comment on them and say why they are important in the poem's overall effect.

Conclusion

Very few poems will use all of these devices, but most will use one or more to get across their ideas and feelings. And, of course, they don't use them in isolation: poems make their effect through complex combinations of all the things mentioned here, and also through the nature of the ideas and feelings they are concerned with.

How to go about putting together the aspects we've discussed in this chapter in order to show how they contribute to the poem's idea, impression or significance, is the subject of the next chapter. But before you go on to that, look closely at the passages and comments below. They are designed to show you how to write on *particular aspects* of poems, such as those discussed in this chapter – a kind of intermediate stage before you go on to write about complete poems.

PRACTICE QUESTIONS

Each of the following passages contains one or more of the features discussed in this chapter. Write about the features and how they contribute to the passages' overall effect.

1   Straight mine eye hath caught new pleasures
Whilst the landscape round it measures

2   And Paris be it or Helen dying,
Who dies soever, dies with pain.

3   From the moist meadow to the wither'd hill,
Led by the breeze, the vivid verdure runs,
And swells, and deepens

4   With blackest moss the flower-plots
    Were thickly crusted, one and all:

5   I have had playmates, I have had companions
In my days of childhood, in my joyful schooldays;
All, all are gone, the old familiar faces

I have been laughing, I have been carousing,
Drinking late, sitting late, with my bosom cronies;
All, all are gone, the old familiar faces.

6   With B.E.F. June 10. Dear Wife,
(O blast this pencil. 'Ere, Bill, lend's a knife.)
I'm in the pink at present, dear.
I think the war will end this year.
We don't see much of them square-'eaded 'Uns.
We're out of harm's way, not bad fed.
I'm longing for a taste of your old buns.

7   I struck the board, and cried, No more.
        I will abroad.
      What? Shall I ever sigh and pine?
    My lines and life are free; free as the road,
        Loose as the wind, as large as store.

8   Woman much missed, how you call to me, call to me
        Saying that now you were not as you were
      When you had changed from the one who was all to me,
        But as at first, when our day was fair.

*   *   *

Thus I; faltering forward,
Leaves around me falling,
Wind oozing thin through the thorn from norward,
And the woman calling

STUDENT ANSWERS WITH EXAMINER COMMENTS

STUDENT ANSWER TO QUESTION 1

This line makes use of an inversion of syntax in that the usual word order is reversed, so that 'straight' comes at the start of the line. This word, meaning 'straightaway' or 'immediately', is thus given more emphasis than it would receive in its usual place.

> **If you don't know the formal words, don't worry – just use more straightforward ones. 'The word order is reversed' would be fine here.**

EXAMINER COMMENT

This is true – a good point. But you need also to say that the second line contains an inversion too. 'It measures' would normally come before 'the landscape'. This change has the effect of putting 'the landscape' in the more important place as the first important word of the line. You could also have mentioned that rhyme performs no special function here, except to give balance and structure to the passage, as it often does in eighteenth-century poetry.

STUDENT ANSWER TO QUESTION 2

This passage makes use of an allusion to Paris and Helen. It says that, even if it is someone as important as they are, whoever it is who dies still suffers pain. The allusion here is used to show that death is painful for everyone, even the great.

> **True – but WHY is this important? What does it add to the poem?**

EXAMINER COMMENT

You have the main point here – this is certainly how the allusion works. You might have said a little more about Paris and Helen, though. Paris was the warrior who carried off Helen, wife of Menelaus, to cause the Trojan war; more important, both were of great physical beauty, so the fact that even they suffer pain at death shows that death is indeed powerful over even the most perfect humans.

Although the answer is incomplete, it shows what can be done by intelligent guesswork when you have to deal with an allusion; it's always worth trying to write in a general way to get across what you think is the point of the reference.

STUDENT ANSWER TO QUESTION 3

This is a piece of grammatical inversion. The subject of the sentence is 'the vivid verdure', which runs, swells and deepens, 'led by the breeze', 'From the moist meadow to the wither'd hill'.

EXAMINER COMMENT

True; but you don't say *why* this is done. It throws more stress on the 'moist meadow' and 'wither'd hill' – two places very different in nature, which emphasises again the distance between them. It also emphasises 'the vivid verdure' by delaying it to nearly the end of the passage, and allows the energy of the movement to be stressed by the flow of 'runs, and swells, and deepens'. Perhaps you could have mentioned the alliteration of 'vivid verdure' – the use of two words each beginning with the same consonant. But this does little except to add to the fluency of the phrase – it isn't the mysterious and important device that very many A-level candidates think!

STUDENT ANSWER TO QUESTION 4

Here, the sounds of the words create an impression of thickness and fullness. The 'ck' sound occurs in both lines, and is echoed in 'crusted'; 'flower-plots' is another word which sounds very rich. Overall the feeling of a garden encrusted and overgrown, as if neglected and still, is created by the sounds here.

EXAMINER COMMENT

An excellent answer – note the very detailed reference to the sounds of the words, and the way that this is *used* to show what it adds to the lines' effect.

STUDENT ANSWER TO QUESTION 5

What about the mood, though?

These two stanzas use a very simple, everyday diction – 'playmates'; 'companions'; 'childhood'; 'schooldays'. The refrain 'All, all are gone, the old familiar faces' creates a tone of sadness and melancholy, which increase with its repetition.

EXAMINER COMMENT

This could say more about the effect of the diction *in combination* with the melancholy of the refrain. The sadness is increased by the use of simple language – it's as if the speaker is a very simple, straightforward person who is bewildered by the loss of his companions. In the whole poem, the effect is much greater, as the refrain appears in each of seven stanzas.

STUDENT ANSWER TO QUESTION 6

Don't be afraid to give your own responses – if you think this is patronising, then say so!

Here the situation is of a soldier writing a letter to his wife from the front line. The first line makes this clear. The diction is an imitation of the language of an ordinary soldier, simple and direct, but saying very little about what is going on and trying to reassure his wife – shown in the general relaxed, almost humorous tone and the claim 'We don't see much of them square-'eaded 'Uns'. In line two, the soldier breaks off to talk to a comrade, asking to borrow a knife with which to sharpen a pencil.

EXAMINER COMMENT

This gets the situation, speaker and tone right. But it could go a little further – what's the effect of all this? I find it really quite moving; here is a man who seems unused to writing letters, writing something which is really a collection of clichés ('I'm in the pink at present') to give reassurance to his wife while he is away fighting. To me this reinforces the idea of the dislocation and suffering caused by war for people who have little or no control over their lives. It's quite appropriate to make a personal response like this in a critical appreciation essay, and the next chapter will say a little more about how you might choose to do it.

STUDENT ANSWER TO QUESTION 7

This is a situation of rebellion, where the speaker makes clear his feelings in a very forthright way. The verbs in the first two lines show this – 'struck' and 'cried', as do the short, decisive sentences of the first three lines. By contrast, the last two lines are much more fluent, showing the freedom he feels now that he has made his rebellion.

EXAMINER COMMENT

A sound, clear statement of how the poem's diction works here. You might have added that the poem's structure, especially the very short second line, reinforces the directness of meaning.

STUDENT ANSWER TO QUESTION 8

> Good on how various elements come together to make the effect here.

In this poem, the speaker is talking in a meditative tone to a 'woman much missed', presumably someone he has known and loved in the past. The lines move slowly, and the sound and rhythm combine to give the end of the first line a feeling of dying away, both in the long sounds of 'call to me' and in the repetition of these three words. That the words rhyme with 'all to me' in the third line is unexpected, and also continues the sense of sadness and loss created by sound and rhythm.

The second stanza has a completely different rhythm. From the rather gentle melancholy or wistfulness of the earlier one, it moves to a rhythm which is stumbling and clumsy, helped by the awkward 'f' sounds in 'faltering forward' and the thin vowel sounds of 'oozing' and 'thin'. That the wind comes from the north and through a 'thorn' – something which is spiky and unsympathetic, and not capable of offering protection – adds to this bleakness. The rhyme of 'falling' and 'calling' reminds us that he still hears, in his imagination, the voice of the lost woman, and it echoes again the way in which the rhymes in the first stanza die out towards the end.

EXAMINER COMMENT

Certainly the main point here is the contrast caused by the last stanza – it's a combination of the use of rhythm and the poem's structure. In the actual poem there are two more stanzas, like the first, before the last one, so the contrast is even more marked. The rhyme in the first stanza is what is known as a 'feminine' ending – the rhyme is on the first syllable of three, with the last two the same in both lines, giving it a weaker sound and the effect of gradually dying away which makes it so much more poignant.

POETRY 2: CRITICAL APPRECIATION IN PRACTICE

GETTING STARTED

Finding individual examples of the use of sound, rhythm, metaphor and all the other techniques mentioned in the last chapter is an essential stage in reading and appreciating poetry. But how do you take this a stage further, to gain an overall grasp of a whole poem? And, once you have that, how do you write about it?

Making the move from spotting and analysing individual features of a poem to writing a coherent, overall appreciation of it is the subject of this chapter. It's particularly relevant to the critical appreciation paper in the exam, but it's also important for many other parts of your study. What it has to say will help you:

- to read, understand and enjoy poetry texts you're studying for other papers;
- to answer questions on set texts of poetry which give you a passage of poetry as an example, and ask you to use it as the basis of general comments about the poet or the anthology studied.

This chapter begins by looking at how you read a poem, by studying each individual part to develop an awareness of how each 'moment' fits into the whole text. Secondly, it looks at how you should consider and develop your own response to the poem – what you think and feel about it. It then gives some advice about how to write about poems in the critical appreciation paper, with plenty of examples for you to work on.

Sometimes, appreciation questions ask you to compare two poems on a related theme. A section of this chapter looks at how to approach such questions, and how to make sure that you really *compare* the two texts rather than discussing first one and then the other.

ESSENTIAL PRINCIPLES

Whenever you're confronted with something to write about in an exam, there's a temptation to feel that you're not *working* unless you're *writing*. But when you are tackling a critical appreciation question nothing is further from the truth. The *real* work is done when you are reading and thinking about the poem or other text, so that, when you come to write, you know what you are going to say and can relax and concentrate only on *expressing* your ideas – not on *finding* them. Ideally, you should spend at least half of the available time in reading and thinking about the text, jotting down notes and planning out ideas, and only the second half in actually writing.

What do you *do* during this reading, thinking and note-making time? For much of it you will be looking for and trying to understand the various *devices* we've looked at in the last chapter. But it may help if you divide the reading process into several clear stages.

1 First reading

When you read through the poem for the first time, try to do so fairly quickly and smoothly, at a regular pace so that you can begin to feel the rhythm and general movement it has. Don't worry about particular details – words, allusions or metaphors that you can't understand at once. Instead, go for an overall idea.

While you are doing this, try very hard *not* to form any firm impressions about what the poem is concerned with, or what it says. At the same time, try very hard to read what is *actually there* and not what you *think* is there. If you misread something the very first time you read it, you will probably continue this misreading and never realise the mistake – a point recognised by perceptual psychologists as a major obstacle in learning. So: read carefully, but keep an open mind as to the text's overall significance.

2 Read it aloud

This isn't something that you can do in the exam, of course – but you can do it while practising. Having the poet's words in your mouth is the best way of getting to know them – their feel and movement as well as their 'meaning'. By doing this you will:

- feel the rhythm of the piece and know which words are given stresses to bring out their importance;
- understand whether the rhythm is being used to create an effect or reinforce a meaning;
- hear the sounds of the words and tell if it reinforces their meaning;
- sense the tone of the speaker's 'voice' and judge how it fits in with the poem's significance.

Although you can't actually read the poem aloud in the exam, you can still go through the motions of reading it – actually shape the words with your mouth so that you *feel* what it's like to read. This may sound crazy and be embarrassing at first, but you'll soon get used to it; you'll also realise that it does help you form an awareness of the poem in the ways listed above. But while you're doing this you should still try to keep an open mind about what the poem says – resist the temptation to come to conclusions about what it's concerned with too soon.

3 Read in detail

This is the stage where most of the work is done. Once you've read the poem to yourself and aloud, you need to go through it more slowly. Try to break the poem into *sections*. Each one could be:

- a stanza;
- a sentence within a stanza;
- a single line containing a complex use of language;
- a paragraph within a poem in one long stanza.

It doesn't matter how you divide the poem, as long as each part *is a complete unit of thought and expression* – don't, for example, stop at the end of a stanza if the sense goes on to the next one, or start at the beginning of a line if a new sentence has started at the end of the line before.

The most important thing to do here is to *ask questions* about every stage of the poem. Here are some that will be useful:

- First – and most important – *questions about uses of language* which strike you as important.
  - Why are they there?
  - What do they do?
  - How do they make their effect?
  - Why do I respond to them as I do?

> ❝ Don't forget that your response is important – so start with the parts you find interesting. ❞

Then, when you've thought about these points, try some more down-to-earth approaches:

- *Questions on meaning*
  Is this meant literally – just what it says – or is it a metaphor of some kind?
  Does this word mean what I think it does, or is there another meaning I've missed?

- *Questions on structure*
  Why is the poem arranged into lines or stanzas in the way it is?
  What does the sound contribute to the line I'm reading?
  What does the rhythm add?

- *Questions on grammar*
  What's the main verb of this sentence?
  Which is the subject and which is the object?
  Is this an inversion of syntax?

Asking questions like these will help you to *recognise* features like those discussed in the last chapter; gradually you will assemble a series of clues as to what the poem is concerned with and how it works.

FORM A WORKING HYPOTHESIS

> ❝ Be willing to change your mind as you read the poem through again. ❞

From what you've read of the poem, you'll be able at this stage to work out a hypothesis – a rough idea of your interpretation of it. This will cover:

- an idea of the poem's *subject* – the point that it is making, the situation it records, the idea that it advances, or any combination of these or other significances;

- an idea of the *techniques* it uses to get its message across;

- an idea of your own response to it.

I've described this as a *working hypothesis* because, once you have a rough idea about these two aspects of the poem, you should always be *reviewing* and *modifying* your overall idea in the light of the answers you get to your questions about individual passages of the poem. Don't reach a final interpretation of the poem too soon – always be prepared to change it in the light of what you're reading.

As you go through this process, you'll find that your hypothesis gradually becomes clearer, and you arrive at a final interpretation of the poem. It may help to think of the reading process in the way suggested by Fig. 5.1: the interpretation gradually develops in the centre as you try to bring together ideas and their expression, individual passages and of course the whole poem.

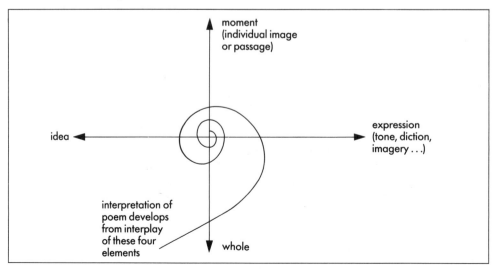

Fig. 5.1 Developing an interpretation

YOUR RESPONSE

Writing an appreciation isn't just a matter of saying what the poem is about and how it works. It's also about making clear your *response* – your own feelings and thoughts about the poem. This is an important part of the process, although it clearly shouldn't overwhelm the essay. A long, gushing statement of how much you like the poem and how moving you find it will not achieve a very good grade; instead you should *demonstrate* those qualities in the poem which you admire or find effective.

By all means make comments on your response while you are talking about *particular features* – you might, for example, say that you find an image particularly effective because it looks at a topic in a new way, or is unexpectedly witty about it. At the end of the essay, write a brief paragraph which draws together your response to the poem. In it, say:

- what features of the poem you like or don't like;
- why you respond as you do.

In doing this, be sure that your response rests on features of the poem itself, not on quite unrelated, personal, factors. Do *not*, for example, say:

I like this poem because it is about horses, and I am very fond of horses.

Instead, say;

I like this poem because it offers a new way of seeing the relationship between the human and the animal world, showing how arrogant people are in controlling animals in the ironic tone it adopts.

> Don't get too carried away with your own feelings – the exam isn't the place for a manifesto!

You don't, of course, have to *like* the poem. If you dislike it, though, you have to give clear and specific reasons. Just saying that you don't like this sort of poem, or that it's 'too analytical', won't achieve very much. Try to pinpoint a failure in the poem's ideas, or an image which does not work because it is too complicated: if you do this directly and state your feelings honestly, your response may well improve the grade you receive for the essay.

WRITING THE ANSWER

> There's no set way of writing an appreciation – as long as you don't just rewrite the poem in prose.

Make notes

Making notes about the poem can be an invaluable help in sorting out your own feelings and thoughts on the poem. Work towards a plan of your final essay – use the techniques discussed in Chapters 1 and 2. Think of key points you want to make about the poem, and go back through it to find evidence and examples from the text to support them. There are two main ways to arrange an essay of this sort. You can structure it according to a series of points – eight or ten features which you consider to be the most important aspects of the poem, arranged in the best logical order, and supported by appropriate quotation or reference.

Alternatively, you can go through the poem from beginning to end, pointing out important aspects such as ideas or features of expression as you do so.

In practice, the best way is often a combination of the two. You might organise your answer like this:

a) short statement of the poem's main ideas and techniques – a paragraph should be enough;
b) body of essay working through the poem, showing how the ideas are developed and expressed, noting changes of tone, diction, development of situation, and growth of argument as appropriate to the individual text, supported by quotation and reference;
c) concluding statement giving your response, based on specific features of the poem.

Your plan should outline your approach, making clear the points and the order in which you make them. When you come to write the essay, you will only have to think about expressing yourself clearly, as the ideas will already be there for you in your plan.

THE FINAL ESSAY

An essay in a critical appreciation paper should follow the same approaches and principles as an essay in any other paper, which were discussed fully in Chapters 1 and 2. But there are some additional points.

- *Don't paraphrase.* Your task is to explain what the poem is about and how it makes its effect, not to paraphrase it in prose. Give a short account of the poem's situation and its main concerns, but don't just write down all that happens: analysis and comment are needed instead.

Point first – then evidence.

- *Identify then explain.* When you are talking about an important feature of the poem, make sure that you follow the pattern suggested in Chapter 4. First identify the feature – say what it is and where it occurs, by line number or brief quotation. Then say what it contributes to the poem's overall effect.

- *Support your points.* By all means begin a paragraph or section with a clear statement of a point, or an assertion about the poem's concerns or techniques. When you do this, though, you must go on to explain where you see it and how it functions in the poem – otherwise it will be just an unsupported assertion, lacking the detailed evidence and analytical argument you need to do the job properly.

- *Quotations.* Keep them short – there's no point in copying out the poem that's in front of you. Refer to specific individual words or short phrases, but when you mention longer passages use line numbers, which will normally be given in the paper.

- *Style.* Keep the style simple, straightforward and clear. Don't go in for pretentious-sounding words or phrases – just say what you mean in a direct fashion, following the advice given in Chapter 2.

PRACTICE QUESTIONS

How does this work in practice? The following are four examples of poems you might well encounter in an appreciation exam, along with essays you might write about them. Write your own critical appreciations of the poems before reading the answers and comments on them – and remember, you don't have to agree with the views expressed here, as long as you support your own ideas by close reference to the poems.

POEM 1

From the drawing-room window
Of my aunt's flat,
you could see lit up at night
the Houses of Parliament,
St Paul's in the distance,
not to mention any number
of City churches.

At the back,
from the scullery,
there was a sheer drop
of 200 feet to an enclosed
well. Here the dustbins
were kept.

My aunt never spoke
of this side of her life,
and was always careful
not to go too near the railing,
lest she become giddy
and fall on hard times.

(Robin Maunsell: 'Two Views')

POEM 2

I am – yet what I am, none cares or knows;
    My friends forsake me like a memory lost; –
I am the self-consumer of my woes; –
    They rise and vanish in oblivion's host,
Like shadows in love's frenzied stifled throes: –
And yet I am, and live – like vapours tost

Into the nothingness of scorn and noise, –
    Into the living sea of waking dreams,
Where there is neither sense of life or joys,
    But the vast shipwreck of my life's esteems;
Even the dearest, that I love the best
Are strange – nay, rather stranger than the rest.

I long for scenes, where man hath never trod
    A place where woman never smiled or wept
There to abide with my Creator, God;
    And sleep as I in childhood, sweetly slept,
Untroubling, and untroubled where I lie,
The grass below – above the vaulted sky.   (John Clare: 'I am')

POEM 3

The apes yawn and adore their fleas in the sun.
The parrots shriek as if they were on fire, or strut
Like cheap tarts to attract the stroller with the nut.
Fatigued with indolence, tiger and lion

Lie still as the sun. The boa-constrictor's coil
Is a fossil. Cage after cage seems empty, or
Stinks of sleepers from the breathing straw.
It might be painted on a nursery wall.

But who runs like the rest past these arrives
At a cage where the crowd stands, stares, mesmerized,
As a child at a dream, at a jaguar hurrying enraged
Through prison darkness after the drills of his eyes

On a short fierce fuse. Not in boredom –
The eye satisfied to be blind in fire,
By the bang of blood in the brain deaf the ear –
He spins from the bars, but there's no cage to him

More than to the visionary his cell:
His stride is wilderness of freedom:
The world rolls under the long thrust of his heel.
Over the cage floor the horizons come.   (Ted Hughes: 'The Jaguar')

POEM 4

I

Hot through Troy's ruin Menelaus broke
    To Priam's palace, sword in hand, to sate
    On that adulterous whore a ten years' hate
And a king's honour. Through red death, and smoke,
And cries, and then by quieter ways he strode,
    Till the still innermost chamber fronted him.
    He swung his sword, and crashed into the dim
Luxurious bower, flaming like a god.

High sat white Helen, lonely and serene.
    He had not remembered that she was so fair,
And that her neck curved down in such a way;
And he felt tired. He flung the sword away,
    And kissed her feet, and knelt before her there,
The perfect Knight before the perfect Queen.

II

So far the poet. How should be behold
    That journey home, the long connubial years?
    He does not tell you how white Helen bears
Child on legitimate child, becomes a scold,
Haggard with virtue. Menelaus bold
    Waxed garrulous, and sacked a hundred Troys
    'Twixt noon and supper. And her golden voice
Got shrill as he grew deafer. And both were old.

Often he wonders why on earth he went
    Troyward, or why poor Paris ever came.
Oft she weeps, gummy-eyed and impotent;
    Her dry shanks twitch at Paris' mumbled name.
So Menelaus nagged; and Helen cried;
And Paris slept on by Scamander side.

(Rupert Brooke: 'Menelaus and Helen')

Note Helen deserted her husband Menelaus to go with her lover Paris to Troy, an action which began the Trojan Wars. Later she returned to Menelaus. Paris was buried beside the River Scamander in Troy.

STUDENT ANSWERS WITH EXAMINER COMMENTS

STUDENT ANSWER TO POEM 1

> **A very good opening summary of how the poem makes its effect.**

This poem is a very skilful mixture of literal and metaphorical. On the surface, the 'two views' of the title are the views to be seen from the front and the back of the speaker's 'aunt's flat'; but on another level they are two views of her life, one public, attractive and carefully organised, the other concealed, with a suggestion of dirt and decay, and presented as something to be avoided and perhaps even feared.

The first stanza is a description of the view 'From the drawing-room window'. The reference to 'drawing-room' suggests that the aunt is a member of the prosperous middle classes, since this is a term used only by people of such a social group. The list of buildings conveys an idea of something metropolitan and sophisticated, because they are all in London, but also something carefully ordered, because they are all very formal architectural structures. Sophistication is echoed in the fact that these are 'lit up at night', suggesting an urbanity to balance the formal nature of the buildings. The language is straightforward, as if the speaker is slowly thinking about the view rather than having a conversation about it.

> **'Stanza' is a formal word for 'verse'.**

The second stanza presents us with the other 'view', the division of the poem into two sections further stressing the difference between them. Straightaway the diction alters; instead of the sophisticated 'From the drawing-room' we have the much bleaker 'At the back', and this use of more down-to-earth words continues with 'scullery' and reaches a climax with the mention of 'dustbins'. This is a very strong contrast with the broad, open view of the first stanza: from the drawing room we look out across London to some of its finest buildings, whereas from the back we look down, seeing only dustbins in 'an enclosed well'. The depth of the well — 200 feet — emphasises the difference still further, and the fact that it is 'a sheer drop' almost introduces an element of fear into the poem which is very different from the confidence of the first stanza.

> **Notice the way that single words and short phrases are quoted — a good way of staying close to the text when making a point.**

The final three lines are important in suggesting that the poem is expressing something about the speaker's aunt in metaphorical, as well as literal terms. That the aunt 'never spoke/Of this side of her life' suggests that it is something rather furtive and improper, to be kept concealed behind a sophisticated façade. There is no open statement of this, but the impression is continued and made much stronger in the final line. The strength of this line lies in its taking a common expression and giving it a new force by taking it literally, 'To fall on hard times' usually means to encounter difficulties of a financial or other nature in one's life. Here, however, the fall is real, as the 'aunt' fears falling into the well. The well and the dustbins thus become an image of her fears of the collapse of the ordered world of her 'drawing-room', and the poet uses the proverbial expression to startling effect in making this clear.

> **Good explanation of how the literal and the metaphorical are combined.**

I like this poem because of its simple and direct diction, and the way in which the poet carefully controls the movement towards a conclusion which is very striking in using a common expression which has both its usual meaning and a strikingly original, literal meaning.

EXAMINER COMMENT

This is a very good answer which makes all the most important points about the poem. Notice that it begins by briefly suggesting the main points to be made later, then moves to a more detailed reading of the poem as it unfolds, and ends with a statement of personal response. Quotation is used sparingly, the words and phrases quoted being incorporated into the text of the answer, and care is taken not to paraphrase or simply describe what the poem has to say, the emphasis instead being on analysing and explaining its effects. An answer like this would gain a very high mark in an exam.

STUDENT ANSWER TO POEM 2

The speaker in this poem is considering himself and his isolation from those around him, to such an extent that he seems to be suffering from an extreme state of exhaustion and despair. The sense of rejection continues throughout the poem but, in the final stanza, is tempered by a longing to find peace and rest in the natural world, far away from human company.

The poem opens with striking directness, the assertion 'I am' being offset against the equally strong claim that 'none cares or knows' what he is. The stanza goes on to an image of the poet as something which has ceased to exist – 'a memory lost' – yet the way that the friends 'forsake' or abandon him is balanced by the way that his 'woes' do not. The speaker is left to 'consume' his woes himself, as they 'rise and vanish like oblivion's host', or like shadows when confronted by the frenzy of love, comparisons which show a great degree of anguish and desperation in the poet.

> Some good teasing out of the poem here – though the image could be read differently.

The last line of the first stanza stresses that, despite this despair, the poet still lives on. A series of images makes clear his sense of emptiness and desolation. The poet compares himself to 'vapours' 'tost into the nothingness of scorn and noise', a very intense vision of negation. 'Vapours' suggests smoke or fumes, in themselves insubstantial, and that they are 'tost' – thrown headlong – into 'scorn and noise' which are themselves described as a 'nothingness' adds further to this idea of the poet's existence in a complete void. This is enhanced by the next line's reference to a 'living sea', which is unreal because made of 'waking dreams', and the seafaring image is continued in the reference to the 'shipwreck' of his hopes. The despair continues in the claim that even those to whom he is closest are 'strange' – 'nay, rather stranger' – so that there seems no hope either of human contact or of the return of self-esteem.

The final stanza is a series of images of scenes for which the poet longs, which are simple and specific in contrast to the empty vastness of those of the second stanza. The poet wants to be somewhere untouched by human grief and simply to be close to 'my Creator, God'. He longs also for the sweet sleep of childhood, contrasting with the 'waking dream' of the second stanza. This he can find only in the open air, away from mankind and close to the natural world.

This is a poem of great intensity of feeling, which uses complex images to express a state of despair and abandonment. Although at the end there is a yearning for peace, there seems little hope that this will be attained. I find this poem very powerful in its intensity, but it is not a poem with which I feel comfortable, since its images and lack of movement towards any sense of hope or resolution are very disturbing.

> It's quite acceptable to say you feel uncomfortable with the poem.

EXAMINER COMMENT

This is not an easy poem. It needs careful thought to work out how the images work, and to write about it with clarity takes much preparation. In places, too, it is hard to decide the exact significance of the images. In the first stanza, for example, 'they' (line 4) could refer to 'my friends' or 'my woes' – you have to make up your own mind and make a case for the reading you prefer, as in this treatment.

Notice that, at the end, the response is one of admiration for the poem's complexity yet without a sense of enjoyment or liking. This is a perfectly valid reaction to a poem of this sort, which is indeed a disturbing evocation of the terrible isolation felt by someone suffering from mental illness.

STUDENT ANSWER TO POEM 3

This poem moves from an account of the stillness of many of the animals in a zoo to the intense energy and power of the jaguar stalking in his cage. It uses this as an expression of the immense power of natural forces which cannot be contained by physical restrictions.

The first stanza has several images of stillness, beginning with an action which suggests tiredness – the apes 'yawning'. The word 'adore' is used to show how they gently stroke their fur to catch fleas, in a caressing gesture which is very relaxed – it is as if they are so tired that removing fleas is something as gentle and unthreatening as stroking a loved one. The parrots, in contrast, are described in terms which suggest heat and – they 'shriek' as if 'on fire'. The comparison to 'cheap tarts' – prostitutes – is suitable because of their very bright colours, suggestion of clumsiness and excessive make-up, and is continued in the bawdy pun on 'nut'.

The laziness continues in the account of the tiger and lion who are 'fatigued with indolence' – worn out through having done nothing. The boa-constrictor is metaphorically seen as a fossil both because a fossil is still, being frozen in time, and because some fossils are coiled shapes which look like the snake sleeping. The remaining lines of the second stanza draw together these images of stillness by saying that many other cages 'seem empty' – presumably because the occupants are so still – or betrays its occupation only by the smell of animals sleeping buried in straw. Here the poet's skill in compression is shown, 'the breathing straw' expressing this very compactly. The final line, likening the scene to a frieze on 'a nursery wall', draws the visual impression together by suggesting a series of separate pictures to correspond with the series of animals in their cages.

By contrast, the third stanza moves much more quickly. Whereas the second has a full stop in the middle of the first line and another in the second, slowing the movement of the words to match the stillness being described, the third is one long sentence which does not end until the first line of the fourth stanza. We are also told about movement – of someone who 'runs', not walks, past these cages. Although the crowd at the jaguar's cage is 'mesmerised', there is still a sense of energy here, conveyed by the force of the animal's movement. The diction here is full of energy: 'hurrying'; 'enraged'; 'drills' and, most energetic of all, 'short fierce fuse'.

The fourth stanza moves us into the world of the jaguar, to show that he is not contained or restricted by the cage. The third line, with its pounding rhythm and repeated b sounds, suggests the vigour of his pacing: the comparison in the opening of the last stanza, suggesting that the jaguar is no more restricted than is a visionary or hermit by his 'cell', makes clear the intellectual energy of the jaguar to balance its physical force. In its mind, the last lines assert, the jaguar is controlling the world, and can see new horizons as it paces its cage.

This is a poem which works very well in moving from an atmosphere of stillness to one of intense energy and movement. The jaguar is portrayed as a natural force which cannot be restrained, and is compared to a human prophet in this. As well as being a literal account of the zoo, it may also be an expression of the boundless power of the natural world. I find it very striking in its control of pace and movement, and also in its expression of energy, although I am not sure whether the comparison with 'the visionary in his cell' really succeeds in expressing the power of nature, since instead it could be taken as seeing the jaguar solely in human terms, which somehow diminishes the strength and vigour of the animal.

> This focuses well on an important detail of the poem and then relates it to the whole.

> Some good comparison here, bringing the two parts together to show their differences.

> Rather weak expression here.

EXAMINER COMMENT

This account goes through the poem explaining how it uses a range of effects to make its point. There is so much in this poem that any essay would probably not be able to include it all – for example, this one has said nothing on the way the poet uses a very free structure, based on a loose four-line stanza, and varies the rhyme scheme to accord with the poem's meaning, 'strut' for example rhyming with 'nut' in the first stanza to give added force to the rude joke.

Notice too the reservation expressed in the response at the end. It is stated clearly and openly and full reasons are given, and so it is quite acceptable in an exam answer. Here, as with any poem set for this kind of analysis, it is for you to reach your own decision: do you think the final comparison works, or does it in some way diminish the energy and power of the jaguar?

STUDENT ANSWER TO POEM 4

> In this poem, the writer is thinking about the contrast between a time of intense passion and activity in the lives of two mythical figures and their old age. Yet he is also concerned with another issue; the way in which a poet concentrates on such intense moments, and ignores the longer reality of the lives of the two figures in their advancing age, when they are no longer vigorous, romantic or attractive.
>
> The poem begins in a very vigorous style to describe Menelaus bursting into 'Priam's palace' to take back his wife, who is described very forthrightly as 'that adulterous whore' because of her desertion with Paris. The vigour is continued in the references to 'red death', 'smoke' and 'cries'. The pace slows, however, as the king arrives at the 'innermost chamber', although he is still described as 'flaming like a god'. The figure of Helen is described with greater gentleness to convey her serene beauty — something the poet prepares us for in the reference to 'the dim/luxurious bower', in which Menelaus is made to seem out of place as he 'crashed' into it.
>
> Helen's 'serene' beauty is shown not only in the actual words used to describe her, but also in the tone; the movement is far slower, the language much gentler here, and this is accentuated by the effect of Helen on Menelaus; 'he felt tired'. The pause caused by the full stop after these words is an important turning point, where he changes from an angry god into a subordinate lover, kissing her feet and kneeling before her.
>
> The poem now changes subject, as is made clear by the line 'So far the poet', in which the writer moves back from what has been said so far, rather like an actor stepping out of character to address the audience directly. He asks how the writer should treat the rest of the story — the life together after the events recorded by mythology. The rest of the poem is concerned to record this by using language which stresses its dull, unexciting nature. Helen's passion gives way to having children, the use of 'legitimate' making this appear boringly legal and proper after the romantic excitement of her affair with Paris. The phrase 'haggard with virtue' has a similar effect. The effects of age on Menelaus are similarly unpleasant; he re-lives the battle by talking to people about it, and instead of being 'bold' is 'garrulous', dealing in words, not actions. The effects of age become worse towards the end of the stanza; she is shrill, he deaf. The final truth is stated in a short, bald sentence which is a depressing contrast to the dynamism of the two in the poem's first part: 'And both were old'.
>
> The second stanza enhances the effects of age: Menelaus wonders why he went to win Helen back, or why Paris stole her away. We are given a picture of Helen in old age which is an appalling contrast to her early beauty; she is 'gummy-eyed and impotent', and at the mention of her former lover 'Her dry' — again the stress on age — 'shanks twitch'. The two are reduced to nagging and weeping while Paris 'sleeps' in death, suggesting that he has come out of the affair best of all.
>
> I like the way in which this poem attempts to show the reality behind a myth, to explore events often left out by a poet. It contains language which is very energetic as well as much which is unpleasant in its description of old age, and it offers a new way of seeing the story of the Trojan wars.

> ❝ What does 'romantic' mean here? Be careful of words like this, which can have many shades of meaning. ❞

> ❝ Good point to show how rhythm is used in the poem. ❞

> ❝ Notice the structure of this sentence. It makes the point, and then lets the poet make it again in his own words: good. ❞

EXAMINER COMMENT

This account covers most aspects of the poem, and certainly grasps its main point about the passing of youthly vigour and the way in which poets seize on the most vigorous, attractive parts of a story while ignoring the less appealing. There are points which it leaves out: it does not, for example, say that the poem's two parts show a desire to present the two views as balancing each other, almost as if to ask which of the two is the true story. It also uses the word 'romantic' twice in a way which is perhaps rather imprecise, and it could say more on the way in which the second part moves in a slow, awkward rhythm to reflect the age of the main figures. Once again, though, it is a complicated poem, and it would be very difficult to include all of these aspects in an account written in the limited time of the exam.

COMPARING POEMS

Appreciation papers quite often ask you to *compare* two poems on a similar theme. Although this may at first sight seem to involve twice the work, it is often actually more straightforward – especially if the poems are very different in style or in the way in which they approach the topic, since each one can help to clarify the other.

There are many ways in which writing a comparison is similar to writing about one poem. For example, you need to read both poems in the way suggested earlier in this chapter, and the general points about planning and writing your answer also hold good. But there are some important new points to be aware of.

> " Always discuss both poems at once. "

Compare features while reading

Instead of spending a lot of time on one poem and then moving on to the next, try to move rapidly from one to the other. Read the first one and then go to the second; while you are asking questions about the first, think about how you'd answer them with reference to the second. Keep glancing from one to the other – in this way you'll find that not only will you notice features of each one, but the *differences* will help to clarify your interpretation of both as individual poems.

While you're doing this, remember the various categories in which differences might occur, in

- meaning,
- figurative language – metaphor, for example,
- rhythm,
- sound,
- grammar and syntax,
- structure,
- the overall impact it has on you.

Think, too, about the attitude that each poem has to its subject. The two will be similar in some ways, but will contain differences in meaning and approach – so try to define these while you are developing your working hypothesis.

Your response

You may or may not be asked directly for your own response. If you are, it will be just as important in a comparison as when you are writing about a single poem. Here you will need to say which of the two poems you prefer, and *why*. As before, your opinions should be supported by *reasons* – the poems' techniques, structures or the ways in which they approach their subject.

Planning your answer

Structure your plan so that you *compare* the poems – bring them together to show similarities and differences, perhaps like this:

> " Try to use structures which make you bring the poems together. "

POEM A	POEM B
Has regular rhythm	Irregular rhythm following flow of action
Uses very formal diction	Uses freer, conversational diction
Classical allusions	No allusions

Making a *table* like this can be very helpful – you may not use all the points that you record, but the discipline of writing notes like this can help to get your mind working to reveal the points of likeness and difference between the two poems. Your response, too, can be added to the plan, so that you are aware of every point you will make in the essay *before* you come to write it.

Writing your answer

Make sure that you bring the poems together, and do not discuss first one and then the other. The best way of doing this is by using sentence structures which bring the two together, like these:

The first poem makes a very personal statement, whereas the second is far more objective . . .

In place of the first poem's rich natural imagery, the second uses a more detached descriptive style . . .

The first poem lacks the urgent tone of the second . . .

Both poems treat the subject with considerable restraint . . .

Keeping this technique in mind will certainly help you to achieve the aim of the question and genuinely compare the texts: make a point of using similar structures when you are writing to make sure that the comparisons you have made when reading and planning receive proper expression.

PRACTICE QUESTIONS

1   Write a comparative study of the following poems, covering matters such as subject, style and form. You are not obliged to say which you prefer, but you may do so if you wish.

A

The Owl

Downhill I came, hungry, and yet not starved;
Cold, yet had heat within me that was proof
Against the North wind; tired, yet so that rest
Had seemed the sweetest thing under a roof.

Then at the inn I had food, fire, and rest,
Knowing how hungry, cold, and tired was I.
All of the night was quite barred out except
An owl's cry, a most melancholy cry

Shaken out long and clear upon the hill,
No merry note, nor cause of merriment,
But one telling me plain what I escaped
And others could not, that night, as in I went.

And salted was my food, and my repose,
Salted and sobered, too, by the bird's voice
Speaking for all who lay under the stars,
Soldiers and poor, unable to rejoice.

Edward Thomas

B

Up-Hill

Does the road wind up-hill all the way?
    Yes, to the very end.
Will the day's journey take the whole long day?
    From morn to night, my friend.

But is there for the night a resting-place?
    A roof for when the slow dark hours begin.
May not the darkness hide it from my face?
    You cannot miss that inn.

Shall I meet other wayfarers at night?
    Those who have gone before.
Then must I knock, or call when just in sight?
    They will not keep you standing at that door.

Shall I find comfort, travel-sore and weak?
    Of labour you shall find the sum.
Will there be beds for me and all who seek?
    Yea, beds for all who come.

Christina Rossetti

2   Write a comparative study of the following two poems, making clear the differences and similarities of style and approach to their subject.

A

London

I wander thro' each charter'd street,
Near where the charter'd Thames does flow,
And mark in every face I meet
Marks of weakness, marks of woe.

In every cry of every Man
In every Infant's cry of fear,
In every voice, in every ban,
The mind-forg'd manacles I hear,

How the Chimney-sweeper's cry
Every black'ning Church appalls;
And the hapless Soldier's sigh
Runs in blood down Palace walls.

But most thro' midnight streets I hear
How the youthful Harlot's curse
Blasts the new born Infant's tear,
And blights with plagues the Marriage hearse.

William Blake

B

Upon Westminster Bridge,
Sept. 3, 1802

Earth has not anything to show more fair:
   Dull would he be of soul who could pass by
   A sight so touching in its majesty:
This City now doth like a garment wear

The beauty of the morning: silent, bare,
   Ships, towers, domes, theatres, and temples lie
   Open unto the fields, and to the sky,
All bright and glittering in the smokeless air.

Never did sun more beautifully steep
   In his first splendour valley, rock, or hill;
Ne'er saw I, never felt, a calm so deep!

   The river glideth at his own sweet will:
Dear God! the very houses seem asleep;
   And all that mighty heart is lying still!

William Wordsworth

STUDENT ANSWERS WITH EXAMINER COMMENTS

STUDENT ANSWER TO QUESTION 1

> **A major difference –
> metaphoric as opposed to literal
> writing.**

Both these poems take as their theme the idea of a journey towards rest and recovery, but treat it in different ways. The journey in the first poem is a real one which has been undertaken by the speaker, whereas that in the second is a metaphor for life. The poems also have differences in structure, the first being presented as a personal narrative, the second as a series of questions.

   The first poem begins with a statement of direct involvement – 'Downhill I came' – and continues with further aspects of the narrator's feeling; 'cold' and 'tired', although he is warm enough to resist the wind, and still able to appreciate the prospect of rest. By contrast, the second poem is concerned with a journey which will happen in the future, with no immediate personal involvement, instead of one that has happened recently to the speaker. Instead of the first poem's feelings, the second poem has physical descriptions about the nature of the journey, expressed in a pair of questions and answers.

> **Look at the different sentence-structures in this paragraph, all of which genuinely COMPARE the two poems.**

There is also a difference in tone and diction between the poems. The first is reflective, as if the speaker is thinking about the implications of his journey; the second is a dialogue between two people, one asking straightforward, factual questions, the other giving reassuring answers. Certainly we learn far less of the emotional state of the second poem's two speakers than we do of the first poem's single one; the 'heat within me that was proof/Against the north wind' suggests a spiritual quality which seems lacking in the second.

The two poems share the idea of rest after a journey in the second stanza. Again, though, the expression is very different, the first poem allowing us to experience the 'inn' through carefully-selected details, with 'food, fire and rest' balancing and curing the speaker's sense of being 'hungry, cold and tired'. Instead, the second poem talks in general terms about 'a resting-place' and protection against the 'slow dark hours'. Instead of this very general idea of night, the first poem has a very powerful image which suggests the exposure and openness of darkness, in the cry of the owl, the melancholy of which – and its saddening effect on the speaker – is made clear by the end of the second stanza and the beginning of the third.

> **A little thin here – more could be said about the two poems. But you have to select points in this kind of exercise. There isn't room to say it all.**

It is the owl's cry which tells the speaker in the first poem 'what I escaped/And others could not'. There is no equivalent sense, in the second poem, of the way in which the speaker alone has shelter while others do not. Instead, there is an idea that the traveller will meet others 'who have gone before'. At this point it becomes clear that the second poem is concerned with the journey through life to heaven, in place of the more literal earthly journey of the first poem – something made clearer in the last stanza which makes clear that no one will be excluded and there will be 'beds for all who come'.

The end of the first poem is not concerned with such a large-scale idea of rest: instead, the speaker's sense of rest is 'Salted and sobered' – made more poignant and serious – by the knowledge that others are out in the cold, 'unable to rejoice'. This gives the first poem a quality of compassion and immediacy which I feel that the second poem lacks, even though it conveys the idea of a firm faith that the journey of life ends with rest in heaven.

> **Precise details are often more effective than general statements about mood.**

Of the two, I prefer the first poem. Although it is about a single, real journey, it moves to a sense of disquiet mixed with gratitude that the speaker has rest while others do not, whereas the feeling in the second poem of a simple faith is altogether too straightforward. Similarly, I find the imagery much more precise in the first than in the second: the reference to the owl's cry is a much more striking way of suggesting the night than the second poem's 'slow dark hours'.

EXAMINER COMMENTS

This study makes clear the essential differences of tone, situation, speaker and structure of the two poems, and also makes clear a preference for one over the other. It could perhaps include a little more detail in discussing the later stanzas of the two poems, but overall it gets across the essential differences and likenesses by comparing the poems – talking about both together rather than looking first at one and then at the other.

STUDENT ANSWER TO QUESTION 2

> **Very good opening point on difference of mood . . .**

These two poems both take a vision of London as their theme, but they treat it in different ways and reach widely different conclusions about the nature of the city. Where the first stresses the negative aspects of the town, the second adopts an almost ecstatic view of its beauty; where the first considers the nature of the people in the city, the second sees it entirely as a visual spectacle as the sun shines over it in the early morning.

> **. . . matched by an equally strong one on the poems' viewpoints.**

A major difference is apparent right at the start of the poems. The first begins 'I wander thro' each charter'd street', showing that the speaker is moving through the city and experiencing it at first hand — an involvement which continues throughout the poem. By contrast, the writer of the second poem is seeing the city from a distance — the title reveals that he is seeing it from 'Upon Westminster Bridge', and is thus cut off from its streets and the people in them. The tone of the second poem is ecstatic and serene, talking about the 'majesty' of the sight and saying that 'Dull would he be of soul' who could 'pass by' so moving a sight. The first poem is much more immediate, telling us where the poet is walking, and stressing the personal experience of seeing the 'weakness' and 'woe' in the faces of the people he meets. Where the second is distant and ecstatic, then, the first is immediate and has a tone of anger.

This anger continues in the second stanza, where the word 'every' is used four times to show the universal presence of the 'mind-forg'd manacles' — a reference to restrictions of their own creation which the Londoners suffer. By contrast, the second four lines of the second poem continue to describe the city in impersonal terms as an object of beauty, listing its features in the second line to show how all are 'bright and glittering in the smokeless air'. Despite the great difference in tone and content, however, there is a similarity in techniques: both these sections make a list of separate elements and then, in the final line, draw them together with a general statement.

The first poem continues in its statement of outrage about the conditions of the Londoners, referring in specific detail to chimney-sweeps and soldiers, whereas the second poem moves on to say that the open countryside never looked as beautiful as the city. Once again, the difference is clear, the second poem regarding the city as an aesthetic object which is the cause of an almost spiritual experience, whereas the first sees in it corruption and exploitation. The second poem reaches a climax at the end with a series of personifications of parts of the city: the river glides 'at his own sweet will', the houses 'seem asleep' and the 'mighty heart is lying still'. The city is thus seen as some kind of organism which is as yet dormant. No such serenity is present in the first poem, which is concerned in the final stanza with how the 'Harlot's curse' blights marriage and the family — presumably a reference to prostitution and its destructive effects in the city. Thus whereas the second poem ends with an image of humanised peace and beauty in the city, the first ends with one of infection and corruption.

Of the two poems, I find the first much more powerful, making as it does a strong statement about the corruption and exploitation of the city and how it is the poor who suffer most as a result. The second poem conveys a vision of the city of much beauty, but the poet's isolation from the people of the city and the ills they suffer is always apparent, being implicit within his position 'Upon Westminster Bridge'.

> " A common technique in poems — look out for it. "

> " Be honest — don't say what you think the examiner wants you to say. "

EXAMINER COMMENT

This study deals with the major point well — the difference in aim and viewpoint. It does leave out some important points, though. The word 'charter'd' in the first poem, stressing the city's incorporation for the purpose of commerce, is not mentioned, so we lose an important further contrast — that the first poem is protesting at the ethic of the city which puts money before people whereas this note is quite lacking in the second.

Nor does the answer mention the difference in diction, the first poem being much simpler and more down-to-earth, while the second is concerned with a mystical experience in seeing the city. 'Fair', 'soul', 'touching' and 'majesty' all show this, and there are many other examples elsewhere in the poem.

Once again, though, remember that you can't be expected to get everything into an essay written in the limited time of an exam. If you read the poems carefully and make clear the main points of difference and similarity between the given texts, that will be more than enough to earn you a good grade.

CHAPTER

POETRY 3: STUDYING COLLECTIONS OF POETRY

APPRAISING A COLLECTION

READING INDIVIDUAL POEMS

GROUPING THE POEMS

SELECTING REPRESENTATIVE POEMS

READING PERIOD ANTHOLOGIES

WRITING ABOUT POETRY

GETTING STARTED

When you are studying a text which is a collection of poems, either by one poet or by several from the same period, there are special difficulties to be met and special techniques to be mastered.

The basis of the process is, of course, critical reading. This helps you to understand individual poems. But how do you get beyond a careful grasp of one poem, and progress to an understanding of the *whole collection*? How do the themes and ideas come together, and how do you get to know the poet's techniques and approaches? If you're studying an anthology, how do you gain an overall view of a group of poems which may be widely different?

When you have solved these problems, you need to know how to write about poems. How do you know which ones to select as examples? How do you quote from poems in an essay? And how do you organise your points about a collection of pieces of writing which may each be very different from the others?

These are the problems fundamental to studying poetry which this chapter addresses. It gives advice on:

- reading individual poems in a collection;
- knowing how to group poems;
- bringing together your work to give a view of the collection;
- sorting out important themes;
- sorting out important techniques;
- selecting poems for detailed reference to the exam;
- dealing with anthologies from different periods;
- separating the 'background' of the poet's life and times from the 'foreground' – the text which is the principal focus of study;
- writing about poetry collections – getting to know how to see them as a whole, and which poems to refer to in essays.

Reading and studying a collection of poems is a demanding, as well as a fulfilling, task. Yet, because it depends on a close knowledge of individual texts, it builds on the foundations laid in your study of separate poems for critical appreciation. This chapter aims to help you make the difficult transition in literary studies from a close reading of a short text to a larger awareness of a complete volume.

In doing this, it leads on to the next chapter, which shows you how the process of writing about poetry collections works in practice. Chapter 7 also covers some of the important themes in the more commonly set poets and anthologies.

ESSENTIAL PRINCIPLES

Before you get down to careful study of individual poems, it's worth just having a quick look at the collection as a whole. For most people, the hardest thing at A-level is moving from close study of one short passage to a knowledge of a whole book – so it's worth going quickly through the collection to see if there's anything that will help you to make this move.

" Use these steps to get a quick idea of a poetry collection. "

- Look at the contents page. Are the poems arranged in any particular way? They could, for example:
  - be grouped under periods;
  - be arranged in themes;
  - consist of various sequences of poems, which could be regarded almost as separate texts in their own right.

- Glance at the introduction to see if particular ideas are suggested. This doesn't mean that you should read the introduction before you read the poems: instead, it means that you should look quickly to see if there are any hints about how the poems might be grouped together according to subject or theme.

" Make a quick first reading. "

When you've done this, you may have some idea about how the collection is put together. Now try to glance quickly through the poems, reading some quickly to yourself to get a very rapid, general idea of subject and treatment. Don't worry at this stage if you don't understand a great deal – later reading will put that right. Instead, just try to gain an overall idea of the main topics, attitudes and structures used by the poet or poets.

This will give you a few ideas to think about while reading the poems in more detail. But don't make up your mind too firmly about anything yet – such as the poet's main preoccupations or the themes about which he or she writes. Keep an open mind, as you would while developing a working hypothesis about a poem or other text in the earlier stages of critical reading.

The essence of studying a collection of poetry is close, detailed reading and analysis of each individual poem. This should be your main goal after you've glanced quickly through the collection in the manner suggested above. The process of *reading* should follow all the stages described in detail in Chapter 1, and you should look out for all the features mentioned in Chapter 4.

" Read each poem using the advice in Chapters 1, 4 and 5. "

This can be rather a daunting experience at first, but with practice it gets easier. Once you gain a little experience of critical reading, and of critical appreciation, you should soon become more confident about (genuinely) engaging with a poem. And remember, once you do become familiar with the work of a poet, it's often easier to read more of his or her poems – though don't assume that he or she will always discuss the same themes or take the same attitudes.

How should you approach this initial reading? There are various ways:

" Ways of reading. "

- *In class.* This is the most straightforward way – you go through a poem in detail, discussing it with the help of a teacher or lecturer, and arrive at conclusions about what it says and how it says it.

- *In groups with other students.* Properly organised, sessions where you read and try to analyse a poem with other students can be very valuable. You need to take them seriously, though, and to make sure that everyone takes part in the discussion. It might be a good idea to appoint someone as a chairperson. The duties may involve reading the poem aloud at the start, making sure that everyone has a chance to contribute to the discussion, summarising the main points you all arrive at, and reading the poem again at the end. This last reading will help to put the poem back together after you've taken it apart for analysis.

- *On your own.* This is often the hardest method to use when you're reading a collection for the first time, but it's something you should try. Reading on your own will help you develop the skills of critical reading, so important for the appreciation paper; it will also help you to remember the points you find of importance in the poem, since something you find out for yourself is always far more memorable than something someone else tells you.

TAKE NOTES

Once you've read the poem critically, you need to take notes about it. You can do this on file paper, or on record cards. If you do this for every poem that you read, you'll have a set of notes which will amount to a critical commentary on the collection. This can be used in a variety of ways, as later parts of this chapter will show.

In your notes you'll need to cover briefly these points:

- *Theme*. What is the poem about? What conclusion, if any, does the poet reach about the topic?
- *Speaker*. Who is speaking in the poem? Is it the voice of the poet, or is he or she adopting a dramatic role?
- *Situation*. Does the poem take place within a particular setting? What has happened before the poem, in terms of events or circumstances, that we need to understand while reading?
- *Attitude*. Does the poet show any attitude to what he or she is describing? If so, how can it be defined? Positive, negative, despairing, cynical, optimistic?
- *Form*. What poetic devices does the poet use, and how do they enhance the poem's effect? If a particular image is used, what does it add to the poem's significance? Does rhyme, rhythm or the larger structure of the poem have any part to play in the poem's effect?
- *Lines to remember*. Note down any lines which are especially memorable, or characteristic of the poet in terms of their ideas or their expression.

For most poems, this can be done in a few lines – far less than it took to describe the process above. The example in Fig. 6.1 shows the kind of notes you might have made after a note-taking session like this.

While you are working through the volume of poems, you should be building up a collection of sets of such notes. Writing them on small record-cards has the advantage that you can read them easily to refresh your memory of individual poems. This will also help you at the next stage – where you arrange them in different orders, grouping the poems together in different ways.

'Mariana'

1 M. is waiting for her lover, in a deserted, decaying house.

2 Narrator speaks to set scene, with refrain spoken by M. herself.

3 No reason given for scene or events; instead poem concentrates on creating desolate atmosphere through description of house and its surroundings.

4 Narrator seems sympathetic, in creating setting to reflect M's loneliness.

5 Makes effect through v. rich, full sounds;
'with blackest moss the flower-plots
were thickly crusted, one and all'

6 Recurrent refrain stresses the <u>stillness</u> — M. is not ever, it seems, to leave the house.

She said, 'I am aweary, aweary,
I would that I were dead!'
NB repetition emphasises boredom and stillness.

Fig. 6.1 Notes on an individual poem

GROUPING THE POEMS

Each poem in a collection or anthology exists as a complete work in its own right. But when you are studying a *collection*, it helps to group poems together, since this allows you to see the volume as a whole, as more than a gathering of separate texts.

When you have completed notes on several poems, start thinking about what they have in common, in any of the aspects mentioned above. Once you've looked at all the poems, of course, you'll be in a better position to group them together – but thinking about *shared features* and contrasts even while you are still reading each one critically in detail, will help you in two ways:

1 It may reveal aspects of the individual poem you're currently reading;
2 It will help you to be more aware of those poems which do, or do not, share common features.

> **Think of different ways to group the poems.**

There are usually several different ways in which the poems in a collection can be grouped together. Think in particular about:

Subject. Do several of the poems discuss the same theme – for example, a particular aspect of love, the idea of suffering, old age, humankind's relationship with the natural world?

Attitude. Does the poet's attitude remain the same in several poems, or does it develop? Are there similarities in outlook in poems which have different themes?

Style. Often the poems in a collection will have similarities in the way they are written. These might be the characteristic features of the poet's style in a collection by one writer; or similarities of style in a particular period of poetry; or ways in which a series of different styles may be seen in a period anthology. Under the heading of 'style' come all features of the expression of poetry – its form, tone, diction, imagery and structure.

Other striking features. Don't restrict your grouping to these areas. If any other aspects strike you repeatedly in the poems, then think about grouping them under that particular heading.

The way to approach the grouping of poems is simply to think about an aspect or feature which you have *seen* several times in the various poems. You can then list the poems which share it under a clear, descriptive heading. This should give you a series of themes or features, each with a number of poems beneath it.

> **Don't assume that your grouping is the only one.**

When you are thinking of themes or features, remember any points that have been made in class about the main features and themes of the poet's work. The introduction to the edition you're using may have some suggestions to make, too. Use these as a way of getting ideas – think for yourself, but be willing to take suggestions from other sources. Try brainstorming, too – sitting down and just making a list of as many characteristic features as you can (see Fig. 6.2). You'll be surprised how many you can find in just a few minutes.

Now take each feature and list the poems which demonstrate it. This will give you a sheet like the one in Fig. 6.3.

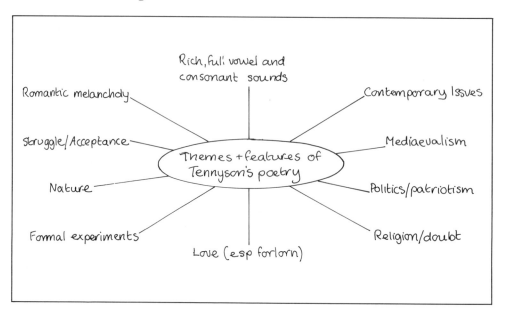

Fig. 6.2 Themes and features of Tennyson's poetry

Features of Tennyson's poetry

1 Rich vowel and consonant sounds
   'Mariana'
   'Claribel'
   'The splendour falls ...'
   'Ulysses' (ending)
   In Memoriam ('Ring out wild bells')

2 Formal experiments
   'Locksley Hall'
   'The Two Voices'
   In Memoriam
   'Maud'
   'Rizpah'
   'Vastness'

3 Mediaevalism
   'Lady of Shalott'
   'Passing of Arthur'

4 Religion and Doubt
   In Memoriam
   'St. Simeon Stylites'

5 Contemporary Issues
   'Passing of Arthur'
   'Locksley Hall'
   'D. of Wellington'
   'Charge of Light Brigade'

Fig. 6.3 Listing Tennyson's poems under particular features

You can now go on to develop this into *more detailed notes* on each feature. Try to keep each set to a single sheet of paper for ease of reference. Each sheet will contain two main elements:

Look at these notes regularly.

1 a description of the feature, attitude or subject;
2 a series of examples from various poems, each of which will:
   – briefly describe the feature;
   – quote a line or lines to show it in practice;
   – explain what is important about the way in which this poem treats the subject or uses the structural device.

When you have done this, you will have a series of single sheets of detailed notes, each on a *particular aspect or feature* of the poet's work (Fig. 6.4).

Struggle versus resignation in Tennyson.

1   Lady of Shalott — perhaps an allegory about consequences of living through art, not life.

2   Lotos-Eaters - dilemma of whether to accept blissful life of 'mild - eyed melancholy Lotos-Eaters' or to struggle with 'sharp distress' of life.

3.   Ulysses - courage to struggle on in old age:
          'Tis not too late to seek a newer world'

     and is positive at end despite earlier doubts:

          One equal temper of heroic hearts,
          Made weak by time and fate, but strong in will
          To strive, to seek, to find, and not to yield.

4   In Memoriam

Fig. 6.4 Detailed notes on a particular feature

You may find that some poems appear on two or three of these sheets, if they display several characteristic features or discuss a particular subject with a particular attitude. You may also find that you can *select* poems on each sheet, as the best examples of the particular feature, to avoid giving endless examples where one or two would be enough.

In this way you will build up a set of notes on the anthology or collection as a whole, which rests firmly on your detailed reading of the individual texts.

A word of warning: don't assume that the groupings you have are the only ones, or that examiners will set questions based on them. They may well have different ideas, so be prepared to think quickly in the exam and to 're-group' the poems according to a topic, theme or idea that may form the basis of an exam question.

> " Learn representative poems or lines – those which demonstrate several features of the collection are most useful in exams. "

CHECKING YOUR THEMES

When you have made your series of notes on themes, you need to check them carefully to make sure that you have covered all the important features and topics of the collection. Check by:

- thinking carefully yourself about the text, reading through it again to see if there are any other topics or features that you've missed;
- discussing the text with other people – your teacher, or fellow-students – to make sure that you haven't missed anything of importance;
- reading the introduction to your edition, to check if the editor mentions important themes or features that you've missed;
- reading critical commentaries for the same reason – though be careful not to be overwhelmed by the interpretations they offer.

SELECTING REPRESENTATIVE POEMS

Once you have gone through these stages, you should have a fairly thorough acquaintance with the poems and the topics they deal with. You can now take your revision a stage further by selecting a number of poems which you can use as the basis of your revision, and which you can discuss in detail in an exam.

Do this by:

- selecting those which are the best examples of each topic or feature;
- looking for poems which appear as examples of several different topics or features.

In this way, you will arrive at a small group of poems, or passages from poems, which you can learn. There's no point in doing this, though, unless you know *why* you are learning them – that is, what features or themes they demonstrate. You can make sure that you do this by copying out a list of passages for quotation and writing next to each one the feature or theme that it demonstrates.

At this stage, you might find that a handful of poems are representative of the poet's work in a manner which conveys almost all the key features or ideas that you've identified. If so, read them very frequently, so that they stay fresh in your mind. This is *not* the same as setting out to learn them off by heart; this achieves little in its own right. But being very familiar with them through repeated reading will help them stay fresh in your mind. You will also be better able to remember important lines and images from them, and to quote passages from them in the exam to support the points you are making when answering the question.

READING PERIOD ANTHOLOGIES

You may be studying an anthology of poetry from a particular period which includes the work of different poets. Working on a text like this is similar in many ways to studying a collection by one poet, but there are certain other points to bear in mind.

> " Grouping poems in anthologies. "

1 *Look for points of contrast*
   Anthologies often include a wide range of poems which discuss the same themes in very different ways. If you group poems together according to subject, make sure that you note the differences between them in style or attitude.

2 *Be aware of individual poets*
   In the exam you may be asked to discuss the treatment of a theme by two or more

poets. Make sure that you include, in your groups of poems, work by individual figures, with notes on their characteristic features of style, subject and attitude.

3 *Note familiarities and differences of style*
In some periods, poetry *shares* features of style and attitude. The early eighteenth century, for example, was a period of much formality in poetry, with a large number of poems written in rhyming couplets of ten syllables to a line. By contrast, the poetry of the nineteen-thirties is very diverse in form, with very few structures in common between poets.

Include in your notes a sheet showing how the styles of the poems you are studying are similar, and a sheet showing their range and diversity, so that you can answer a question on these aspects should it arise.

4 *Beware of 'background'*
When studying an anthology of work from a particular period, it's easy to get carried away with 'background studies'. Reading about the social history of the thirties, or the conditions in the trenches in the first world war, can become more absorbing than reading the poems themselves.

Be careful about this. If you find the period interesting, by all means read about it; but make sure that this doesn't become a substitute for the close study of the poems themselves. This should always be the main focus of your work, and the background should never change into the 'foreground' of your work.

> By all means read about the period of the poems – but remember: the poems are the main focus.

WRITING ABOUT POETRY

> Organising ideas when writing about poetry.

If you have read the chapter on the critical essay (Chapter 2) and the two chapters about the critical appreciation of poetry (Chapters 4 and 5) you should have a good idea of what's required in essays about poetry. The key points to remember are those that were made in these chapters:

- read the question carefully and know what you are asked to do;
- marshal your knowledge of the text and relate it to the question;
- organise your material in concepts – a list of eight or so points which directly engage the question;
- support each point with a quotation or close reference to a text.

> Don't quote a poem unless you use it to support a point.

As well as these points, remember that simply quoting a poem will achieve nothing unless you *use* it – relate it to a critical point which directly answers the question. Remember, too, that quotations which are longer than a few words should be set out as they are in the printed poem – as separate lines, usually with a capital letter at the start of each.

Finally, remember that your knowledge of the poems will achieve little unless you actually answer the question; you must make everything relevant. This means leaving out biographical or 'background' material, and points which, while perfectly valid about the poems, do not engage with the question.

What you *can* do, however, is to make clear your own opinions. If you are asked to discuss the effectiveness of a poet's work or treatment of a theme, give your opinion clearly and directly. Simple statements of liking or disliking are clearly out of place, but a *reasoned evaluation* of the work *is* a valid part of your response, so don't be afraid to make it.

POETRY 4: WRITING ABOUT POETRY

TYPES OF QUESTION

PRACTICE QUESTIONS

GETTING STARTED

This chapter is concerned with putting into practice the advice given in the last chapter about how to study and write about poetry. It contains a series of exam questions, with student answers and examiner comments. Try to answer those which are set on the texts which you are studying before you look at the answers. Perhaps time yourself. This will help you to gain practice in writing in the limited time you'll have in the exam.

Even if you're *not* studying the texts discussed here, it's still worth looking closely at the questions and answers. They'll suggest ways of writing about poetry which you'll be able to use for the texts which *are* part of your syllabus, so helping in your preparation for the exam.

ESSENTIAL PRINCIPLES

Questions on poetry will be of three main types.

1   Questions which give you a *complete poem*, with an accompanying question

Generally, this will ask you to comment on the features of the poem which are typical of the poet's work, or of an aspect of the anthology's nature if it comes from a collection by many poets.

Tackle these by reading the given text carefully, identifying its representative features and then finding examples of these elements elsewhere in the collection. Always make sure that you *relate* the poem to the whole collection in this way, otherwise you will end up writing a study of just one poem.

2   Questions based on a *quotation*

In most cases, the quotation will be specially invented for the question, and will be a statement which is partially true about the poetry.

Your first task here is to look carefully at both the quotation and the question itself. Make sure that you know what the question means, perhaps by concentrating on key words and concepts in the manner discussed in Chapters 1 and 2. You should then marshal your ideas by writing a *plan* which makes a series of relevant points, supporting each one with a textual reference or quotation. Having done this, you can write the essay.

3   Questions which ask you to discuss a *particular aspect* of the poetry

These are generally more straightforward than quotation questions, but still demand close reading to define precisely the task they set you to complete.

Once again, you should make a plan with a series of points, each supported by a quotation or reference, making sure all the time that you are *relating* your knowledge to the question. When you are sure that you have done this in the plan, write the essay.

1   How effectively does Marvell convey his enjoyment of natural scenery and beauty?

2   Discuss the view that Eve only becomes a recognisably human figure after she eats the apple in *Paradise Lost* Book IX.

3   'Wordsworth's strength lies not in describing people and places, but in the way he uses these descriptions'. Discuss this statement with reference to Books IX and X of *The Prelude*.

4   Write a critical appreciation of the following poem, showing how it is typical of 'Victorian' qualities you have found in *The Penguin Book of Victorian Verse*.

> The sea is calm to-night.
> The tide is full, the moon lies fair
> Upon the straits; – on the French coast the light
> Gleams and is gone; the cliffs of England stand,
> Glimmering and vast, out in the tranquil bay.
> Come to the window, sweet is the night-air!
> Only, from the long line of spray
> Where the sea meets the moon-blanch'd land,
> Listen! you hear the grating roar
> Of pebbles which the waves draw back, and fling,
> At their return, up the high strand,
> Begin, and cease, and then again begin,
> With tremulous cadence slow, and bring
> The eternal note of sadness in.
> Sophocles long ago
> Heard it on the Ægæan, and it brought
> Into his mind the turbid ebb and flow
> Of human misery; we
> Find also in the sound a thought,
> Hearing it by this distant northern sea.

The Sea of Faith
Was once, too, at the full, and round earth's shore
Lay like the folds of a bright girdle furl'd.
But now I only hear
Its melancholy, long, withdrawing roar,
Retreating, to the breath
Of the night-wind, down the vast edges drear
And naked shingles of the world.
Ah, love, let us be true
To one another! for the world, which seems
To lie before us like a land of dreams,
So various, so beautiful, so new,
Hath really neither joy, nor love, nor light,
Nor certitude, nor peace, nor help for pain;
And we are here as on a darkling plain
Swept with confused alarms of struggle and flight,
Where ignorant armies clash by night.

5   Show the ways in which the following poem is typical of Hardy's poetry in the selection
you have studied.

In time of 'The Breaking of Nations'

I

Only a man harrowing clods
    In a slow silent walk
With an old horse that stumbles and nods
    Half asleep as they stalk.

II

Only thin smoke without flame
    From the heaps of couch-grass;
Yet this will go onward the same
    Though Dynasties pass.

III

Yonder a maid and her wight
    Come whispering by:
War's annals will cloud into night
    Ere their story die.

1915

6   'Nature and humanity are the basic elements of the poetry of Edward Thomas'. Show
how these aspects are present in the poems.

STUDENT ANSWERS WITH EXAMINER COMMENTS

STUDENT ANSWER TO QUESTION 1

> Be careful with 'obvious' –
> you still need to say *why* it's so
> clear.

> A good long quotation – if
> you can remember passages of
> this sort you'll get a good
> grade.

It is obvious from even a rapid reading of the poems that Marvell derived intense
enjoyment from nature. This is unusual in many of the poets of his time, the
metaphysical poets more often being concerned with philosophy or scientific
advances. Marvell is often opposed to progress and praises the wild, sensual beauty of
nature:

> Then as I careless on the Bed
> Of gelid Straw-beryes do tread,
> And through the Hazles thick espy
> The hatching throstles shining eye.

These lines suggest that he is only happy in the beauty of a hot balmy day with birds
singing and rich fruit at his feet.

Marvell violently opposes man's interference in the natural order of life in, for example, experimenting with tulips to produce blooms exotic in colour and ridiculous in size:

> Luxurious man, to bring his Vice in use,
> Did after him the world seduce,
> And from the fields the Flow'rs and Plants allure,
> When nature was most plain and pure.

Marvell here seems to be advocating a return to man's natural state, shedding the sophistication of his new-found scientific power. It is interesting to note that, when Cook discovered Tahiti and brought back one of its inhabitants, the cult of the 'noble savage' received widespread popularity in England.

Marvell mocks man's efforts to enslave flowers in a ridiculously disciplined array:

> In fragrant Vollyes they let fly;
> And to salute their Governess
> Again as great a charge they press.

Here the flowers are compared to a rank of soldiers who let fly with their powerful scents when their commander walks past in a natural 'salute'. The satirical tone used here about man's efforts to improve the landscape shows Marvell's love of nature in a natural, unmodified form.

Marvell reveals his great love of nature most effectively of all in his poem 'Bermudas', which represents what he considered to be the ideal circumstances of life, with a few companions on a beautiful island far away from the struggle of everyday life. The poem begins with an account of the pilgrims' approach to the isle and continues with a song about the island which is a paeon of praise for the natural world. The song shows that Marvell sees nature as the product of a benevolent God, as it refers to God's generosity in giving man the spring which 'here enamells every thing', and gives a catalogue of the fruits of the island, including oranges, pomegranates, and concludes:

> He makes the Figs our mouths to meet;
> And throws the Melons at our feet.
> But apples plants of such a price,
> No tree could ever bear them twice.

Here, the reference to the pineapple comes as the climax of a richly sensuous account of the pleasures of life close to nature and its bounty.

The close of the poem makes an important point about Marvell's view of man's place in the ideal, natural world:

> And all the way, to guide their chime,
> With falling oars they kept the time.

Here, it is not necessary for man to work; all is done for him by a sympathetic nature.

Marvell's delight in nature, then, is based on a strong awareness of its sensuous beauty and its existence as evidence of God's love and generosity. He is far happier with nature in its original state, unimproved by man, than he is with the large-scale, formal gardens of the time. Another aspect of his delight comes from his seeing nature as a retreat from the complexities and pain of normal human life. This has already been noted in 'Bermudas', but is perhaps best shown in these lines from 'Appleton House':

> How safe, methinks, and strong, behind
> These trees have I encamp'd my Mind...
> And where the World no certain Shot
> Can make, or me it toucheth not.

Margin comments:

"Note how the point is made before the quotation and clarified after it – a sound piece of writing."

"Interesting, yes; relevant, no."

"Do we know this was his ideal? Is it relevant to the poem?"

"Better here because it analyses HOW Marvell regards nature."

"You don't think there's an element of satire here, in using the language of the Fall?"

"Finishing with a quotation which demonstrates your point is a strong way of ending."

EXAMINER COMMENT

This is an essay which has several strengths. It shows a good knowledge of the text and includes many quotations. But it also has weaknesses. It doesn't say much about *how*

Marvell expresses his delight in nature – although the question does not explicitly ask for this, it would have improved the depth of the essay to include some mention of it. It also omits Marvell's famous line about 'a green thought in a green shade' – understandably, as it's hard to comment on, but nevertheless it should have been included in an ideal answer.

STUDENT ANSWER TO QUESTION 2

> Nothing wrong with disagreeing with the question – but you need to know the material well and have a strong case prepared.

> Looks as if it's going off the point . . .

> . . . but it gets back to the question here.

> True – if not quite the view of obedience Milton had when writing the poem.

> All this is true – but it isn't explicitly relevant.

> Again, the writer pulls the answer back to the question and shows that what he said before is relevant.

I disagree with this view of Eve in Paradise Lost. I think that, although Eve is more human after eating the apple, she shows clear signs of being fallen and human before this happens.

Before she eats the apple, we feel that she has her own reasons and instincts for wishing to be equal to God and, even though she shows Satanic elements in her false reasoning, these instincts are clearly human ones which we can share. Satan knows that she wants to be immortal, and exploits this rather than creating it. That this is so is shown in the heat of eating the apple when we are told that 'Nor was Godhead from her thought'.

One of the basic elements of religion is the hope for immortality or heaven. Eve had the former but didn't appreciate it, and so wanted the latter. In a strict sense this was pride, since it made her go against and above God's law, but it didn't involve the hatred of God felt by Satan. It was innocent, natural ambition of the kind that people still have today. It would have taken superhuman courage and trust for Eve to have acknowledged this 'pride' and ignored it in herself – it's certainly something we can't do. Here again she is recognisably human before the fall.

As Satan sits on the tree of Life, we are told, in Book IV,

> so little knows
> Any but God alone to value right the good before him.

In the same book Adam says

> Needs must the power that created us
> And for us this ample world, be
> Infinitely good.

This sounds hollow and too good for a fallen human, but when Eve questions God's restrictions and intentions we hear our own doubts and fears. That God 'Forbids us good, forbids us to be wise' implies, as Satan says, 'Not just, not God. Not feared then, nor obeyed'. Eve's appraisal of this ignorance leads to the arrogant and sarcastic questions 'what fear I then? Rather what know to fear?'. The logic of Eve's 'For good unknown sure is not bad' is contrasted with the illogicality of Adam's

> The danger lies within us
> Yet lies within our power.

Trust is overpowered by curiosity and ambition – again suggesting man after the fall.

What Milton recognised was the state of mind of fallen man. The fallen reader appreciates Eve's desire to eat the apple and know more, as well as sympathising with Adam's very human reasoning or instinct which made him link his fate to his wife's for 'bliss or woe'. The reader is led to make the same mistakes that Adam and Eve made, and only in Adam's earlier statements about God's goodness is the reader made to see things from a more critical viewpoint, where Eve's actions are wrong because they lack trust in God's will.

Milton also impresses the nature of fallen mankind on the reader by showing the actions of Adam and Eve immediately after the fall. The cunning of Eve, the insatiable lust, the shame and the following mutual accusation all show the nature of fallen man. Yet within this lies the hope for man, because we still have knowledge of 'good' even though it is 'bought dear by knowing ill'. Although we are revolted, we hope that the fall may be fortunate as we realise Adam's tenderness to Eve, and thus the foreshadowing of fallen mankind in Eve's earlier character is in part vindicated.

Eve is not only recognisably human after her fall but also before it. Milton thus implicates us in the fall by making us feel sympathetic towards her. In doing so he reveals how completely we, too, are 'Defaced, deflowered and now to death devote'.

EXAMINER COMMENT

This is a very good essay, which is interesting because it goes against the statement made in the question but argues its case very strongly. Of course, there is a counter-argument to most of the ideas raised here, but this is very often the case, and the arguments are advanced very clearly and with copious textual reference. In places perhaps the essay drifts away from the idea of Eve before the fall – it certainly does not advance a simple case based on detailed study of Eve's behaviour. Instead, it talks about how Milton involves us in the process of the fall and thus makes it – and the nature of Eve – much more convincing. It is therefore a good example of how you can disagree with a statement in a question and still do well in the exam.

STUDENT ANSWER TO QUESTION 3

> Clear explicit opening claim which engages directly with the question.

Wordsworth does not simply describe people and places in the manner of a more conventional autobiographer. Instead he uses them to reveal various facets of his own personality, political and social philosophy, and his relationship with the natural world.

The clearest example of this is the portrait of Beaupuy. Wordsworth presents the man very much as a reflection of his own feelings of liberalism, to recreate the youthful optimism of the scene. Feelings of individual friendship here combine with a philosophy of universal brotherhood which Beaupuy is seen to exemplify. The young Wordsworth's optimism that an egalitarian state can exist is shown when he says that, despite Beaupuy's aristocratic birth,

> unto the poor
> Among mankind he was in service bound.

The 'bravest youth' of the revolution, and the academic community from whom he gains many of his ideas, are presented in similarly idealised terms, and are used to reveal his enthusiasm.

> Good points on how the poet's own ideas are shown in the two portraits.

Two portraits reveal Wordsworth's own sensibility, drawn to picturesque individual incidents rather than larger, more general social wrongs. He talks of the girl leading the heifer and, although he sees her as an image of larger exploitation of the political state in France before the revolution, he does not offer a solution; instead, we are left with the vision of her which is almost as picturesque as the many other characters in his poetry who are close to the natural world. The officer who is 'blighted' by the times is similarly treated; there is individual compassion but no larger, carefully-developed political theory about how such tragedies should be avoided, and so Wordsworth reveals his own nature clearly here.

He does, however, write skilfully about the aristocracy, showing satirically how they have little knowledge of the real state of the nation or any political awareness. The army officers in Blois are similarly used to stand as representatives of a corrupt system, especially in their lack of fear of 'bad becoming worse'.

> Again a clear explanation of the use the poet makes of the references.

Wordsworth is skilful at conveying the nature of places, such as the celebration in Arles, his room in Paris after the massacres and various other aspects of France in the revolution. Here again, though, these details reveal his own nature – he reads late at night 'with unextinguished taper' in his room, showing how political action is in him transformed to academic or creative energy. There are occasions, however, when Wordsworth describes not only the place but the atmosphere; the 'hissing Factionists with ardent eyes' suggests very well the air of intensity of the times, and his summing up of Paris after the revolution, 'defenceless as a wood where tigers roamed' shows this too. Yet both images suggest that he is looking on the events not as a political realist but as an idealist, seeing in them immense poetic richness and an experience as intense as any he had with the woods and plains in earlier parts of *The Prelude*.

This quality continues in the account of Leven Sands, which suggests the harmonious peace and state of unity achieved by leaving nature to its own course, rather than changing it as the events of the Revolution in France had done – perhaps revealing the innately reactionary character of Wordsworth which was to become increasingly apparent later in his life. The longing for unspoiled nature is continued in the accounts of the woods around the Loire, where he envisages an earlier mystic 'In Sylvan meditation undisturbed'.

Wordsworth uses people and places very powerfully and very revealingly in this part of *The Prelude*. His attitude towards them tells us much about his own political and social feelings, and perhaps undercuts the revolutionary zeal which is often the outward subject of the book.

EXAMINER COMMENT

The degree to which Wordsworth's revolutionary sympathies were real and active is something which critics have disagreed on for some time. What matters is that you are aware that, in this book of *The Prelude,* he is using the descriptions of people and places for far more than descriptive purposes: the book is much more than a travelogue.

An essay of this sort can very easily turn into a series of lists of examples, so be sure to *select* what you are going to say. Possibly this essay could do with a little more quotation and be more analytical to support and argue through the points made, but overall it is a good example of the need to select and use material when faced with an exam question which asks you to 'discuss'.

STUDENT ANSWER TO QUESTION 4

> If you can, it helps to identify the poem, but don't spend ages trying to remember it.

> Rather a thin statement – more references to other poems would strengthen it.

> Still general: what is the precise nature of the difference?

> This is tighter, as it shows how other poets *use* images of nature.

> Another thin point – you need to say much more about *how* this works, and compare it with similar techniques in other poems.

This poem, 'Dover Beach' by Matthew Arnold, is typical of Victorian qualities in *The Penguin Book of Victorian Verse*. This is mainly true in its main theme; the great feeling of loss when, as a result of the theory of evolution, it was no longer possible to believe in the story of the creation as presented in the Bible. This sense of doubt is presented in the way the poem discusses the sea in literal terms, and then moves on to say that 'The Sea of Faith/Was once, too, at the full', but now there is nothing more than an empty world, devoid of meaning because it is no longer a symbol of God's love. The concern for religion, whether in the form of belief or doubt, is seen in many poems in the collection, including 'Rizpah', although the serious philosophical treatment it receives here has few equivalents in the collection.

The despairing tone of the poem is something that is found in many other poems in the anthology. Browning's 'Child Roland's Pilgrimage' suggests a similar sense of desolation, again by using a landscape, even if it is a very different one. The same poet's 'Caliban upon Setebos' has a similar mood, discussing the question of whether pain ends with death. A. E. Housman, too, shares the mood of despair, often as a result of looking at the natural world. Tennyson, in 'The Passing of Arthur', suggests a sadness that one age has come to an end, which is similar to Arnold's feelings at the loss of Christianity.

The poem is also typical in its close observation of nature. Many Victorian poems depend on this as their main topic, even though they often use the natural world as a symbol for something larger. Tennyson, for example, uses the world as a reflection of the mood of his characters in, for example, 'Mariana', as does Hardy in 'During Wind and Rain'. Arnold himself explores the theme further in the excerpts from *Balder Dead*, where the discussion of the idea of the death of God in a Pagan society allows him to make points about the contemporary situation. A similarity of subject but a difference of attitude can be seen in the poems of Gerard Manley Hopkins, who sees in the beauty of the natural world the proof of the love of God which is quite absent in Arnold's poem.

The poem is also representative in finding solace from the troubles of the world in love. Browning's 'Meeting at Night' presents this theme in a strikingly similar setting, with its creation of mood in 'a mile of warm-scented beach'. The final image, of warfare, is one that is frequent in Victorian poetry, coming in many of Tennyson's poems, as well as Arnold's own 'Sohrab and Rustum'.

The technique of the poem, in using sound and rhythm to suggest mood and underline meaning, is something that many Victorian poems share. Hopkins does this, although in a different way to recreate different moods, as do Tennyson and Hardy. In all, then, the poem is typically Victorian in its mood and in its expression, although there are many poems in the anthology which do not share its attitude towards life.

EXAMINER COMMENT

This is an essay of acceptable quality, but not one which would pass very well. Although it does link the poem with others, it does not quote specific lines or show similarities in any depth. Closer analysis of the poem itself, and more study of other poems, would help this to gain a far higher grade than the D or C it's currently worth.

It's worth mentioning in this context that, if you're feeling very confident, you can always go against the question and say that you *don't* think the poem is typical of the anthology. To support this you could say that the mood is much darker than those of most other poems, and that the sense of a lost faith isn't really reflected elsewhere in the collection. As it happens, there are many other poems from this period in which it *is* reflected – much of Tennyson's *In Memoriam*, for example – but, in this collection, the poem is slightly unusual for the religious stand it takes. Be careful, though: you shouldn't attempt such a disagreement unless you are very sure of your facts and the arguments, and have available the textual evidence to support them.

STUDENT ANSWER TO QUESTION 5

This poem is typical of Hardy's poetry in both theme and expression. It is concerned with the relationship between man and the natural world, which is a common preoccupation of Hardy in his poems. The central idea is the fact that, even though the poet is writing 'In time of "The Breaking of Nations"', certain processes which are age-old will continue: the man 'harrowing clods', the burning of couch-grass, and the maid being courted by her 'wight' are all ways in which natural processes, and man's involvement with them, will go on despite the fall of dynasties or the coming of war.

> This would be stronger if you hadn't started a new paragraph before the point was complete.

This awareness of the passage of time, and man's place within it, is a major aspect of Hardy's personality which is revealed in this poem. Very often Hardy gives the impression of seeing mankind from an immense distance, and considering him within a very large time-span. Here the reference to the passing of dynasties – whole families of kings – while the ancient processes of farming continue shows this very well. So too does the statement that 'War's annals will cloud into night' – the story of the present war will be forgotten – before the process of a man and woman in love dies out. This contrast between the perpetual processes of man and nature and the present circumstances is seen elsewhere in his poetry, most clearly perhaps in 'The Convergence of the Twain'.

> Good – but you take a long time to get to this point!

Here, as in other poems such as 'The Darkling Thrush', we feel that Hardy is gaining some consolation from the permanence of the processes of nature, finding comfort in the fact that they will continue whatever mankind does, and perhaps using this to offset the confusions and uncertainties of contemporary life, especially during the First World War. Topical references are, however, not unusual in Hardy's poetry, even though he finds refuge from them in the longer processes of nature.

> Two more sound points, but 'not unusual' is rather too vague.

Typical of Hardy is the use of words which are either from a country dialect, or are unusual because they are archaic. The reference to 'couch-grass' in the second stanza is an example of the first; 'wight', a word used by Chaucer to mean 'man', is an example of the second. Many of the more familiar words of the poem are concerned with nature and natural processes, and this is another frequent technique of Hardy's. The references to the man harrowing, for example, and that to the burning of couch-grass, show a familiarity with working life in the country which often supplies the basic situation, as well as important symbols of continuity, in Hardy's poems.

> The writing's stronger on form than on ideas here – always aim for a balance.

The form of the poem is also typical of Hardy's poems. Hardy rarely uses the same verse form more than once, preferring to create structures which are suitable to the individual poem he is writing. Here, instead of a regular or traditional pattern, Hardy uses a simple four-line stanza. Typical, too, is the meditative tone of the poem; it is as if the spectator is leaning against a farm-gate watching what is going on, thinking about it, and then recording his reflections – as indeed he does in 'The Darkling Thrush', which shares the meditative tone of this poem and many others in the anthology. Thus in both theme and treatment the poem reveals many facets of Hardy's poetic style and outlook.

EXAMINER COMMENT

This is a straightforward handling of the poem, identifying the main features of the poet's work and showing that they are typical of his work. One of the problems of this kind of answer is knowing how much reference to make to other poems. You are not, after all, asked to say where else these features appear, but only to say which ones are typical of the poems you've studied. In this answer, a couple of other poems are mentioned; reference to one or two more would have made the argument more convincing – although, if the features really are 'typical', you could mention any number of other poems to prove a point and the essay would become simply a catalogue. The main aim is to list clearly a series of typical themes, approaches and techniques, and this answer achieves that with clarity and directness.

STUDENT ANSWER TO QUESTION 6

> **A very general opening which could easily lapse into the biogaphical: mercifully it doesn't.**

Edward Thomas was a very personal poet who wrote of the fears, doubts and loves which possessed him. He was also deeply concerned for the countryside. These two elements are the basis of his work.

The most striking feature of Thomas' work is his closeness to and knowledge of nature. 'As the Team's head-brass', for example, shows detailed knowledge of the technical terms involved in the process of ploughing, and also shows his direct personal involvement with the natural world:

> I sat among the boughs of the fallen elm
> That strewed the angle of the fallow, and
> Watched the plough narrowing a yellow square
> Of charlock.

Thomas is very observant, and notices the most minute detail of the natural world, as in these lines:

> Its cloudy foliage lowers
> Ahead, shelf above shelf

The poem 'But these things also' contains delicate, fragile descriptions of nature:

> **Some good quotations, but little analysis or comment.**

> The shell of a small snail bleached
> In the Grass; chip of flint, and mite
> Of chalk

Yet despite this closeness to nature there is an atmosphere of isolation and loneliness in a great deal of his work. The reader often feels that Thomas is alone in the world with only nature as a companion. Often, this induces a note of sad reflection. This is the subject of the poem 'Melancholy';

> The rain and wind, the rain and wind raved endlessly
> ...and melancholy
> Wrought magic so that if I feared the solitude
> Far more I feared all company

> **Much stronger here; the passage explains how the poem works and shows some of the poet's larger concerns.**

The opposite to this idea of isolation is found in poems which stress the idea of continuity in the natural and human world. 'As the Team's Head Brass' shows this twofold continuity in the ploughing which will create new crops and in the lovers who will create new generations: 'Then the lovers came out of the wood/The horses started...'.

The infallibility of nature is important, too: man cannot manipulate the seasons or the activities of the land. 'March the third' shows this when Thomas says:

> This day unpromised is more dear
> Than all the named days of the year

In 'Rain', Thomas furthers this link between human and natural elements by writing about a storm which cleanses everything, but is also a storm so dreadful that death will be a release from it:

" A limited reading of this poem; there's more to it than this . . . **"**

" . . . and the writer shows his uneasiness by hurrying to end the essay **"**

> I shall die
> And neither hear the rain nor give it thanks
> For washing me cleaner than I have been
> Since I was born into this solitude.

It is clear, then, that both natural and human worlds are of essential importance to Thomas in his poetry and that, in his finest poems, he brings the two together in both literal and symbolic ways.

EXAMINER COMMENT

This again shows a good knowledge of the poems by supporting points with quotations, but its range is rather limited. It could, for example, have said more about Thomas's very personal poems – the poems to his family, especially 'And you, Helen', are striking omissions here. There are also some rather shaky interpretations.

Discussing a limited number of poems need not be a limitation, as some questions will ask you to discuss an idea with reference to three or four poems. If this is the case, choose them carefully: selecting the wrong ones – that is, ones which are only marginally relevant to the ideas of the question, can seriously limit your grade before you even start writing the essay.

CHAUCER

THE RIGHT TEXT

APPROACHING THE LANGUAGE

STUDYING THE TEXT

REVISING THE TEXT

PRACTICE QUESTIONS

GETTING STARTED

Many exam papers stress the study of 'major authors', and one of the foremost among these is Geoffrey Chaucer. In the great majority of cases, this means the study of parts of *The Canterbury Tales*, usually either 'The General Prologue' or one of the separate tales of which the collection is composed.

Students often have difficulty with Chaucer because the language in which it is written, Middle English, is not instantly accessible. With care, however, it is not too difficult to understand the meaning and to appreciate the qualities of sound, rhythm and association in which Chaucer's writing is so rich. Approaching Chaucer's language is one of the main topics of this chapter.

For many, the nature of the language poses special problems when reading, studying and revising Chaucer texts. This chapter discusses ways in which these problems may be overcome, and suggests approaches in which the usual techniques of study and revision may be adapted so that you can approach the exam with a sound and full knowledge of the text.

Questions on Chaucer take one of three forms. First there are detailed analyses of passages, which may ask you to write detailed notes on the use of individual words, the use of imagery, allusion or other aspects of language, and the discussion of themes. Secondly, there are questions which give you a larger passage and ask you to describe its features and themes to show how it is representative of the whole work from which it is taken. Finally, there are the more traditional essay questions, where you are given a quotation or statement about the text to discuss, or a particular theme of the work to explore.

This chapter looks at techniques appropriate for all three kinds of question, and ends by giving student answers to examples of them so that you can see exactly what is required of you in the exam and gain practice in achieving it.

ESSENTIAL PRINCIPLES

THE RIGHT TEXT

Having the best edition available is important for every text you are studying, but it is even more so for Chaucer. You need a text which has:

- the text itself based on authoritative sources, clearly and accurately presented;
- a glossary, so that you can look up unfamiliar words;
- full explanatory notes;
- an introduction covering themes and ideas raised in the text.

The tales which are most frequently set are all available in single volumes which have all these elements. Your school or college may already have these volumes; if not, they should be available from a library or you might prefer to buy them.

You may be tempted to buy an edition of the text which 'translates' Chaucer's original into more recent English. Don't. No paraphrase of Chaucer can convey the full effect of the original because it changes the syntax and abandons the sound and rhythm of Middle English. It may, it is true, help you to understand what is happening in the tale – but this is a very meagre advantage, since the best way of gaining this is to read the text in its original form.

> **Always study Chaucer in the original language.**

Reading the text in the original will not be easy at first, but with perseverance you will find that you will soon get accustomed to the language. A translation won't help you with the meanings of individual words, and it certainly won't help you get the feel of the language so that you can discuss Chaucer's effects or quote short passages to support points in an essay. Overall, reading a paraphrase is more trouble than it's worth – so get hold of a good text in Middle English and stick with it.

APPROACHING THE LANGUAGE

There are many ways in which Chaucer's language is like present-day English. Many words have the same meanings, and (with some notable exceptions) the rules of grammar and syntax are similar. But don't take anything for granted. Many words which look familiar are actually different in meaning, and so you need to be on your guard. A good principle is always to read with an eye on the notes and glossary so that you can look up things which aren't clear. If you find you have difficulties with a line, try looking up a word which seems very familiar – it's often the words that you think you know which have new meanings.

While you are reading, try to split the text up into passages of between ten and twenty lines. In the General Prologue, this is easy – the account of each pilgrim takes about this space, and you can work on one at a time, checking notes and glossary to make sure that you understand what's being said.

Be careful about *syntax*. Middle English very often inverts the syntax, with the order *object subject verb* instead of the more common *subject verb object* of today's language. For example, Chaucer writes

> With him ther was his sone

instead of

> His son was with him

> **Think carefully about Chaucer's word order – it's not what you expect.**

Always read carefully to sort out the syntax, and to make sure that you know what word is the *subject* of the sentence; this can save a lot of mistakes and frustration.

Many people suggest that you write down the meanings of words which are strange to you, perhaps in the margin next to the words themselves. If you can't remember them in any other way, by all means do this; but you will find it easier in the long run to try to remember Chaucer's words, using them when talking about the passage and when writing essays about it. This has two advantages:

- it makes you appreciate the sound, rhythm and other qualities of the word, which makes the tale more immediate to you as well as helping you to write about the poetic qualities of Chaucer's writing;
- because you are constantly using the word, you come to remember it.

Taken together, these two points mean that you gradually build up a vocabulary of Chaucerian words, and so using them in the exam will be that much easier. Of course, you may have to sit down and learn some of the words, too – but reading in the original language and basing all your studies on the original text will mean that you are far more familiar with it right from the start of your work on Chaucer. You might also try using Chaucerian language in everyday conversation, especially with other people who are studying the text!

STUDYING THE TEXT

Studying Chaucer is very much like studying any other text, so you should follow all the advice given in Chapters 1 and 2. But there are some extra points which you need to be aware of.

> Try to think about Chaucer as you'd think of any other poet.

- *Don't let the language overwhelm the whole thing*, by spending all your time sorting out meanings. If you find the language element difficult, try to allot extra time to it at a very early stage of your studies, just to get to grips with meanings and syntax so that you can become familiar with the text.

- *Don't get too absorbed in 'background' studies*. There are lots of very good books which discuss Chaucer's world, some lavishly illustrated – it can be much easier to read these than to read the text itself, so be careful.

- *Think about the poetic qualities* of the text as you are reading it. Sound, rhythm, association and all the other techniques are used by Chaucer in much the same ways as they are by most other poets. While you're reading, then, consider the use he makes of them. This will not only enhance your knowledge of the text, and make it stick in your mind – it will also prepare you for questions which ask you to look closely at a particular passage and say how it is typical of Chaucer's writing.

- *Consider important themes* which the tale discusses. If necessary, make a list of these themes and note against each one the places where points of particular importance are made about them. Chivalry in *The Franklin's Tale*, true and corrupt religion in the 'General Prologue', sovereignty in marriage in *The Nun's Priest's Tale*, are all examples of themes which you need to be aware of as the basis for essay questions in the exam.

REVISING THE TEXT

Once again, the usual advice applies, but with the following additional points.

- Make a list of short passages to learn so that you can quote them in the exam. Remember, you won't get extra marks just for quoting – but you will receive credit for *supporting* your points with quotation or close reference. Between eight and a dozen passages of a line or two in length, each one demonstrating a range of points, will be a useful armoury with which to approach the exam. Each one should be important in several ways:

  - to demonstrate a theme;
  - to show the attitude or contribution of a character to the tale;
  - to exemplify an important image;
  - to show Chaucer's own opinion, whether directly or through ironic implication.

  Just going through the text *looking* for short passages like these will also help you a great deal in getting to know the text quickly while you are revising.

> – or make a pattern map like the one in Chapter 1.

- Make a 'map' of the tale to show where various events or discussion of themes occur. This will help you find your way around the tale quickly when you need to check a point. Here, for example, is the start of such a 'map' for *The Franklin's Tale*

LINES	SUBJECT	NOTES
1–22	Franklin tells Squire about his tale	File 1, p1
23–36	Franklin talks to Host	NB diction of F and H
37–56	Franklin introduces his tale and claims he is 'burel', knowing nothing about rhetoric	Untrue – F later shows *does* know about it

Notice that this not only gives the lines and the content of each section but also has a 'notes' column. You can use this, as in the first line, to show where your notes on that section are, referring to a file or notebook page. Alternatively, you can make a brief note about the main significance of the passage, as the second and third sections do here.

- *Test yourself on the meanings of words.* If you do this with a friend, it can bring variety into your revision, as well as telling you very quickly just how much you know.
- *Give yourself a 'critical appreciation' exercise on part of the text* – you can either get a friend to choose one for you or choose one yourself. Make sure that you've rubbed out any notes you've made on this passage, and go through it, asking yourself questions like these:
    - How does Chaucer use the poetic qualities of this passage to help make his main points?
    - What does the passage contribute to the discussion of key themes?
    - What does it reveal about the character of the speaker?
    - What use, if any, does Chaucer make of irony here? (a question of essential importance in reading the 'General Prologue', of course).

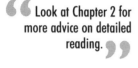

Look at Chapter 2 for more advice on detailed reading.

These are all approaches which you will find useful when reading and revising Chaucer. In addition, of course, you will have your *own notes* about the themes and ideas discussed in your text, the techniques Chaucer uses to discuss them, and the varieties of language employed to make the characterisation, themes and situations convincing. These will form the basis of your revision, together with single-sheet topic plans prepared in the manner suggested in Chapter 2.

- As a relaxation, try thinking about some present-day equivalents of the pilgrims in the 'General Prologue'. Chaucer's irony and satire is directed against timeless human failings, remember – so there's plenty of scope. Perhaps the Pardoner is alive and well selling the Eiffel Tower for scrap metal, or peddling junk bonds in the City. I have a feeling, too, that the Man of Law probably has a hand in some rather shady offshore investment deals. The Merchant drives a BMW with a personalised number plate; while the 'povre persoun' is still the same, other-worldly and quite, quite broke.

PRACTICE QUESTIONS

Here are a number of typical exam questions. Try to write answers to them yourself before looking at the student answers and examiner comments which follow them.

1 Read the following passage carefully and then answer the questions beneath it.

> By this gaude have I wonne, yeer by yeer,
> An hundred mark sith I was pardoner.
> I stonde lyk a clerk in my pulpet,
> And whan the lewed peple is doun yset,
> I preche so as ye han herd bifoore, 5
> And telle an hundred false japes moore.
> Thanne peyne I me to strecche forth the nekke,
> And est and west upon the peple I bekke,
> As dooth a dowve sittynge on a berne.
> Myne handes and my tonge goon so yerne 10
> That it is joye to se my bisynesse.
> Of avarice and of swich cursednesse
> Is al my prechyng, for to make hem free
> To yeven hir pens, and namely unto me.
> For myn entente is nat but for to wynne, 15
> And nothing for correccioun of synne.
> I rekke nevere, whan that they been beryed,
> Though that hir soules goon a-blakeberyed!

i) Explain 'hir soules goon a-blakeberyed' (line 18).
ii) Comment on the Pardoner's use of the word 'bisynesse' (line 11).
iii) Comment on the effect of rhymes and rhyming couplets in lines 10–18.
iv) What attitude towards his congregation does the Pardoner reveal here?

2 Read the following passage from *The Franklin's Tale* carefully and then answer the two questions below.
   a) Show what this passage reveals about the character of Dorigen and what methods it uses to do so.

b) What is the importance of the passage in the tale as a whole?

> "Eterne God, that thurgh thy purveiaunce
> Ledest the world by certein governaunce,
> In ydel, as men seyn, ye no thyng make.
> But, Lord, thise grisly feendly rokkes blake,
> That semen rather a foul confusion   5
> Of werk than any fair creacion
> Of swich a parfit wys God and a stable,
> Why han ye wroght this werk unresonable?
> For by this werk, south, north, ne west, ne eest,
> Ther nys yfostred man, ne bryd, ne beest;   10
> It dooth no good, to my wit, but anoyeth.
> Se ye nat, Lord, how mankynde it destroyeth?
> An hundred thousand bodyes of mankynde
> Han rokkes slayn, al be they nat in mynde,
> Which mankynde is so fair part of thy werk   15
> That thou it madest lyk to thyn owene merk.
> Thanne semed it ye hadde a greet chiertee
> Toward mankynde; but how thanne may it bee
> That ye swiche meenes make it to destroyen,
> Whiche meenes do no good, but evere anoyen?   20
> I woot wel clerkes wol seyn as hem leste,
> By argumentz, that all is for the bestes,
> Though I ne kan the causes nat yknowe.
> But thilke God that made wynd to blowe
> As kepe my lord! this my conclusion.   25
> To clerkes lete I al disputison.
> But wolde God that alle thise rokkes blake
> Were sonken into helle for his sake!
> Thise rokkes sleen myn herte for the feere."
> Thus wolde she seyn, with many a pitous teere.   30

3 'Instead of a random collection of individuals, Chaucer presents us with a single literary work'. How does Chaucer make 'The General Prologue' into a unified whole?

4 How does the introduction of Pluto and Proserpine add interest and significance to *The Merchant's Tale*?

STUDENT ANSWERS WITH EXAMINER COMMENTS

STUDENT ANSWER TO QUESTION 1

> i) This phrase means that their souls have gone wandering in hell, or are damned: he does not care where they go.

EXAMINER COMMENT

Notice that this very short explanation does not translate the phrase, but rather makes clear its importance within the general meaning of the passage as a whole.

> ii) The word here refers to his vigorous display in the pulpit while he is preaching. He behaves in a very 'busy' way, moving rapidly as the earlier lines explain.

> " Notice that there's no reference to 'business' in its modern use: don't be caught out by words that look familiar. "

EXAMINER COMMENT

Once again, this isn't a simple translation: the aim is to show the effect as well as the meaning. The word is a good example of how a word which seems familiar actually has a meaning different from its present-day equivalent.

> **Here the effect of the rhyme is important: there's no point in listing words that rhyme unless you say why they matter.**

iii) One of the main effects here is to link opposites in the words which rhyme – 'bisynesse' and 'cursednesse', 'free' and 'me', 'wynne' and 'synne'. This reflects the way that the Pardoner's purpose is the exact opposite of what it seems when he is preaching. There is also a rather glib, or even smug, air to the lines; it is as if the Pardoner has said this several times before.

EXAMINER COMMENT

A very thorough answer. Notice that this shows how the rhyme is *used* – always an important aim, but especially so here for the reasons given in the answer.

iv) The Pardoner is very patronising to his audience, making clear that he uses them as a source of income, and that he is concerned for his own gain, not their redemption. Yet it is also clear that he relies on his audience, working hard to perform in front of them to gain the most money from them.

EXAMINER COMMENT

Another sound answer. Notice that the 'audience' here is the congregation in church and *not* the audience of pilgrims. Make sure that you sort out subtle distinctions like this before answering: a wrong answer can gain very few marks in this kind of question.

STUDENT ANSWER TO QUESTION 2

> **You don't have to reach a decision; Chaucer can mean either or both of these things.**

a) This passage shows very well the character of Dorigen at the beginning of *The Franklin's Tale* where she is greatly worried about the safety of her husband Arveragus.

  The character of Dorigen is revealed as very caring and loving, as she is so concerned about the rocks. Yet she is also very religious, as lines 4–5 reveal a trust in God's love and his purpose in creating everything in the world. Perhaps she reveals not much understanding in the way that she does not understand why the rocks were created or perhaps Chaucer is using this to discuss an essential moral problem, the nature of evil. Her attitude towards the rocks is shown when she stresses the complete absence of good it does for anyone in the long list in lines 12–14, and by repeating the question at the very end of the passage. Chaucer thus skilfully uses her simple, incredulous questioning to create a picture of a loving, caring wife who has religious faith but cannot understand the presence of evil in a world created by an all-loving God. We are told that she speaks 'with sorweful sikes colde' to reinforce the impression of misery.

> **Good use of the sounds of language here to reinforce the point – but you could say much more on diction and tone.**

  The diction and tone of the passage reinforce Dorigen's sense of outrage at the rocks. The phrase 'grisly rokkes blake' sounds hard and dry, suggesting the appearance of the rocks and their threat to shipping. The rather tentative tone, twice using the word 'seem' (lines 8 and 20) reinforces her nature as gentle and caring.

> **Sound summary of main points at the start**

b) The passage has much to contribute to the tale on several levels. First of all, it presents the problem which is the cause of great concern to Dorigen and thus furthers the plot, since it leads her to say that she will take pity on Aurelius' longing for her if he can remove them so that Arveragus can return safely.

  As well as this major narrative function, it plays a part in the moral theme of the book in introducing the presence of evil in a world created by a loving God. As a physical embodiment of a moral and philosophical problem it brings together the two levels of the tale very well.

A further function that it performs is in revealing the nature of Dorigen, as detailed above, through the kind of language used and the ideas she expresses. In this, it contributes also to the variety of the tale, since Dorigen's speech is different from those of the other characters, so that overall we are given the impression of a genuine dialogue taking place which makes the tale convincing. These are the main functions of the passage in the tale.

EXAMINER COMMENT

The two parts are both of a pass level, but could do with a little more depth to raise them to a higher grade. The first could say more about the tone and diction of the passage, and also about its structure – the way in which Dorigen keeps asking the same question in different ways, and how this shows the puzzled desperation with which she approaches the rocks.

The second part could go further in discussing the place of the rocks as a representative of the natural world in contrast to the magic that is to come later on, although it does give three solid, clear functions and is a sound pass. Notice that it does not repeat the points about Dorigen made in the first part: in questions of this sort it is quite acceptable to refer to an earlier answer in this way.

STUDENT ANSWER TO QUESTION 3

Chaucer holds together 'The General Prologue' in a number of ways so that, although at first reading it may appear like a series of character sketches, on further study it does reveal itself as a carefully linked whole.

One of the ways in which he achieves this is in the structure of the Prologue. It starts with the invocation to spring and the account of the circumstances in which the pilgrims met; it then moves on to describe each of them in turn; and it ends with the suggestion that they should tell stories and the account of their departure. Within the central section, the pilgrims are carefully grouped. He begins with the courtly characters, and then moves on to the first group of religious pilgrims. Then come the professional middle classes – the Merchant, Clerk and Franklin, for example, before a short group of people of lower status such as the five gildsmen. The Doctor of Physic and the Wife of Bath then balance each other well, with the Parson coming at the very centre of the Prologue, matched by his brother the Plowman. A further group of middle-class people follow, in ascending order of corruption, until at last we have the greatest evil in the Summoner and the Pardoner. Thus the order gives a sense of progression and unity to the Prologue.

Chaucer also achieves unity by having certain themes which recur in the Prologue. The nature of love, for example, is often referred to. The Prioresse's knot with the text 'Amor Vincit Omnia' represents a worldly kind of love which is close to that of the Wife of Bath. The idea of love is also mentioned in the portaits of the Monk and the Friar, the Doctour, the Plowman and the Pardoner. All display the quality to some degree, whether sacred or profane, and this forms an important link in the Prologue. The same is true of the theme of greed, which occurs in many of the pilgrims. The Friar and the Merchant are both concerned with making money, the latter's talk always being to do with 'the encrees of his winning'. The Miller has 'a golden thombe', meaning that he takes more than his share of the flour he grinds, and the Doctour has an illicit trading practice with a pharmacist. The climax of this theme is reached in the Pardoner's corruption, in particular his use of fake relics to collect money for himself.

The church is a major topic in the Prologue. The discussion of the true nature of religion begins with the mild corruption of the Prioress and continues with the slightly greater evil of the monk and friar; the climax is reached with the thorough evil and avarice of the Summoner and Pardoner. At the very centre of the Prologue, however, is the moral goodness of the Parson, who acts almost as the standard by which the other pilgrims are judged.

In all these ways, then, Chaucer succeeds in uniting the Prologue and making it something more than a simple list of people. If we add to that the similarity of purpose of all the pilgrims in going on a pilgrimage, and the fact that all the characters are described not as individuals but as timeless types, then it is clear that the Prologue succeeds as a unified literary work.

> **A major point which deserves much more detailed treatment.**

EXAMINER COMMENT

This makes a number of sound points, although it rather lacks detail and depth. Some more quotation to show the way in which themes are discussed would help. So, too, would more mention of Chaucer's moral purpose in showing types and not individuals. The passing mention at the end reads like an afterthought here, whereas it deserves more depth and explanation.

A more important flaw is that no mention is made of the presence of the character Chaucer adopts as the pilgrim-narrator – sometimes called Chaucer-the-Pilgrim. The presence of this straightforward, rather gullible man who observes a great deal but criticises very little, and whom Chaucer uses as a mouthpiece so that he can make ironic points by what the narrator leaves unsaid, is a very important element of unity which this essay really should have included.

STUDENT ANSWER TO QUESTION 4

The entry of Pluto and Proserpine in the tale is important both to the plot and in introducing a new level of action. The two are introduced near the end, just after January has tried to win back May's affections by promising that she will be well off when he dies. She listens without interest, knowing that she is about to be unfaithful to him when Damian enters the garden, as previously arranged. While Januarie and May are walking in the garden after she has beckoned Damian to come in, the scene changes to Pluto and Proserpine. This shift of scene thus provides the first reason for their presence: to introduce suspense by delaying the final events of the story.

> **Be consistent – use either 'January' or 'Januarie'. The latter is better as it's Chaucer's original.**

The two characters begin by talking of marital strife — the major theme of the whole tale. Pluto begins by quoting Solomon on the fickleness of women. This contributes to the earlier arguments, particularly the recent ones between Placebo and Justinus, in which Placebo has already referred to Solomon. The fact that Pluto took his wife by force, only to have her reclaimed for six months of the year by her mother Ceres, adds further resonance to the marriage debate; theirs is hardly an ideal marriage.

> **Good point – notice how this isn't simple narrative, but *uses* the reference to what happened earlier to make a point.**

Prosperpine refuses to admit Solomon's wisdom, whereupon Pluto promises to take action which intervenes in the plot of the tale, making clear another reason for their introduction. He will, he says, restore Januarie's sight so that he can see his wife's adultery in the tree. Proserpine answers that she will

> yeven hire suffisant answere,
> And alle woman after, for hir sake

January's sight is indeed restored at the psychological moment, but May says she has only committed adultery to restore his sight, showing that Pluto and Proserpine have considerably influenced the plot at the ending of the tale.

Another function of the couple's introduction is to bring a completely new level of action, moving from the Rabelaisien tone and action of the tale to a level of mythology. This is matched by a different tone of language, which is more lyrical and free than the preceding narrative, thus enriching the whole tale. In addition, it contributes to the discussion of marriage in the manner already stated.

> **An example of this new language would make this much clearer.**

Another function is to provide a metaphor of the whole tale. Pluto is another version of Januarie, old and besotted, whereas Proserpine is May, ostensibly sweet and innocent but inwardly cunning and vindictive. In turn, the story of May and Januarie is a metaphor for that of Pluto and Proserpine. May's affair with Damian represents her six months above ground, in contrast to the winter in the underworld which May spends with Januarie. That humans and Gods behave in the same way is comic, as well as adding to the serious debate in the tale.

Another function is to underline the theme of fertility which is important in the tale. May's craving for a pear possibly suggests that she is pregnant, and Januarie is obsessed with virility, dosing himself with all kinds of aphrodisiacs. The idea of Proserpine as symbol of the summer, the daughter of Ceres, goddess of fertility, stresses this aspect of the tale at another level. In all these ways, the presence of the god and goddess adds a great deal to *The Merchant's Tale.*

EXAMINER COMMENT

This begins with what is perilously close to a narrative of the appearance of the god and goddess in the tale, but recovers just in time and gives a creditable account of the reasons why they are there. Notice that there is not a great deal of quotation here: textual reference to the place at which the two appear is generally sufficient, although a line or two to support the suggestion that their presence adds a different tone of language after the Rabelaisian qualities of the body of the tale would have strengthened the essay considerably.

GETTING STARTED

Many critical appreciation papers include a passage from a play as well as a poem and a piece of prose for you to write about. In such papers, you will be able to choose two of the three pieces offered but, as it's impossible to predict the nature of the passages, you need to be able to write about all three if you are to produce the best answer in the exam.

Writing about drama is in many ways similar to writing about poetry. There is a strong possibility that the passage set will be dramatic verse rather than prose and, even if it is in prose, you will still have to consider elements familiar from the critical process with poetry. Diction, imagery, situation and the nature of the speaker or speakers are, if anything, more important in dramatic writing than in poetry, and your experience in writing critical appreciation of poems will certainly help in your work on passages from plays. So, too, will the experience of reading closely, in the manner described in Chapter 4. Overall, then, there are many ways in which writing about unseen passages of drama is similar to writing about poetry.

There are also some new techniques to develop, which are dealt with in this chapter. They include looking, for, and writing about:

- the situation of the action and characters;
- how things change in the course of the passage;
- the nature of individual characters;
- what the characters contribute to the themes and ideas of the passage;
- dramatic interaction between characters;
- the importance of staging and physical action.

As well as advice on how to handle these topics, this chapter gives you some sample passage and answers to study and suggests ways in which you can develop the skills of close textual reading to make sure that you understand dramatic passages fully and can write clearly and critically about them in the measured time of the exam.

CHAPTER

9

DRAMA 1: CRITICAL APPRECIATION TECHNIQUES AND PRACTICE

FEATURES TO NOTE

READING A DRAMATIC PASSAGE

COMPARING PASSAGES

PRACTICE QUESTIONS

ESSENTIAL PRINCIPLES

While you are studying a passage from a play, you need to look for a number of features. These are listed below. They aren't presented here in order of importance: you should try to be aware of them all as you read, gradually developing your own interpretation of the passage in the way suggested for reading a poem in Chapter 4.

Meaning and situation

Sometimes, you will be given a brief note before the passage explaining something about the situation of the scene – who the characters are, what has just happened, and any other information essential to a grasp of the scene. More often, however, you will have to work this out from a careful reading of the passage itself.

Do this as you would with a passage of poetry – by making an initial interpretation which you will modify and confirm by careful and repeated reading, making your final interpretation only when you are sure that you have taken everything into account.

Setting

> **Try to SEE what happens on stage while you're reading.**

The actual, physical location where the scene takes place may not be of much importance to the action or main themes which the passage discusses, but you should look out for any clues which will help you establish where the scene is taking place. A close reading of the passage may give clues to this – look for:

- references to specific places;
- references or kinds of language which suggest a particular historical period;
- kinds of language which reveal a particular country or area.

Diction

One of the key elements to look for in dramatic passages is not only what the characters say but the words they use to say it. This tells you about:

- the individual characters – for example, whether they are aristocratic or educated or speak in a popular dialect; whether they speak in a regional accent and so reveal their place of birth; if they use language related to a skill or profession; or whether they are serious or comic in the way they speak;
- the setting of the play – the country or part of the country in which it is set, and the historical period;
- the relationship between characters, which may be indicated by the way in which they address each other; formally or informally; using terms of endearment; coldly; with language suggesting a professional relationship; as old friends; or in any other way which reveals something about why they are together.

A close reading of the *kinds of words*, then, is just as important as noting what the characters actually say, in gaining an awareness of the situation and the overall significance of the passage.

Tone

In poetry, the tone of voice in which the lines are spoken can often reveal as much as the words themselves. This is even more true in dramatic writing, since at its heart is the exchange of *ideas and feelings* between the characters. In everyday life, we communicate as much by the tone of our voices as by our words – so tone is of great importance in the theatre.

> **Always read stage directions to see HOW people speak in plays.**

The tone of a speech can be indicated in various ways. The simplest is a stage direction, making clear how a character is speaking, like this:

DUNOIS [*furiously disappointed*]: Is that all? You infernal young idiot; I have a mind to pitch you into the river.

THE PAGE [*not afraid, knowing his man*]: It looked frightfully jolly, that flash of blue. . .

But more often, you'll have to work out the tone for yourself. Think about the setting, situation and what you have so far worked out about the characters and their relationships. Be aware, too, that a character might be using sarcasm or irony – meaning the opposite of what he or she is saying. A careful reading of *all* the aspects of a scene, then, is necessary to arrive at an understanding of the tone of voice a character is using – and an awareness of the tone will help you to understand the overall importance and significance of the scene.

Mood

A dramatist will use language in the same way as a poet to create a mood or atmosphere. Read carefully therefore to work out, for example, whether the mood is tense or relaxed; uncertain or clear; reflective or dynamic – that is, whether it is concerned with thought or with movement and action. For example, many scenes of Peter Schaffer's *Equus* have a very great tension; O'Casey's plays about the Irish troubles show a dynamic mood, shifting rapidly from comic banter to tragic suffering; and Shaw's *Widowers' Houses* changes from romantic exchanges to moral discussion.

While reading to discover the mood of the scene, think about the rhythm and sound of the words, to see if they are used to help convey the effect. This will not always be a part of the dramatist's technique, but it's worth asking yourself whether the choice and movement of the language is used to reflect the mood of the scene.

Action and movement

> **Think about what's happening on stage – don't stop at the words.**

While you are reading, you will of course aim to gain an idea of what is actually *happening* in the scene. Sometimes the stage directions will help here – but more often you will need to work out what is going on from the words of the characters.

Look especially for signs of *movement* and *development* during the scene – how far things have changed from the situation at the beginning to that at the end. Sometimes action will be rapid, as in the short battle scenes of Shakespeare's history plays, or the comic scenes in Marlowe's *Doctor Faustus*. In other plays, for instance Shaw's *Heartbreak House*, there's less action than a series of views of a current phase of civilisation.

Dramatic interaction

This is one of the most important ways in which writing about passages from plays differs from writing about poems or pieces of prose. You need to explore the ways in which the dramatist allows the characters to *exchange* ideas and thoughts, so that there is a genuine sense of people interacting with each other in a real, convincing situation. In *Look Back in Anger*, for example, the interaction between Jimmy Porter and his wife's friend Helena begins with violent abuse and ends in a passionate physical relationship; in Beckett's *Endgame*, the interaction between all the characters shifts in a repetitive, almost random way from tenderness to nostalgic remembrance to aggression and personal dislike.

Look especially for ways in which emotions, ideas and relationships change during a passage. Ask yourself questions like these:

- Are these two characters closer to each other at the end than at the beginning?
- Has an idea been developed or made clearer?
- Has a particular statement modified the actions or thoughts of another character?

When you find that something like this has happened, try to work out the reason *why*. Is it because of the use of a particular kind of language; the statement of a particular idea or feeling; or the announcement of some new information? Asking questions like these will help you understand the interaction between the characters and also the *movement* of the passage, which is one of the essential features of dramatic writing.

Characters

> **Remember: the characters are all created by a dramatist, who controls their speech and action.**

One thing that you should *not* do in an exercise of this kind is simply to write about each of the characters in turn – in the way that you might gossip about a friend. Dramatic characters are *not* real people, and can't properly be considered outside the theatrical texts of which they are a part. One of the most common reasons why people do badly in exams – when writing about their set texts as well as in critical appreciation papers – is that they use this approach, so make sure that you *avoid* it!

Despite this, you do need to think carefully about the nature of each of the characters who speaks or takes part in the scene you are given for critical appreciation. Do this by studying the following:

- *What they say*. This is the essential information for understanding a character and his or her contribution to the whole play. Look at the kinds of words; the tone and diction of the speeches; the structure of the sentences; the frequency with which he or she speaks; stage directions which accompany the speeches; and the meaning of what he or she actually says and its significance within the situation of the scene. All of these will tell you a great deal about the character.

■ *What others say.* What the characters say to and about each other will reveal much about their relationships. Remember, though, that each character will look at things from his or her own viewpoint – so don't assume that they are giving a full or unbiased commentary on each other.

> **Think about characters who DON'T speak. What are they doing?**

■ *How the characters behave towards each other.* Look to see if one character is persistently ignored, or if his or her remarks are treated with respect and immediately acted on. Look, too, at what actions, if any, take place between the characters, since these too will reveal much about their relationships.

Themes and ideas

Just as a poem may be concerned with one central theme or idea, so a scene of a play may wish to get across a particular concept. It might, for example, be a discussion of the nature of justice; or the futility of armed combat; or a point about the nature of love or human relationships. While reading, think carefully about this and keep asking yourself whether the passage does have a subject of this sort, or whether the action is its main concern.

This does not mean that you should seek to identify one theme for the passage. Shakespeare's *Measure for Measure* is concerned with justice, but that does not prevent it from having some very funny scenes of bawdy comedy: many of Shaw's plays contain debates about intellectual, social or moral issues, but they still contain striking scenes about personal relationships.

READING A DRAMATIC PASSAGE

> **Ways to bring a dramatic passage to life.**

While you are reading the passage, you will be looking for the above features and trying to assemble an overall interpretation in the manner suggested for reading a poem in Chapter 5. To help you arrive at your interpretation, try the following approaches while reading:

Visualise the scene

Always try to *see* what is going on, as if it were being performed in the theatre in front of you. Visualise the actions of the characters and, if it helps, imagine the scene and costumes too. All this will make the passage real *as a theatrical event*, not just as a passage from a novel or a story. And this will help you become more aware of how the passage makes its effects *in the theatre*.

Imagine yourself as director

Pretend that you are directing the scene. How would *you* ask the cast to play it? What advice would you give your actors about speaking their lines, in terms of which words to emphasise, what gestures to make, where and when to move? Think of all these things as ways of making the scene clearer.

While you are doing this, you will be thinking about what the passage is fundamentally concerned with – a theme or idea, if there is one. And this will help you to understand how the passage works in putting across its main concerns, and what effects the dramatist is using to do this.

'Cast' the passage

If it helps to make the scene real, try giving the parts to individual actors whom you know. This can make a lot of difference – it can bring the scene to life for you and help you to understand its overall effect and significance. But don't get too carried away – an essay which tells the examiner who you think would play each part best, isn't going to do very well in the exam!

Try to respond as you would in the theatre

> **Your own response is important.**

When you've imagined yourself as the director, think about how you'd react as a member of the audience if you saw the play for the first time. Would you be filled with anger, or moved to pity? Would you laugh and, if so, why and at what? Would you be caught up in the suspense of the scene, wanting to know what happens next? All of these are questions which are useful ways of evaluating the passage – thinking about how well it works in the theatre.

Look at the question

Many questions about dramatic passages ask you to consider a particular aspect of the scene. It might ask, for example, why it is funny, or how the dramatist builds suspense; how the poet uses language to convey ideas or emotions, or how a dramatic exchange develops and changes. Make sure, when you are reading the passage, that you have this firmly in your mind: it's easy to forget that the question has a specific target of this sort, and to write instead a general critical appreciation of the scene – especially if you have just done the same about a poem or piece of prose. Be sure, then, that you know *exactly what you're asked to do* in a question of this sort.

> ❝ Try not to get TOO involved – remember to keep a critical distance. ❞

There is one more important point which you must bear in mind while reading a dramatic passage. Remember that the whole sequence of events has been created by one person – the writer of the play. It is *not* just a series of encounters or events which happened in real life and were then written down. Each speech and action has been prepared, corrected and revised as carefully as each word in a poem, so that they all come together to give the effect the dramatist desired. Your task as a critic – which is essentially what you become in this exercise – is to see what that effect is and to say how well the passage achieves it.

All of these points will be going through your mind while reading. As with a poem, try to relate the individual 'moment' – a line, or speech, or image – to the whole thing, and the expression – diction, tone and other elements – to the idea or emotion being put across. At the same time, try to relate this to the main topic raised by the question, unless you are being asked for a general appreciation of the passage.

Gradually, as you do this, you will find that your initial response or hypothesis will grow and clarify until you have a complete reading or interpretation of the passage and can set about writing your answer, using the techniques and the advice given in Chapter 5.

COMPARING PASSAGES

> ❝ Look at the advice on comparing poems in Chapter 5. ❞

Sometimes a question will ask you to compare two passages of dramatic writing. When you are doing this, you need to read each passage closely using all the approaches suggested here. In addition, though, you need to *bring the two together*. Always think about one passage in the terms of the other. Ask yourself:

- Which of the two is more effective on stage, and for what reasons?
- Which has the more effective characterisations?
- Which shows more complete interaction between characters?
- How do the settings and situations of each differ?
- What similarities and differences are there of themes and ideas?
- What similarities and differences are there in the kind of language the passages use?
- How do all these similarities and differences change and develop in the course of the passages?

Make sure, too, that you cover:

- any specific area which the question mentions;
- your own response to the two passages, with reasons.

If you follow this advice, as well as the general points about comparing passages given in Chapter 4, you should be able to produce clear passages of comparison about pieces of dramatic writing. Remember, too, that it's often easier to write about two passages than about one: as with two similar but contrasting colours, they are clearer when placed against each other.

PRACTICE QUESTIONS

Here are some questions which are typical of those appearing in critical appreciation papers. Answer them for yourself before turning to the student answers and examiner comments which come at the end of the chapter.

1   Write a critical appreciation of this passage, paying particular attention to the relationship between the two women and the ways in which the scene is comic.

> GWENDOLEN . . . Of course you are quite, quite sure that it is not Mr Ernest Worthing who is your guardian?
>
> CECILY: Quite sure. [*A pause.*] In fact, I am going to be his.

GWENDOLEN [*inquiringly*]: I beg your pardon?

CECILY [*rather shy and confidingly*]: Dearest Gwendolen, there is no reason why I should make a secret of it to you. Our little county newspaper is sure to chronicle the fact next week. Mr Ernest Worthing and I are engaged to be married.

GWENDOLEN [*quite politely, rising*]: My darling Cecily, I think there must be some slight error. Mr Ernest Worthing is engaged to me. The announcement will appear in the *Morning Post* on Saturday at the latest.

CECILY [*very politely, rising*]: I am afraid you must be under some misconception. Ernest proposed to me exactly ten minutes ago. [*Shows diary.*]

GWENDOLEN [*examines diary through her lorgnette carefully*]: It is very curious, for he asked me to be his wife yesterday afternoon at 5.30. If you would care to verify the incident, pray do so. [*Produces diary of her own.*] I never travel without my diary. One should always have something sensational to read in the train. I am so sorry, dear Cecily, if it is any disappointment to you, but I am afraid I have the prior claim.

CECILY: It would distress me more than I can tell you, dear Gwendolen, if it caused you any mental or physical anguish, but I feel bound to point out that since Ernest proposed to you he clearly has changed his mind.

GWENDOLEN [*meditatively*]: If the poor fellow has been entrapped into any foolish promise I shall consider it my duty to rescue him at once, and with a firm hand.

CECILY [*thoughtfully and sadly*]: Whatever unfortunate entanglement my dear boy may have got into, I will never reproach him with it after we are married.

GWENDOLEN: Do you allude to me, Miss Cardew, as an entanglement? You are presumptuous. On an occasion of this kind it becomes more than a moral duty to speak one's mind. It becomes a pleasure.

CECILY: Do you suggest, Miss Fairfax, that I entrapped Ernest into an engagement? How dare you? This is no time for wearing the shallow mask of manners. When I see a spade I call it a spade.

GWENDOLEN [*satirically*]: I am glad to say that I have never seen a spade. It is obvious that our social spheres have been widely different.

[*Enter* MERRIMAN, *followed by the footman. He carries a salver, table cloth, and plate stand:* CECILY *is about to retort. The presence of the servants exercises a restraining influence, under which both girls chafe.*]

2   Write a critical appreciation of this scene, showing the way in which control over the events passes from one character to another.

The executioner takes a set of steps from the cart and places it ready for the prisoner to mount. Then he climbs the tall ladder which stands against the gallows, and cuts the string by which the rope is hitched up; so that the noose drops dangling over the cart, into which he steps as he descends.

RICHARD [*with suppressed impatience to Brudenell*]: Look here, sir: this is no place for a man of your profession. Hadn't you better go away?

SWINDON: I appeal to you, prisoner, if you have any sense of decency left, to listen to the ministrations of the chaplain, and pay due heed to the solemnity of the occasion.

THE CHAPLAIN [*gently reproving Richard*]: Try to control yourself, and submit to the divine will. [*He lifts his book to proceed with the service.*]

RICHARD: Answer for your own will, sir, and those of your accomplices here [*indicating Burgoyne and Swindon*]: I see little divinity about them or you. You talk to me of Christianity when you are in the act of hanging your enemies. Was there ever such blasphemous nonsense! [*To Swindon, more rudely*] You've got up the solemnity of the occasion, as you call it, to impress the people with your own dignity—Handel's music and a clergyman to make murder look like piety! Do you suppose *I* am going to help you? You've asked me to choose the rope because you don't know your own trade well enough to shoot me properly. Well, hang away and have done with it.

SWINDON [*to the chaplain*]: Can you do nothing with him, Mr Brudenell?

CHAPLAIN: I will try, sir. [*Beginning to read*] Man that is born of woman hath—

RICHARD [*fixing his eyes on him*]: "Thou shalt not kill."

The book drops in Brudenell's hands.

CHAPLAIN [*confessing his embarrassment*]: What am I to say, Mr Dudgeon?

RICHARD: Let me alone, can't you?

BURGOYNE [*with extreme urbanity*]: I think, Mr Brudenell, that as the usual professional observations seem to strike Mr Dudgeon as incongruous under the circumstances, you had better omit them until—er—until Mr Dudgeon can no longer be inconvenienced by them. [*Brudenell, with a shrug, shuts his book and retires behind the gallows*]. You seem in a hurry, Mr Dudgeon.

RICHARD [*with the horror of death upon him*]: Do you think this is a pleasant sort of thing to be kept waiting for? You've made up your mind to commit murder: well, do it and have done with it.

BURGOYNE: Mr Dudgeon: we are only doing this—

RICHARD: Because you're paid to do it.

SWINDON: You insolent—[*he swallows his rage*].

BURGOYNE [*with much charm of manner*]: Ah, I am really sorry that you should think that, Mr Dudgeon. If you knew what my commission cost me, and what my pay is, you would think better of me. I should be glad to part from you on friendly terms.

RICHARD: Hark ye, General Burgoyne. If you think that I like being hanged, you're mistaken. I don't like it; and I don't mean to pretend that I do. And if you think I'm obliged to you for hanging me in a gentlemanly way, you're wrong there too. I take the whole business in devilish bad part; and the only satisfaction I have in it is that you'll feel a good deal meaner than I'll look when it's over. [*He turns away, and is striding to the cart when Judith advances and interposes with her arms stretched out to him. Richard, feeling that a very little will upset his self-possession, shrinks from her, crying*] What are you doing here? This is no place for you. [*She makes a gesture as if to touch him. He recoils impatiently*] No: go away, go away: you'll unnerve me. Take her away, will you.

JUDITH: Won't you bid me goodbye?

RICHARD [*allowing her to take his hand*]: Oh goodbye, goodbye. Now go—go—quickly. [*She clings to his hand—will not be put off with so cold a last farewell—at last, as he tries to disengage himself, throws herself on his breast in agony.*]

SWINDON [*angrily to the sergeant, who, alarmed at Judith's movement, has come from the back of the square to pull her back, and stopped irresolutely on finding that he is too late*] How is this? Why is she inside the lines?

SERGEANT (*guiltily*): I dunno, sir. She's that artful—can't keep her away.

BURGOYNE: You were bribed.

SERGEANT [*protesting*]: No sir—

SWINDON [*severely*]: Fall back. [*He obeys.*]

RICHARD [*imploringly to those around him, and finally to Burgoyne, as the least stolid of them*]: Take her away. Do you think I want a woman near me now?

BURGOYNE [*going to Judith and taking her hand*]: Here, madam: you had better keep inside the lines; but stand here behind us; and don't look.

Richard, with a great sobbing sigh of relief as she releases him and turns to Burgoyne, flies for refuge to the cart and mounts into it. The executioner takes off his coat and pinions him.

3 In the following passage, the speaker has sold his soul to the devil and is making his final speech at the end of the play. Read it carefully and then comment on its style and dramatic effectiveness.

FAUSTUS:

Ah Faustus. Now hast thou but one bare hour to live,
And then thou must be damned perpetually.
Stand still, you ever-moving spheres of heaven,
That time may cease and midnight never come.
Fair nature's eye, rise, rise again, and make   5
Perpetual day. Or let this hour be but
A year, a month, a week, a natural day,
That Faustus may repent and save his soul.
O lente, lente, currite noctis equi.
The stars move still, time runs, the clock will strike.   10
The devil will come, and Faustus must be damned.
Oh, I'll leap up to my God: who pulls me down?
See, see, where Christ's blood streams in the
   firmament.
One drop would save my soul, half a drop. Ah, my   15
   Christ!

Ah, rend not my heart for naming of my Christ!
Yet will I call on him. Oh, spare me, Lucifer!
Where is it now? 'Tis gone:
And see where God stretcheth out his arm,   20
And bends his ireful brows.
Mountains and hills, come, come, and fall on me,
And hide me from the heavy wrath of God.
No, no. Then will I headlong run into the earth.
Earth, gape! Oh no, it will not harbour me.   25
You stars that reigned at my nativity,
Whose influence hath allotted death and hell,
Now draw up Faustus like a foggy mist
Into the entrails of yon labouring cloud,
That when you vomit forth into the air   30
My limbs may issue from your smoky mouths,
So that my soul may but ascend to heaven.
        The watch strikes.
Ah! half the hour is past,
'Twill all be past anon.   35
Oh God, if thou wilt not have mercy on my soul,
Yet for Christ's sake whose blood hath ransomed me,
Impose some end to my incessant pain.
Let Faustus live in hell a thousand years,
A hundred thousand, and at last be saved.   40
Oh, no end is limited to damned souls.
Why wert thou not a creature wanting soul?
Or why is this immortal that thou hast?
Ah, Pythagoras' *metempsychosis*, were that true
This soul should fly from me, and I be changed   45
Unto some brutish beast.
All beasts are happy, for when they die
Their souls are soon dissolved in elements,
But mine must live still to be plagued in hell.
Cursed be the parents that engendered me!   50
No, Faustus, curse thyself, curse Lucifer,
That hath deprived thee of the joys of heaven.
        The clock strikes twelve.
Oh, it strikes, it strikes! Now body turn to air,
Or Lucifer will bear thee quick to hell.   55
        Thunder and lightning.
Oh soul, be changed into little water drops
And fall into the ocean, ne'er be found.
        Thunder. Enter the DEVILS.
My God, my God, look not so fierce on me.   60
Adders and serpents, let me breathe awhile.
Ugly hell, gape not, come not, Lucifer!
I'll burn my books. Ah, Mephistophilis!
        Exeunt with him.

Notes
1   '*O lente, lente currite noctis equi*' (line 9) Literally 'O slowly, slowly run ye horses of night'.
    The line is a quotation from Ovid, where it expresses a lover's wish that night be prolonged
    so that he may lie longer with his mistress.
2   *Pythagoras' metempsychosis* (line 44): his theory of the transmigration of souls.
3   *Quick* (line 55): Alive.

4   Both of these speeches are given by military leaders before battles. Write a critical
    comparison of them, showing their differences in aim, style and any other features you
    find interesting.

                              A

Now crouch, ye kings of greatest Asia,
And tremble when ye hear this scourge will come
That whips down cities and controlleth crowns,

Adding their wealth and treasure to my store.
The Euxine sea, north to Natolia;
The Terrene, west; the Caspian, north north-east;
And on the south, Sinus Arabicus;
Shall all be loaded with the martial spoils
We will convey with us to Persia.
Then shall my native city Samarcanda,   10
And crystal waves of fresh Jaertis' stream,
The pride and beauty of her princely seat,
Be famous through the furthest continents.
For there my palace royal shall be plac'd,
Whose shining turrets shall dismay the heavens,
And cast the fame of Ilion's tower to hell.
Thorough the streets, with troops of conquer'd kings,
I'll ride in golden armour like the sun;
And in my helm a triple plume shall spring,
Spangled with diamonds, dancing in the air,   20
To note me emperor of the three-fold world;
Like to an almond tree y-mounted high
Upon the lofty and celestial mount
Of ever-green Selinus, quaintly deck'd
With blooms more white than Herycina's brows,
Whose tender blossoms tremble every one
At every little breath that thorough heaven is blown.
Then in my coach, like Saturn's royal son
Mounted his shining chariot gilt with fire,
And drawn with princely eagles through the path   30
Pav'd with bright crystal and enchas'd with stars
When all the gods stand gazing at his pomp,
So will I ride through Samarcanda streets,
Until my soul, dissever'd from this flesh,
Shall mount the milk-white way, and meet him there.
To Babylon, my lords, to Babylon!
   Exeunt.
Notes
1 *Selinus* (line 24): town in Sicily.
2 *Herycina* (line 25): Venus.

B

*Alarum. Enter the King, Exeter, Bedford, Gloucester,
other lords, and soldiers with scaling-ladders*

KING HENRY:
Once more unto the breach, dear friends, once more,
Or close the wall up with our English dead!
In peace there's nothing so becomes a man
As modest stillness and humility:
But when the blast of war blows in our ears,
Then imitate the action of the tiger;
Stiffen the sinews, conjure up the blood,
Disguise fair nature with hard-favoured rage;
Then lend the eye a terrible aspect;
Let it pry through the portage of the head   10
Like the brass cannon; let the brow o'erwhelm it
As fearfully as doth a gallèd rock
O'erhang and jutty his confounded base,
Swilled with the wild and wasteful ocean.
Now set the teeth, and stretch the nostril wide,
Hold hard the breath, and bend up every spirit
To his full height! On, on, you noblest English,
Whose blood is fet from fathers of war-proof! –
Fathers that, like so many Alexanders,
Have in these parts from morn till even fought,   20
And sheathed their swords for lack of argument.

Dishonour not your mothers; now attest
That those whom you called fathers did beget you!
Be copy now to men of grosser blood,
And teach them how to war. And you, good yeomen,
Whose limbs were made in England, show us here
The mettle of your pasture; let us swear
That you are worth your breeding – which I doubt not;
For there is none of you so mean and base
That hath not noble lustre in your eyes.   30
I see you stand like greyhounds in the slips,
Straining upon the start. The game's afoot!
Follow your spirit, and upon this charge
Cry, 'God for Harry, England, and Saint George!'
Exeunt. Alarum, and chambers go off

STUDENT ANSWERS WITH EXAMINER COMMENTS

STUDENT ANSWER TO QUESTION 1

Good summary of your points at the start – this will get you some marks even if you don't have time to finish.

How would this refinement be shown on stage?

A good passage on the changing tone of the exchange.

The essence of this passage is the confusion between two characters, who both think that they are engaged to be married to the same man. The comedy arises in part from this misunderstanding but far more from the way in which their intense dislike for each other is concealed beneath social politeness. In many cases, this produces remarks whch are extremely comic because of the way anger and rudeness is hidden by apparently sophisticated language and terms of endearment in Gwendolen's speeches. In contrast, Cecily's statements are more straightforward, and she comes much closer to open expression of anger and resentment.

It is apparent from early on that the setting is one of genteel refinement and order, with references to the engagement and its announcement in newspapers, the names of the characters, and the polite tone that both adopt initially. It is the contrast between this refinement and the strong feelings of the two women that creates much of the comedy.

The first instance of this comes when the two women support their claims that Ernest has proposed to them by showing each other their diaries, as if simple documentary evidence of this sort will resolve the issue. Gwendolen's greater poise and assurance is shown by her witty remark about always having her diary with her as 'something sensational to read in the train' – an assurance which continues in her next sentence, which shows that, to her, there is no question that it is she who is to marry Ernest.

Cecily's elaborate statement of her concern for Gwendolen in the next speech – 'it would distress me more than I can tell you' – continues the comedy, which is here caused by the way that both women strive to be polite, and even affectionate, towards each other when underneath they are really very angry and dislike each other. Cecily's tone here is politely patronising, as if explaining something quite simple to a child who cannot understand it: as a result, she gains the upper hand by her tone of superiority, and the result is comic. Gwendolen, however, regains control by suggesting that 'the poor fellow' may have been 'entrapped' into a 'foolish promise', from which it is her duty to free him. This not only gives her the initiative – it also suggests that Cecily has been unscrupulous in luring Ernest away from her. Once again, the combination of angry and even offensive ideas with very restrained, genteel expression is richly comic.

In contrast, Cecily is much more serious, as shown by the stage direction 'thoughtfully and sadly'. Yet she, too, is capable of being genteelly offensive, referring to what has happened as an 'unfortunate entanglement', which succeeds in making Gwendolen more openly angry. Her statement that speaking one's mind is not only a duty but also 'a pleasure', however, shows that she can still control her anger and give it a comic surface. Cecily, however, seems less able to do this, making a reference to 'calling a spade a spade'. This is a fatal mistake: it allows Gwendolen to seize on the expression and make her wonderfully comic remark about never having seen a spade, and thus claiming great social superiority over Cecily.

The appearance of Merriman the butler at this point is comic because it reminds us of how incongruous the argument is: the two are apparently meeting for afternoon tea. This is a very formal, polite occasion, and the appearance of all the formal mechanisms of the butler, footman and tea things at this point makes the whole scene almost ridiculously funny. The fact that Cecily instructs that tea be laid 'as usual', while the two women 'glare at each other' is a final comment on the way in which the scene's comedy works.

Overall, the relationship is one based on dislike and mistrust, in which each of the women is constantly trying to get the upper hand, by showing greater control over her feelings and a prior claim to Ernest. It is comic largely because of the way that polite behaviour is used to conceal deep anger and animosity.

> " Fair summary – but more is needed on how the play works in the theatre. "

EXAMINER COMMENT

This answer begins and ends with a general statement of the scene's effectiveness, with special reference to the concerns of the question, and spends most of its time explaining the working of the scene as it unfolds. Notice how there is reference to the ways in which first one woman and then the other gains control of what is happening, showing an awareness of the changing nature of the relationship which is an important aspect to clarify when writing about dramatic passages.

One thing that the answer lacks is explicit mention of the way that the scene would be far more comic on stage, with the gestures and tones of voice of the women adding much to the comedy. Although the final reference to the appearance of tea things goes some way in this direction, the point needs to be made earlier on that the stage presence and behaviour of the two women are essential to the comedy of the scene.

STUDENT ANSWER TO QUESTION 2

This passage is striking because of the way in which Richard, who is just about to be executed, frequently overcomes his fear and takes over control of the proceedings from his executioners. This is shown right at the start, where he tells the chaplain that 'this is no place for a man of your profession'. This is effective because it rejects the idea of the administration of justice which lies behind the presence of a clergyman at an execution, instead seeing it as an act of violence. Swindon realises this, but makes an appeal to Richard, trying to restore formality and dignity to the proceedings and, in so doing, regain control over them. This continues when the chaplain asks Richard to 'submit to the divine will' – a chilling phrase which provokes an angry response from Richard. In his reply he calls the executioners 'accomplices' of the chaplain, making clear his feeling that they are committing a crime. He makes his contempt quite clear when he says that talk of Christianity at a hanging is 'blasphemous nonsense', and says that Swindon's purpose is only to impress people with his 'dignity'. Here Richard is angry and forthright – the stage direction asks him to speak 'more rudely', and he regains control of the scene – but his anger perhaps also shows that he is upset and disturbed, not unnaturally considering the situation.

> " Good point on Richard's rejection of the usual order of things. "

The conflict continues in the next exchange. The chaplain begins to read the burial service, and Richard interrupts with one of the ten commandments, 'Thou shalt not Kill'. The chaplain is confused, and Richard then presses home his advantage by answering his question with 'Let me alone'. This again shows his mixture of control and despair – he tries to take control of the situation but is really upset and perhaps frightened. Burgoyne takes over, speaking 'with extreme urbanity', using sophisticated language and tone to regain control, and saying with a detachment that again stresses the fact that he is in charge, 'You seem in a hurry, Mr Dudgeon'. Richard's reply again shows his dual attitude: he speaks 'with the horror of death upon him', yet he still speaks with defiance in saying 'You've made up your mind to commit murder', showing that he doesn't recognise their authority.

> " How would this come across in the theatre? "

Burgoyne then tries to reason with Richard by explaining why they are executing him, but Richard interrupts, saying that they are doing it 'Because you're paid to'.

This is very effective, in that Swindon almost loses his temper before he 'swallows his rage'. Burgoyne, however, answers more calmly and takes control, by being very detached and talking about how much he paid for his commission in the army. This cynicism is his way of taking control, but Richard is understandably not amused by it.

He does, however, manage to reply with a kind of patronising humour which again gives him the advantage, when he says that he doesn't 'like being hanged', even if it is 'in a gentlemanly way'. He is also sure that he is in the right, saying that Burgoyne will 'feel a good deal meaner than I'll look' after the hanging. The appearance of Judith at this point almost upsets Richard's composure, as the stage-direction make clear and as he, too, indicates by saying 'You'll unnerve me'. The presence of Judith may almost unnerve Richard, but it also shows the corruption of the army, since Burgoyne knows that the Sergeant has been bribed to let her near. Richard's composure is still present when he asks Burgoyne if he wants 'a woman near me now', but almost goes when she leaves: he breathes 'a great sobbing sigh' and turns to the cart. It is almost as if he finds being executed less of a strain than bidding farewell to Judith, but it also shows his courage.

66 Good comparison of Richard's changing feelings here. 99

This passage shows very skilfully the way in which the initiative and control passes from Richard to his executioners and back again, yet also reveals Richard's understandable fear and anger. The mood is at times comic, as for example when Richard says 'Because you're paid for it', and at others very serious, as when Judith throws herself at Richard. It is very effective in controlling the reactions of the audience, especially when the mood and controlling character change very rapidly.

EXAMINER COMMENT

This answer charts well the changes of control and mood in the passage, and supports its points well by brief quotation. Again, though, it could say more about how the passage works on stage, with the presence of the executioner and the gallows adding a constant, gruesome reminder of what Richard is about to suffer.

Notice how, although it goes through the passage in chronological sequence, it avoids simply telling the story by first *commenting* on the events and then quoting a short phrase to support it – a version of the point made in Chapter 2, which stresses that you should first state a concept and then give evidence to support it.

STUDENT ANSWER TO QUESTION 3

This passage is dramatic because it shows how Faustus' feelings change and develop at the very end of his life, as he grows more fearful about what will happen when the devil comes to collect his soul. He feels regret and remorse, and draws us into these feelings as they mount to climax at the end of the speech.

When the passage starts we are told that Faustus has 'one bare hour to live' before he will be 'damned perpetually'. He appeals to 'heaven' for the planets to stop moving, already passionately wishing for more time. His quotation of Ovid is very ironic, since he is pleading now for more time of life itself, not for more time for sinful pleasure.

Faustus next turns to Christ in his longing for life. First he turns to Christ, then asks forgiveness of God, and finally in line 18 cries out 'O spare me Lucifer', suggesting that he still places more faith in the devil than in God, showing his blasphemy and confusion at the approach of death. This confusion helps us to share the scene, making it dramatically real as it unfolds before us. Faustus presents us with a literal picture of God bending over him with 'ireful brows', and this and his appeal to the stars to draw him up 'like a foggy mist' make the scene very compelling.

66 How does the writer make one person talking dramatic? 99

The stage direction of line 33 continues the dramatic movement. In the speech the space of an hour is compressed into a few moments, yet this is dramatically convincing because of the intensity of the scene; it also helps to show Faustus' growing panic as the time left him diminishes so quickly. As the time slides away, Faustus' panic increases. He asks for some end to his torment in hell, if pardon is not possible, pleading for 'a thousand years' or even 'a hundred-thousand, and at last be saved'. In his panic he curses his parents and asks why he has an immortal soul. Then a kind of calm comes on him as he realises, in lines 51–2, that he alone is responsible for his own damnation.

The dramatic compression of time continues with the striking of the clock at this point, and in desperation he asks to be turned into drops of water: he is prepared to accept anything to avoid eternal damnation. Faustus' psychological torment changes into physical form when Faustus is carried off by devils; Faustus' panic shows that these are real and terrifying to him.

The style of the writing helps us to share the dramatically evolving horror and despair felt by Faustus. Lines 1 and 2 state his realisation of damnation; lines 6 and 7, in their mounting speed, show his growing despair, and the ungrammatical start to the sentence in line 6 – 'Or' – shows his panic. But Faustus realises his damnation is inevitable, and shows this by the logical sequence of events that is presented in lines 10 and 11. The style lets us share Faustus' vision of Christ's blood, in the desperate way he adds that 'half a drop' would save his soul; we are also drawn into his feelings by the immediacy of 'Where is it now? 'Tis gone'.

The simple style of lines 34–5 shows how inevitable his death is – the time is half gone, and the remaining half will pass quickly too. As the time goes, Faustus speaks in shorter and shorter sentences and fragments of language, in lines 49–52, making the pace quicker and letting us share Faustus' anguish.

I find this a very effective piece of dramatic writing since, even though there is only one character on stage, we are drawn into the action because the style of speech, as much as the words themselves, draws us into the mind of the character and lets us share his anguish.

> **Note use of line numbers instead of quotation – to save time.**

> **Not so much 'simple style' as clear logical progression.**

EXAMINER COMMENT

This answer chooses to approach the passage in rather a different way from the previous one. It first goes through the passage to clarify actions, and then makes comments on the style. Although the points are made well, I think that the answer would be more effective were it to draw together the points and make them in a single sequence, to show the way that style and other facets come together to create the effect of the passage.

Bear this in mind when writing on passages: very often the way that you organise a response can make the difference between a pass and a good pass, so it's worth planning and structuring your answer carefully and precisely.

STUDENT ANSWER TO QUESTION 4

These two speeches share the situation of being given before a battle, but they are different in circumstances, diction and tone.

In the first, the speaker is talking in general terms about his own greatness and power which will shortly be demonstrated in battle, telling the 'greatest kings of Asia' to 'crouch' and 'tremble' before him. In the second, the speaker is talking to his own army, encouraging them and rousing them to 'Stiffen the sinews' and 'conjure up the blood'. This difference of circumstance perhaps accounts for the difference in tone and diction. Whereas the first is full of rich sounding words, names of countries which the speaker says he will conquer, and is sure in tone, as the speaker meditates his coming victories, the second is much more down to earth, urging the soldiers forward in language which, while rousing, is far more straighforward.

Much of the effect of the first is made through the exotic sounds of the place names – Euxine Sea, Natolia, Sinus Arabicus, Samarcanda. It is as if the speaker is intoxicated with them. On the other hand, the power of the second speech comes from the way the speaker gives courage to the listeners – by stressing the need for warlike action in strong, direct images such as those of the forces of nature in lines 10–14.

The difference in language reflects the difference in aim of the two speeches. The second is given with the intention of rousing the troops to action by playing on their ideas of nobility and patriotism. This is first stated in line 17, which refers to 'you noblest English' and goes on to compare their fathers to 'so many Alexanders', an

> **Notice that right from the start the answer COMPARES the two passages.**

> **Look at the way the expression and sentence structure helps to make the comparison more direct here.**

allusion to the classical hero which stresses the bravery of the ancestors of the soldiers. References to 'good yeomen' and a plea that the soldiers 'Dishonour not your mothers' – bring disgrace on their parents – complete the way in which the soldiers' patriotism is played upon by the speaker here.

By contrast, the first speech seems to have as an aim the simple glorification of the speaker. He tells how 'my native city, Samarcanda' shall 'Be famous through the furthest continents', and how his palace will 'cast the fame of Ilion's power to hell' – an allusion to the renown of Troy, which will be as nothing in comparison to the speaker's fame. Instead of the simple directness of the second speech, the first is full of rich and exotic sounds and images, all of which are there to stress the grandeur of the speaker, lines 17–21 showing this quality very clearly.

A difference in aim is shown in the climactic passages of the two speeches. The first is concerned with the triumphal entry of the speaker into Samarcanda, which is described in terms of great richness, achieved through a comparison to 'Saturn's royal son', a Greek god, and the rich description of the chariot 'gilt with fire' drawn by 'princely eagles' through a path 'Pav'd with bright crystal and enchas'd with stars' and admired by 'all the gods'. In place of this richness, the second passage is concerned with urging the English soldiers to fight – a far more practical end. It begins by flattering the men, saying that none of them 'hath not noble lustre in your eyes' and that they all stand like greyhounds straining to race off – far more vigorous and dynamic images than those of imperial pomp created in the first passage. The final line is a stirring battle-cry with which, having roused the soldiers to a fury, the leader sends them off to war.

The two passages are thus very different in aim and style. The first is rather a self-indulgent view of the glory to be gained by victory for a single great leader; the second, a practical exercise in rousing troops to fight again in battle. Both are very powerful, but in strongly different ways, and both use language in a manner quite appropriate to their purposes.

> Magical language can be part of the effect of theatre.

> 'Self-indulgent' could be expressed more clearly – self-centred, perhaps, or egocentric

EXAMINER COMMENT

These two passages are both very rich and very complex so that even if each was set for critical appreciation on its own, it's unlikely that anyone would be able to say all there was to say about them. Here, the answer rightly concentrates on those elements singled out for comment by the question – the differences in aim and style. Such limitation is necessary in the exam – you'd certainly not be able to explain and discuss every aspect of language and imagery in both passages, but instead should single out the most striking ones, as has been done here.

CHAPTER 10

DRAMA 2: STUDYING DRAMA

READING A PLAY

MAKING NOTES

CONSOLIDATING

WRITING ABOUT PLAYS

CONCLUSION

GETTING STARTED

Studying a play is in some ways like studying poetry. But in many other ways drama is very different: it has a life and world of its own, as a continuously changing and developing theatrical reality. Trying to bring the two together can be confusing. Should you think about the feelings and responses of individual characters, or consider instead the larger issues and themes the play discusses? Should you think about how the play works on stage, as a combination of movements, speech and responses between a group of characters, or should you think about it as a series of separate poems or chapters of prose? And just what is it that makes something inherently dramatic, rather than poetic or literary, like a novel or piece of descriptive or analytical writing?

All of these questions are of central importance to the business of reading and studying plays. And, in addition, there are the more familiar areas to be thought of – sorting out how the language makes its effects, what the main themes are, and the structural techniques which are important in any literary work. But there is one problem which is fundamental to studying plays which doesn't arise elsewhere: how do you make sure that your study covers both the language of the play *and* its stage presence?

This chapter looks at the whole process of studying dramatic texts and writing about them in the exam. It covers:

- reading through a play to get to know what's going on;
- detailed reading and textual analysis;
- the production elements – how a play works on stage;
- making notes on dramatic texts;
- how to talk about characters;
- distinguishing between plots, sub-plots and themes;
- planning and writing essays about plays;
- the language of dramatic criticism.

Studying a play is demanding in very special ways, since it needs both the ability to grasp features of language and the skill of visualising the play as a continuing performance on stage. It includes some familiar territory – the principles of detailed reading and critical analysis covered in Chapters 1, 3, and 9 are all important. Moving from the close study of individual passages set for critical appreciation is one of the most important changes of perspective and approach you have to make in your literary studies. This chapter helps you to make this shift, and prepare you for the next chapter, which looks in detail at some exam questions on plays frequently set for study and suggests ways in which you might answer them.

ESSENTIAL PRINCIPLES

READING A PLAY

> Plays exist IN THE THEATRE – never forget this.

When you are looking at a collection of poems, the main focus is on the individual poems which make up the collection. When you're reading a play, the balance is rather different: you have to be aware of what's going on at each moment, but you also need a larger awareness of the play's development and its growth – the life of the play as a changing reality in the theatre.

This means that, as well as the close textual reading needed for any literary work, there are other techniques that you need to master when studying a play. Critics talk of the division between the study and the stage – the way in which some people look upon a play as something to be analysed, while others see it only as something to be performed. Your task as a student of dramatic literature is to see that *both* aspects are covered fully, and that each one clarifies and complements the other. Throughout your studies, then, try to bring literary analysis to bear on stage performance, and vice versa.

First steps

You should always remember that plays are written to be performed – taken in by the audience visually and aurally, within the confines of a theatre. That means that they are both 'real' and 'artificial' – real in the sense of presenting a sequence of actions resembling those of actual life, and artificial in the sense of being a product of artifice or creative skill. We become involved in the action to the extent of *thinking* it real – yet we only have to look at the borders of the stage to realise that this is a vision of reality, not reality itself. Reading a play, then, should help you to maintain this dual awareness.

As soon as the curtain goes up, a performance gives you a lot of information that reading a play doesn't. It tells you, visually and directly, for example, the ages of the characters, and the nature of the place where things happen. You can supply this information when you're reading by looking carefully at two important parts of the play:

> Think of the characters both as individuals and as creations of the dramatist.

- The *dramatis personae* or list of characters.
  This will tell you about the main characters – names, relationships, and perhaps ages and something of their characters. If there isn't a separate list of characters, each one may be described on his or her first appearance. Read these details carefully: they're not part of the 'text' in the sense of being part of the dialogue, but they are just as important in the overall nature of the play. Careful reading will help you to understand the characters and to grasp the action and themes of the play more quickly.

- The *opening stage direction*.
  Plays vary in stage directions. Some playwrights, like G. B. Shaw, write very full, complex stage directions; others, especially those from the sixteenth and early seventeenth centuries, give very few, although these are often supplemented by modern editors.
  Whatever the extent of the first stage directions, read them carefully. They will help you to follow what's going on, and to see the action imaginatively – the next best thing to seeing it in the theatre.

> Stage history and production illustrations can help you visualise the play.

Your edition might also include illustrations of productions, stage designs or costume drawings. If so, look closely at them, as they too will make the play more real to you. It's also very likely that your edition will contain a critical introduction to the play, stating its main themes and ideas and other points of critical and theatrical interest. Although it's tempting to read this first, to get some idea of what the play is about, it's much better not to. If you go straight on to the play, you'll be able to form *your own* ideas about it first, instead of having your first impression inevitably coloured by those of the editor. Save the introduction for later; put yourself in the place of the audience for the first night of the play, and let it speak for itself.

First reading

> In the first reading, imagine that you're seeing the play.

Once you've looked at these two essential preliminaries, you should read the play itself. Try to read it quickly, so that it takes you about as long to read as it would to see a performance. At this point, don't worry too much if there are things you don't understand – though clearly keeping an idea of how the plot progresses will help.

While reading, try to hear the different characters speaking in separate voices. If it helps, 'cast' the play with actors familiar from plays or television series you've seen. Try, too, to visualise it – see the events unfolding on a mental stage in your mind. If you can, get together with some other people and give each one a part to play – though try to make sure that your friends can read fluently and clearly, as otherwise the reading may be rather destructive. Alternatively, you might be able to read the play quickly in class – though this is difficult to do at a single sitting.

However you read the play for the first time, you should try to respond to it as fully as you can, while still keeping an open mind about it. Think about various interpretations, or different themes which the play might discuss – but be prepared to accept new ones when you come to study it in more depth. It may help at this point just to *jot down* your impressions of the play in a brainstorming session. Don't worry about explaining the story or plot: you'll soon become familiar with that and almost take it for granted. Instead, think about:

> **What to look for at first.**

- Language – especially in the ways it makes the play work in the theatre;
- Characters – especially what they contribute to the plot;
- Staging – any points especially striking about the play's action;
- Structure – the way the play unfolds, in terms of what we see and what we don't, the dramatist's use of suspense, points of climax, or other similar matters;
- Themes and ideas – any topics which the play seems to be discussing, either openly or by less obvious suggestion such as symbolism.

Try this approach – you'll be surprised how much you can find to write as an intitial response. Often the very process of writing helps to define your ideas. The moment when you've just read a play, and your mind is full of various impressions of it, is full of possibilities for this kind of activity.

Detailed reading

> **Study should complement what happens in performance.**

This is the process covered in Chapters 1 and 2. While there is no substitute for it if you are to gain the knowledge of the text that you need in order to pass the exam, the process is rather different for a play. The difficulty is that you need to bring together a full knowledge of the text, with all its stated and unstated significances, with an awareness of how it works in the theatre. This doesn't mean that *either* the study or the stage should dominate: instead, that you should make the two constantly reflect and deepen each other.

When reading in this way, look for:

> **Always relate the language to how the play works in the theatre.**

- *Features of language.* This applies especially to plays written in verse – plays of the Elizabethan and Jacobean period, which will often use very rich figurative language as well as prose which has many poetic qualities in its use of rhythm, sound and allusion. Think about the dramatic qualities of the language:
  – the effect it has on other characters;
  – how it is related to the action of the play, and develops the plot;
  – how it is related to the themes of the play and clarifies their unfolding on stage;
  – how the audience will respond to it.
- *Themes and ideas of the play.*
- *Aspects of structure* – whether, for example, the play grows to a climax, or uses suspense or other techniques to hold the audience's interest or build tension.
- *What's happening on stage.* What action is a character performing while talking? How is this related to what he or she says, and to the play's themes? Is there ever action without words and, if so, what is its effect? Think, too, about the characters who are *not* speaking. Ask yourself what they are doing, in particular how they are responding to the speaker and what he or she is saying. This can often reveal much about a theme or aspect of a play.

> **Try to read a play with other people, each person taking a part.**

Reading with care in this way can be greatly enhanced if you do it with other people. Reading and discussing parts of a play in class is one way to do this – another is getting together with some fellow–students to talk over a particular scene.

MAKING NOTES

GENERAL OR COMMENTARY NOTES

These are notes you can make during or just after the process of close reading. It's really a matter of going through and noting down points of importance in any of the areas mentioned above, and on any other topics or points which strike you as important or interesting.

In this way you'll produce a set of notes which are more or less a commentary on the scene, showing points of importance in various areas. As well as this, you can annotate your text in the way shown in Chapter 1. Be careful about this, though. If you're allowed to take the text into the exam with you, you may have to erase such marks. And notes in a text are often less clear than those you make on paper! Whatever method you use, make sure that your notes are clear – both in the sense of being well expressed and in the sense of being easy to read – you'll have to work from them later on when you come to revise, remember.

At the end of a session of detailed reading and note-taking, you'll end up with a sheet of general commentary notes like those shown in Fig. 10.1. Keep them carefully and use them as a guide when reading through the text later on, and as the basis for revision and further notes.

> Don't rely too much on these notes – they're no substitute for the text itself.

Duchess of Malfi

Act I

127 Conventional exposition, Antonio and Delio. Satire on court life (incidental)
"He rails at those things which he wants;/ Would be as lecherous, covetous, or proud,/ Bloody or envious, as any man,/ if he had means to be so."
(Antonio on Bosola)

128 "He and his brother are like plum trees that grow crooked over standing pools; they are rich and overladen with fruit, but none but crows, flies and caterpillars feed upon them" (Bosola on Cardinal and Ferdinand)

129 Bosola feels cheated by Cardinal/Comparison of Court strata to hospital.

130 Obsequiousness of courtiers Rod and Chris.

131 Character of Cardinal: very jealous and vindictive
Character of Ferdinand: very perverse and turbulent
Animal imagery – spider – imagery of devils and gods etc.
Duchess: divine beauty and sweetness to wake the dead.

133 Beginning of plots of Card. & Ferd.
Imagery of plants – the oft shaking of the cedar tree fastens it more at root.

134 "Familiar" use of witchcraft imagery (devilishness) – hell etc.

135 Bosola should be "like a politic dormouse" –
Some classical imagery "Subtler than Vulcan's net".

136 Hint of incest about persuasions to Duchess not to remarry
– later motive of money appears.

138 Imagery of death – making will etc.

140 "'Tis not the figure cut in alabaster/ kneels at my husband's tomb".

141 Comparison of married bliss to harmony of the spheres.

142 Already Duchess described as mad – later madness imagery vital.

Act II

142 Satire on court behaviour

143 Imagery of decay of human beings – a false façade presented to the world. – also animal imagery.

144 "You would look up to Heaven, but I think/The devil, that rules i'the air, stands in your light."
(Antonio of Bosola)

146/147 Bosola's tricks to get her to eat the apricots show she is pregnant.

148 Devil imagery "the devil takes delight to hang at a woman's girdle".

149 Cover story of robbery to conceal the delivery

150 II/III – use of animal imagery – Ant. calls Bos. a mole who undermines him.

Fig. 10.1 Commentary notes

TOPIC NOTES

Once you've made your commentary notes, you'll find that particular *topics* will emerge as important in the play. They could be:

- themes or ideas;
- particular kinds of language or imagery;
- theatrical effects such as the use of suspense;
- contributions of characters to the growth of the plot;
- aspects of the theatrical nature of the play – the use made of sets, costumes, or action which is largely visual rather than verbal in nature.

One way of making these notes is to go through your commentary notes and to mark off each topic with a separate colour or number. You can then go back and write a separate sheet of notes on each topic. Fig. 10.2 does this for *Imagery* in *The Duchess of Malfi*. In this way you'll end up with a collection of single sheets which cover the main aspects of the play.

Imagery of <u>The Duchess of Malfi</u>
Death, madness, witchcraft, sorcery, religion, animals, precious metals/
jewels, (Classical)
<u>Death, madness and illness</u>
i) Scene where madmen play before the Duchess' murder
ii) When D. wants to marry A., he is summoned "to make a new will".
iii) "This is flesh and blood, sir; / Tis not the figure cut in alabaster/
   kneels at my husband's tomb"
iv) D's marriage = a terrible illness (Ferd + Card) – treated with "desperate
   physic".
v) Constant references to death – create atmosphere
→ Used to build up atmosphere of gloom, underline final madness
   of Ferdinand, insane world etc.
<u>Witchcraft, sorcery and superstition</u>
i) Bosola = Ferdinand's "familiar"
ii) Ruined castle gives atmosphere (as does moonlit palace)
iii) Wolves digging up graves (cf <u>Wasteland</u>)
iv) Cariola dislikes disguise of flight to Antonio as a religious pilgrimage
→ Used to underline evil character of Ferd. + Card., gives atmosphere,
   textual 'thickening'.
<u>Religion</u>
i) References to heaven, hell and the devil
ii) "You would look up to heaven, but I think/The devil that rules i'the air,
   stands in your light".
iii) Movement of spheres, influence of heaven's rule on earth etc
iv) "What devil art thou that counterfeits Heaven's thunder?"
v) Used chapel of Loretto – shows power of religion with three characters.
vi) Character of priest is full of imagery, almost condoning and encouraging
   D. + Ant.
→ Atmosphere – char. of D. (v. religious), char of Ferd + Card. (irreligious).
<u>Animals</u>
i) Underlines baseness of character – B. = "a political dormouse".
   Shows insignificance and baseness of men's actions and motivations.
<u>Precious Metals and Jewels</u>
i) Opulence and greed – Ferd. + Card. shown in this light
ii) Also shows hypocrisy + deception of F. + C. "Why dost thou wrap thy poison
   pills/In Gold and sugar?" D. of M.
<u>Classical</u>
– "Subtler than Vulcan's net" – less important than others.
<u>General</u>
i) V. forceful in nature – an integral part of play & built up + used almost as 'leitmotif.'
ii) Without it D/M would be less interesting seen as tragedy
iii) Creation of atmosphere, including characters, is main function of imagery.

Fig. 10.2 Student notes on imagery of *The Duchess of Malfi*

CONSOLIDATING

❝ Ways of reinforcing your work. ❞

❝ Be careful about productions of plays. Some are very good, some aren't... ❞

❝ ... and the same is true of films and television versions. ❞

❝ Visualise when reading. ❞

At this stage you can begin to *consolidate* and reinforce your work on the play by considering the views of *other people*. This might include:

- Reading critical interpretations of the play, including the introduction to your edition of the text. Remember the advice given about this process in Chapter 1, though – don't be overwhelmed by critical readings, but instead try to absorb them into your own overall interpretation of the play.

- Discussing it with other people who have different interpretations. Once again, though, don't be too easily led into believing what they have to say – stand your ground and argue your own interpretation.

- Seeing productions. In an ideal world, it would help to see two or more contrasting productions of each play you study, but in practice that's rarely possible. If you can see a single production, that's fine – it will bring together your work, and perhaps give you some new ideas. Once again, don't be led into thinking that this is the *only* way of interpreting the play – the way you have originally visualised it is just as valid, and might be a much sounder reading.

  By all means watch film or television adaptions of the play too, but be careful – very often such adaptations change the action from the original. Remember, too, that the effect will be very different from that in the theatre; you'll be able to see the faces of the actors in close-up, so the director will be aiming your attention towards certain parts far more than in the theatre. The action, too, may well have been changed to allow for the greater potential of film: scenes may be cut or added, and material set indoors moved outside to give greater visual variety. So always make sure that you know just how closely the version you see is based on the play itself.

  If you can't see a production, don't worry. Thinking carefully about how you'd *like* to see it produced can often be just as valuable, if not more so. Consider the stage design, lighting, costumes, movement and any other aspects of the written text which are important. For example, if there are any particularly difficult scenes, ask yourself how you would make them 'work' on stage. If you're also studying art, try doing some designs.

  Activities like these can be very rewarding, but make sure that they don't take over from the study of the play's text – as a blueprint for stage performance – which should always be the main focus of your attention.

- Read about the stage history of the play. Many editions of plays have a section on this, giving dates and brief descriptions of important productions. Knowing about its stage history can often help you to broaden your knowledge of how the play works in the theatre.

When you follow any of these approaches, make a few notes and keep them in your file with the commentary and topic notes. You may find that an aspect of a production will help to clarify a general point, and once again bring together the study and the stage. Always make a note of the date of the production, and who directed or mounted it – a useful detail which adds precision if you need to refer to it in support of a point in the exam.

WRITING ABOUT PLAYS

❝ Chapters 2 and 3 will help here. ❞

The business of writing about plays is similar to writing about poems or novels – it's the same process of defining the question, thinking of points which are related to it, and then supporting them with evidence from your knowledge of the text.

There is, however, one particular problem which is more apparent with plays than with other kinds of writing. Dramatic criticism makes use of a number of *words* which are in everyday use, but which have very specific meanings. If you use them in the rather imprecise way that we all do in normal speech, you run the risk of not gaining the credit for what might be a perfectly good point. So make sure that you are happy about the meanings of the following words when you use them in an exam essay.

- **Absurd** While this normally means ridiculous, in the theatre it refers to a particular kind of play, written in the middle of the twentieth century and concentrating on making moral or philosophical points through plots that are 'absurd' – for example, a giant corpse which keeps growing or a choir of weighing-machines. Much better to avoid its use apart from in this very specific way.

- **Action** This refers to whatever is happening on stage, not only something which is 'active'. It's quite valid, therefore, to talk of the 'action' of a play even in those of, say, Samuel Beckett, where very little actually 'happens'.

- **Business or Stage-business** This is a term used to refer to parts of the action which call for the characters to perform certain physical acts. In John Arden's *Serjeant Musgrave's Dance*, for example, there is a lot of 'business' which includes assembling a Gatling gun. It's easy to overlook this kind of action, as it's only described in the stage directions. But remember that a paragraph of description may take several minutes to perform on stage – so don't overlook *stage business* in your study of a text, and make sure that you use the term properly when writing about it.

- **Character** This is generally used to mean 'a person in a play'. Try not to use it to mean 'what a person's like'; otherwise you end up talking about 'the character of a character'. Try using 'nature' instead.

- **Comedy** In popular speech, this simply means something that is funny. In the theatre this is not always the case. Shakespeare's comedies, for example, are not always 'funny'. Instead, the word refers to a particular kind of play. Shakespearean comedy generally moves from confusion and uncertainty about identity and love to a conclusion in which confusions are resolved, lovers are united and there is a feeling of progression and resolution. *Comedy of Manners* is a general term for later seventeenth and eighteenth century plays which make their effect by satirising sophisticated behaviour, generally with a strong love interest; and *Social Comedy* is a term often used to describe later writing on a similar theme, such as the plays of Oscar Wilde.

- **Comic** This has two meanings in the theatre: the usual, everyday sense of something funny, and the sense of 'referring to a comedy' in structure or tone. Because this can be confusing, it might be better to use the term 'comedic' when you mean the latter; it may sound a little fussy, but it makes the meaning absolutely clear.

- **Drama** Generally this means a play or story, or even an event in real life, that is serious or sensational in some way. In its strict sense, it is simply a label for a type of art, like 'poetry' or 'prose', so try to avoid the popular sense.

- **Dramatic** This is even more confusing. We talk about 'dramatic events' as those which are surprising, or violent, or unexpected – like a sudden change of course in someone's life, or a bank robbery, or somebody making an announcement which comes as a shock to everyone who is listening. Used properly, it is simply an adjective for drama – meaning 'to do with the drama or theatre'. If you use it, make sure you use it properly – expressions like 'Gwendolen then makes a very dramatic entrance' really say very little; as you're writing about a play, *every* entrance is dramatic. On the other hand, used properly it can be used to stress the nature of a scene as something which could only be done in the theatre, as opposed to in a novel or poem.

- **Dramatic irony** This is used to describe scenes when the audience knows something that the characters don't. It can be a very successful way of increasing suspense in a play and so making it intensely effective in the theatre.

- **Farce** A very special kind of comedy which depends on mistaken identities, rapid entrances and exits, concealments and similar devices. It's unlikely that you'll study a farce – which is a pity, since writing them is an extremely skilled art which demands theatrecraft of a high order. Using the term simply about something which is very funny is imprecise and confusing: it's far better to use the word 'amusing' or 'comic' and then to go on and explain why the scene makes its effect.

- **Melodrama** Originally, in the ancient Greek theatre, melodrama was a special kind of play in which spoken words were accompanied by music which created atmosphere. It then became associated with eighteenth and nineteenth-century popular plays which did the same, often dealing with sensational crimes or highly emotional themes. As these developed and the music was omitted, the word came to be given to any highly sensational action. Nevertheless, it is a weak use of the term to describe events in a play as melodramatic, and you'll do far better to describe simply the effect that is being created in the audience.

- **Naturalism and Realism** Two specific terms used in the modern theatre in ways which are not quite what you might expect. 'Naturalism' refers to a play which is concerned with re-creating external, everyday life in great detail – for example, a scene in Terence Rattigan's *Flarepath* which calls for a reproduction Lancaster bomber to be produced on stage.

'Realism' is rather different: it concentrates on issues of life and death which are fundamental to human existence – the purpose of life, the reality of God, or similar large philosophical matters. Make sure that you know the difference between these two and use them correctly if you are writing about a twentieth-century play, or wish to use the terms to describe an aspect of an earlier work.

- **Play** Remember to use this word when you are writing about a play. If you frequently refer, as many students do, to 'the book', then you will suggest to the examiner that you have no understanding of how the play works *on the stage*. This may or may not be true – but don't give the impression of ignorance by a mistake which can so easily be avoided.

- **Plot and Sub-plot** The 'plot' is the main line of action of the play. This doesn't mean that it is everything which happens – plot and story are not necessarily the same. It is the main force which drives the play along; for example the spiritual and physical struggle of Joan of Arc in Shaw's *Saint Joan*. The 'sub-plot' is a secondary level of motivation – in *Saint Joan*, for example, the struggle between the English and French.

- **Role** People very often talk about a role that is played by something in everyday life – the City of London plays a role in the national economy, for example, or youth unemployment plays a role in football violence. The only things that play roles in plays are actors; if you start talking about the role played, for example, by Davies in *The Birthday Party*, you complicate things greatly. Instead, talk about the *contribution* a character or theme makes to the play.

- **Theatrical** Rather like 'dramatic', this is used popularly to mean something very flamboyant or unusual. If you use it of a play, it will be unclear whether you mean this, or 'pertaining to the theatre', its strict meaning. This will make things unclear for the reader and confuse or obscure a point in your essay. Avoid such ambiguity and possible loss of marks by using 'theatric', or by talking about how the play works in the theatre.

- **Tragedy** This is perhaps the most misused word of all in this group. In common speech, a tragedy is an unfortunate or distressing event – the sinking of a ship, say, or the early death of a brilliant man or woman. In the theatre, it means something very different. There are many theories about what the word means: in Elizabethan theatre, for example, it can be said to refer to the gradual fall of a hero as a result of his or her own actions or a nature which, though great, is also impaired or limited. If you use the word, make sure that you know what specific meaning you are giving it: if you read it in an exam question, make sure that you know how it is being used there. Never use it in its everyday sense when writing about a play; this could make all the difference between a pass and a fail grade on that question.

CONCLUSION

> Always think of the play's effect in the theatre.

Studying and writing about plays demands the skill of being able to see how the written text works on stage – just as a blueprint is the basis of a finished building, or a score for a symphony. You need to be able to write about literary elements when discussing a play – but you also need to be able to capture the life of the play as it grows and develops on stage. And you need to relate these two features to each other, and to the question, supporting your argument by close reference and quotation. The advice given in this chapter should help you do this: the next chapter goes on to show how the process works in practice.

DRAMA 3: WRITING ABOUT DRAMA

TYPES OF QUESTION

PRACTICE QUESTIONS

GETTING STARTED

This chapter takes the techniques of reading, studying and writing about drama discussed in Chapter 10 and puts them into practice, with a series of exam questions, student answers and examiner comments. Some of these may cover texts which you are studying – if so, try to write an answer to them before you look at the ones given later in the chapter.

Those answers which discuss texts which you are *not* studying will still be of interest to you. Read them carefully, as they will suggest ways of writing about plays which you will be able to apply to the drama texts on which you're working, so helping your revision.

ESSENTIAL PRINCIPLES

Questions on drama will be of four main types.

1   Short questions on passages

Some papers may give you a passage from a play with a series of short questions on its expression, contribution to the play's themes and action and other aspects of its importance within the movement and growth of the play. These are most often set for Shakespeare's plays, but may also come up on other papers.

To find out whether such questions will appear in your exam, check your syllabus and past papers carefully. For advice on how to answer them, read Chapter 3.

2   Questions about a scene or part of a scene, which ask for comment on its place in the play as a whole

These questions usually appear in 'plain text' papers – those which allow you to take an unmarked copy of the play into the exam. Once again, you should check carefully with your syllabus to see if you can do this. You can practise referring to the text quickly and accurately. This is really the only difference between plain text papers and others; you can consult the text for quotations and references, instead of your memory.

3   Questions based on a quotation

These are just the same as those on a poetry paper, and will contain a quotation – generally specially created for the paper – which makes a statement about the play. Usually it will be a comment which is only partly true, and you will then be asked to discuss its validity.

When answering such questions, make sure that you understand the quotation, by looking carefully at the key words and trying to relate its judgement to the text itself. Next look at the question which follows it. It might simply be 'Discuss'; but it might be something longer, asking you to show how far the statement is true, to say whether or not you agree with it, or perhaps even to show that it is only a partial view of the text.

Once you have defined both quotation and question, you should *plan* your answer in the usual way by making a series of points which engage with the question, supporting each one with a quotation or close reference. It's quite acceptable to do this by referring to a scene by number – Act IV scene ii, or IV.ii – and then perhaps by adding a sentence to show the way in which what happens in it supports your point. When you're sure that all your points are relevant and in the best order, you can then go on and write the essay.

4   Questions about a particular aspect of the play

These need careful reading, to make sure that you arrive at a precise understanding of the meaning of the key terms they use and the tasks they set you. Once you have done this, you can make your plan, check it for relevance and order, and then write your essay.

1   Is Marlowe's Edward II worthy of being called a tragic hero?

2   'In the force of its imagery lies its strength.' Discuss this view of *The Duchess of Malfi*.

3   Write about the ways Milton presents Comus and the Lady in lines 243–332 of Comus. *Note* In the exam, you would refer to your own 'plain text' for this question, but to make things easier it is reprinted here.

Song

Sweet Echo, sweetest nymph that liv'st unseen
Within thy airy shell   230
By slow Meander's margent green,
And in the violet-embroidered vale
Where the love-lorn nightingale
Nightly to thee her sad song mourneth well.
Canst thou not tell me of a gentle pair   235
That likest thy Narcissus are?
    O if thou have
Hid them in some flowery cave,
    Tell me but where

Sweet queen of parley, daughter of the sphere.   240
So mayst thou be translated to the skies,
And give resounding grace to all heaven's harmonies.
COMUS: Can any mortal mixture of earth's mould
   Breathe such divine enchanting ravishment?
   Sure something holy lodges in that breast,   245
   And with these raptures moves the vocal air
   To testify his hidden residence;
   How sweetly did they float upon the wings
   Of silence, through the empty-vaulted night
   At every fall smoothing the raven down   250
   Of darkness till it smiled: I have oft heard
   My mother Circe with the Sirens three,
   Amidst the flowery-kirtled Naiades
   Culling their potent herbs, and baleful drugs,
   Who as they sung, would take the prisoned soul,   255
   And lap it in Elysium, Scylla wept,
   And chid her barking waves into attention,
   And fell Charybdis murmured soft applause:
   Yet they in pleasing slumber lulled the sense,
   And in sweet madness robbed it of itself,   260
   But such a sacred, and home-felt delight,
   Such sober certainty of waking bliss
   I never heard till now. I'll speak to her
   And she shall be my queen. Hail foreign wonder
   Whom certain these rough shades did never breed   265
   Unless the goddess that in rural shrine
   Dwell'st here with Pan, or Sylvan, by blest song
   Forbidding every bleak unkindly fog
   To touch the prosperous growth of this tall wood.
LADY: Nay gentle shepherd ill is lost that praise   270
   That is addressed to unattending ears,
   Not any boast of skill, but extreme shift
   How to regain my severed company
   Compelled me to awake the courteous Echo
   To give me answer from her mossy couch.   275
COMUS: What chance good lady hath bereft you thus?
LADY: Dim darkness, and this leafy labyrinth.
COMUS: Could that divide you from near-ushering
   guides?
LADY: They left me weary on a grassy turf.   280
COMUS: By falsehood, or discourtesy, or why?
LADY: To seek i' the valley some cool friendly spring.
COMUS: And left your fair side all unguarded lady?
LADY: They were but twain, and purposed quick return.
COMUS: Perhaps forestalling night prevented them.   285
LADY: How easy my misfortune is to hit!
COMUS: Imports their loss, beside the present need?
LADY: No less than if I should my brothers lose.
COMUS: Were they of manly prime, or youthful bloom?
LADY: As smooth as Hebe's their unrazored lips.   290
COMUS: Two such I saw, what time the laboured ox
   In his loose traces from the furrow came,
   And the swinked hedger at his supper sat;
   I saw them under a green mantling vine
   That crawls along the side of yon small hill,   295
   Plucking ripe clusters from the tender shoots,
   Their port was more than human, as they stood;
   I took it for a faëry vision
   Of some gay creatures of the element
   That in the colours of the rainbow live   300
   And play i' the plighted clouds. I was awe-struck,

And as I passed, I worshipped; if those you seek
It were a journey like the path to heaven,
To help you find them.
LADY: Gentle villager   305
What readiest way would bring me to that place?
COMUS: Due west it rises from this shrubby point.
LADY: To find out that, good shepherd, I suppose,
In such a scant allowance of star-light,
Would overtask the best land-pilot's art,   310
Without the sure guess of well-practised feet.
COMUS: I know each lane, and every alley green
Dingle, or bushy dell of this wild wood,
And every bosky bourn from side to side
My daily walks and ancient neighbourhood,   315
And if your stray attendance be yet lodged,
Or shroud within these limits, I shall know
Ere morrow wake, or the low-roosted lark
From her thatched pallet rouse, if otherwise
I can conduct you lady to a low   320
But loyal cottage, where you may be safe
Till further quest.
LADY: Shepherd I take thy word,
And trust thy honest-offered courtesy,
Which oft is sooner found in lowly sheds   325
With smoky rafters, than in tap'stry halls
And courts of princes, where it first was named,
And yet is pretended: in a place
Less warranted than this, or less secure
I cannot be, that I should fear to change it,   330
Eye me blest Providence, and square my trial
To my proportioned strength. Shepherd lead on . . .

4 Shaw speaks of 'high tragedy' and also of 'an element of comedy' in *Saint Joan*. Give examples of how his characters can be serious and comic.

5 Show the effectiveness of Act II of O'Casey's *The Shadow of a Gunman*, relating it to what you understand to be the main concerns of the play.

6 Discuss the view that the main dramatic appeal of *Murder in the Cathedral* lies in the moral growth of the chorus.

STUDENT ANSWERS WITH EXAMINER COMMENTS

STUDENT ANSWER TO QUESTION 1

" Good opening list of tragic attributes . . . "

" . . . but this soon gives way to speculation. Avoid the 'perhaps' school of criticism! "

Edward has many of the qualifications of a tragic hero: he is of noble birth and inherits the throne from his father in an orthodox manner. He is surrounded by avaricious and ambitious men who are common in most tragedies of this period. He has committed no 'unnatural' act such as the deposition or murder of his father and he appears to be a rather negative character, at least in the opening scenes of the play. Perhaps the lords would have overthrown any king because of their own greed and ambition; but if this is not so, and they are incensed solely by the king's love for Gaveston, why do they not kill *him* and find other ways to gain the king's favour? They are consumed by greed, and perhaps seek to conceal this beneath an ideal of purity in kingship which they wish to uphold. But they plan their greed badly, at the end finding themselves ruled by the king's son, who has at last realised the awful nature of their crime. It is unlikely that they will receive money or lands from him.

This is only one view of tragedy – don't take it for granted.

An impressive claim, but it needs evidence: why do they sound like this?

A useful comparison to another tragedy.

Although this paragraph looks a little thin, it does convey a sound point and support it well.

Some more useful comparison.

Like all tragic heroes, Edward has the tragic flaw of character that leads him into disrepute, downfall and death, but his flaw is not clear-cut like Macbeth's ambition or Othello's jealousy. At first sight it appears that his love for Gaveston is his only fault. Certainly he commits errors of judgement, in failing to realise the seriousness of what they say, thinking they are just bluffing to get more land from him. It is probably true to say that he is too kind and gentle in the early part of the play, instead of taking on the more ruthless nature of a typical monarch of the times.

At times he does behave with the dignity expected of a king, and several times has outbursts to prove his authority, as when he says 'I bear the name of king'. But these give the impression of responses learnt as part of his training as future monarch, not the natural authority expected of a monarch and a hero. Nearer the end of the play he appears weak and vacillating, but perhaps this is because of the influence of Mortimer and his associates, which makes Edward confused. Yet at these times he produces some fine pieces of rhetoric, almost becoming a tragic hero: Edward's mind is so confused, we feel, that there are many different ways of seeing his behaviour, all of which may be supported by textual evidence. For this reason it is difficult to reach a firm conclusion about his tragic stature. The play's ending adds to the uncertainty, with Mortimer being executed, the Queen suffering a similar fate at the hands of Prince Edward, now king. In no true tragedy do the evil ones suffer retribution to such an extent.

Yet despite these confusions, Edward does grow in stature during the play, as is shown in these lines nearer the end:

> I'll not resign, but whilst I live
> Traitors be gone, and join you with Mortimer,
> Elect, conspire, install, do what you will,
> Their blood and yours shall seal these treacheries.

This point of climactic rhetoric is similar in some ways to Lear's speeches to the storm on the heath; both men seem to realise their shortcomings and shout defiance against the forces opposing them.

Yet does Edward really come to an awareness of his faults? It is hard to say, since at the time when he should by all the conventions come to his senses he is being held prisoner under conditions which may well have affected his reason. Sometimes he seems certain of his own innocence and blames all his suffering on chance and the heavens:

> heaven and earth conspire
> To make me miserable...

and talks of 'these innocent hands of mine'. Only a short while later, however, he has realised his faults:

> Make me despise this transitory pomp
> And sit for aye enthronised in heaven.
> Come death, and with thy fingers close my eyes,
> Or if I live, let me forget myself.

Later still he again changes his mind:

> Yet how have I transgressed.
> Unless it be with too much clemency?

This view is fairly consistent; that Edward's sole fault was in being too kind and generous. But if Edward suggests this himself, surely he does it to impress the others (and possibly himself) of the goodness of his character? The arguments on both sides are convincing, and the character is enigmatic.

There is no clear point of recognition of guilt and repentance, as there is with Othello and Macbeth: Edward dies seemingly without deciding about his own nature. This may be further evidence of his weakness: but is this weakness a natural part of his character? Or is it created by his imprisonment and torture? He is certain that his duty on earth was solely to rule: he keeps saying to his antagonists, why do you plot against your sovereign, how can you bring yourselves to do it? This shows that his faith in divine right was almost absolute and remained with him to the end — an unswerving strength we would expect of a tragic hero:

> I know that I am a king; and at that name
> I feel a hell of grief: where is my crown?
> Gone, gone! and do I remain alive.

A fair limitation of the question in the conclusion.

But after all the arguments, a decision has to be made. Edward comes very close to the idea of a tragic hero, but essentially remains apart from the traditional view of one. However, if the alternative is to see him as powerless and blind, then he is a tragic hero. The evidence for this is considerable, and thus one is led to believe that, despite his shortcomings, Edward is a tragic hero at the end of the play.

EXAMINER COMMENT

Don't just tell the story when you show qualities like these, though.

This has some strong points, particularly in the way that it *considers* the question, weighing up points for and against Edward's nature as a tragic hero, with some awareness of the growth in his stature as the action develops. Yet it has gaps too. There should be more on whether Edward's judgement is lessened by the influence of Gaveston, and more on the way that his 'greatness' is shown largely at the end of the play. The references to other tragedies help to show the difference between Edward and more conventional tragic heroes, but perhaps a brief but explicit definition of what one actually *is* would help – it's often a good idea to give a brief definition of a key term in the question in this way. Overall, then, an answer with some basic strengths which could have been stronger with more concentration and more explicit argument in places.

STUDENT ANSWER TO QUESTION 2

A sound opening list.

Good link between language and action, showing how the play works in the theatre.

The imagery of *The Duchess of Malfi* is of vital importance in creating the dark mood of the play. The main kinds of imagery refer to death and madness, witchcraft and sorcery, religion, animals, and precious metals and jewels. Classical imagery is also used but to a lesser extent, with less importance to the play's growth.

Images of madness and death occur very often, and spill over into the action of the play in the scene where the madmen play before the Duchess shortly before she is murdered. Every aspect of the play, it seems, is linked with death; when the Duchess summons Antonio to tell him of her wish to marry, she says

> This is flesh and blood, sir;
> 'Tis not the figure cut in alabaster
> Kneels at my husband's tomb.

Imagery of madness again becomes part of the action of the play when Ferdinand realises his crime and goes insane. The Duchess' marriage, when discovered by the brothers, is described as a terrible illness which must be purged by 'desperate physic', and the Duchess' incarceration with mental patients shows that they see this as a disorder of the mind.

The constant references to death set the mood of the play and create a suitable atmosphere for the final events. The atmosphere is also created by frequent use of images of witchcraft, sorcery and superstition. When Ferdinand sets Bosola to spy on the Duchess, Bosola talks of himself as Ferdinand's 'familiar', a term used in witchcraft to describe someone who aids a witch. The settings of the play — the ruined castle and the moonlit palace — add to the atmosphere of sorcery. Superstitions about wolves digging up graves are mentioned, and when the decision is made to disguise the flight to Ancona as a pilgrimage Cariola says:

> I do not like this jesting with religion,
> this feign'd pilgrimage.

66 A comprehensive list of images, carefully selected and concisely expressed. 99

These images contribute to the thickening of the texture and darkening of the mood of the play.

Images of religion, with frequent reference to heaven, hell and the devil, are also important. Talking of Bosola, Antonio says:

> You would look up to heav'n, but I think
> The devil, that rules i'the air, stands in your light.

There are also many references to heaven and the way in which it rules events on earth. The movement of the spheres is used as a metaphor during the discussion of marriage, and lines such as the following are common:

> What devil art thou that counterfeit'st Heaven's thunder?

The use of the chapel at Loretto is in a way an image of the power of religion over the characters, and the chant of the priests is full of religious imagery almost encouraging and condoning the actions of Antonio and the Duchess. Once again, imagery and action are very closely linked, showing its importance in the play's growth and effectiveness on stage.

66 Good explanation of how the images work here, and to what effect. 99

Imagery concerning animals is used to a great extent, to show the baseness of the characters, their actions and instincts. Bosola is advised to be 'a politic dormouse' and described as a 'mole' who undermines Antonio's actions. Such images draw man down to the level of animals, something the contemporary audience would feel very strongly because of their hierarchical concept of creation.

Imagery of precious metals and jewels also comes frequently, often in connection with corruption and evil to give an effect of richness and decay. Just before her death, for example, the Duchess asks

> Why dost thou wrap thy poison pills in
> Gold and sugar?

Classical imagery, though used ('Subtler than Vulcan's net'), is not so important in creating atmosphere and reinforcing themes as are the other kinds noted here.

All the imagery is very forceful, concerned as it is with death, madness, witchcraft and similar phenomena. Its strength makes it an integral part of the play, contributing to the creation of atmosphere and reinforcing the settings and events. It also adds to the rich quality of the language, giving the poetry a distinct quality of corrupt richness.

66 This could be explained a little more fully – what does 'corrupt richness' really mean? 99

The imagery is not wholly responsible for the strength of the play but without it the drama would be much less complex, lacking its unique atmosphere and the unity that is supplied by the frequent return of similar images. The imagery is also important in establishing the characters. The Duchess uses much religious imagery, talking at length about heaven, hell and the devil, whereas her brothers talk of witchcraft, madness and death. The quality and frequency of the imagery, and its integral place within the plot, characters, action and settings of the play, is thus a major force of the drama's overall effectiveness.

EXAMINER COMMENT

66 Look back at the notes on imagery in Chapter 10, from which the essay's points have been selected. 99

Another strong essay. The problem here is knowing what to leave out rather than what to put in. Notice that the examples of each kind of imagery have been carefully selected, and as well as the two or three line quotations there are several individual words and short phrases slipped into the text of the answer. Notice too the stress on the way the imagery is linked to settings, action and characters: this prevents the play being discussed just as a poem, and stresses its effect in the theatre.

STUDENT ANSWER TO QUESTION 3

> *Clear opening statement of the major point of the essay*

The main technique Milton uses to present the two characters is by the kinds of language they use, revealing the sensuality of Comus and the innocence and purity of the Lady. This is clear from the very start of the passage, where Comus' reaction to the Lady's song shows that he feels her to be of immortal nature, in its references to Circe and the Sirens. His opening image of her song moving the air to reveal 'his hidden residence', and the following lines showing how the song floated through the darkness both create a mood of exquisite and other-worldly stillness which makes us think of the Lady as far above human life and beauty. Comus' manner of address to her, as a 'foreign wonder', continues these thoughts by showing how out of place she is, a 'goddess' among 'bleak unkindly fog'.

> *This looks as if it's going astray, but comes back to the question of Milton's techniques at the end of the paragraph.*

The Lady is strongly practical in reply, and this reveals her own nature as more straightforward. In many ways Comus represents evil and the Lady chastity, so her refusal to be enchanted by his flattering speech suggests a simple purity quite appropriate to her nature. There follows a rapid exchange of questions and answers in which the reason for the Lady's desertion is shown, which Milton uses to show her simple purity again.

In his account of the brothers, Comus once more talks of the supernatural, seeing them as 'a faery vision'. Here Milton is again using very imaginative language to reveal the nature of Comus, as concerned with sensuality and unreality as opposed to the straightforward, honest virtue of chastity which the Lady reveals in her more direct language. When Comus says that accompanying her to find her brothers would be 'like the path to heaven' she merely responds that it will be difficult to find the way without guides, again showing the difference in their natures through their language and attitude.

> *A strong, clear point well supported by an example from the text.*

The sensuality of Comus is again revealed in his next speech where he talks of how well he knows the wood, and here it is as if Milton is linking Comus to the natural world, which has no conception of virtue, in contrast to the greater control and practicality of the Lady. Her willing acceptance is further proof of her simple goodness, as is her belief that 'honest-offered courtesy' is more common 'in lowly sheds' than in 'tap'stry halls/And courts of princes': once again, simple honesty and avoidance of show reveal her straightforward, virtuous nature.

Throughout this passage, Milton uses language to show the difference between Comus and the Lady. Comus speaks of rich sensual things — classical gods, the magical world of faery, and the sensuality of the wood and nature at night. The Lady, by contrast, is simple and practical, revealing the strength of her virtue. In this way the difference between them is made clear, and the plot advanced, since the very innocence of the Lady allows her to be led astray by the sensual Comus.

EXAMINER COMMENT

This covers most of the important points in the passage, in particular the use of different kinds of language to reveal the different natures of the two characters. Notice that some use is made of quotation to support points: references to line numbers would have been just as valid.

The essay could have been improved by some references to action outside this scene, just to hint at how the techniques used here are employed elsewhere, or perhaps how the scene works as an introduction to later developments. But this would not be essential to a pass. Perhaps more important is the fact that this essay goes through the passage in chronological order, instead of making separate points and then supporting them from the text. In a question of this sort, where the passage is there for you to consult, you would not lose marks for doing this. But when discussing a text without such help, it is usually better to structure your answer around a series of points than to follow the order of events in the text.

> *Structure answers according to concepts, not chronology. . .*

STUDENT ANSWER TO QUESTION 4

In Saint Joan Shaw weaves comic and serious elements closely together, so that it is often not easy to separate them. Yet the technique is particularly clear in the character of de Stogumber, the chaplain to the English army.

The fanatical patriotism of de Stogumber creates both comic and disturbing elements. Much of what he says appears comic, for example this speech:

> Englishmen heretics!!! ... How can what an Englishman believes be heresy?

In the theatre we laugh at this, but a little later realise that it is not funny, as the speaker means it quite seriously: it is attitudes like these which cause wars. This quality of fanatical patriotism is shown in a much more disturbing way later on when he says that Joan 'will not slip through our English fingers even if the whole city be on her side'. However, at the end of the scene, when he has seen Joan's execution, his tone changes considerably, and he is deeply disturbed by what he has seen and the truth it reveals to him. The simplicity of what he has to say is made more moving and striking because of its sharp contrast to his earlier smugness:

> If I had known, I would have torn her from their hands ... O God, take away this sight from me! ... She is in Thy bosom; and I am in hell for evermore.

This is certainly a tone of great seriousness, perhaps appropriate to the 'high tragedy' of which Shaw spoke.

There are characters who are mainly serious, but who are at times deflated by the comic speeches of others. Warwick and Cauchon, for example, have a seriousness which is constant, but there is a satirical tone in several of Warwick's statements which presents a serious point – about contemporary England as much as about the time and characters depicted in the play – in a comic fashion. When de Stogumber accuses Cauchon of being a traitor, Warwick placates him by saying that in England the word means 'simply one who is not wholly devoted to our English interests'. A similarly satirical technique is used to make something serious appear comic when de Baudricourt talks of the horrors of war to Joan, only to have her reverse the situation and try to comfort him by saying 'You must not be afraid, Robert'. The incongruity of the retort makes the scene comic, especially when one remembers the difference of the two characters on stage, the one large, imposing and perhaps in armour, the other small and apparently defenceless. Yet it is a serious point: Joan has no fear because of her faith, whereas Robert, without her vision, is a prey to fear. Joan's ability to take control of a scene by using comic means is also shown in the trial scene, where she makes the inquisitors appear ridiculous by saying that the tower from which she is supposed to have 'flown' has 'grown higher every day'. Once again, this is comic but also serious.

The epilogue also combines comedy and tragedy: the Dauphin hiding under the bedclothes is ridiculously comic, but also shows his weakness in comparison to Joan's strength. The tributes to Joan from the other characters in this scene also suggest the tragic movement of the play, going from the rejection and torture of the central character to a full realisation of her stature. Yet a comic statement follows closely, when Joan asks of her statue 'Is that funny little thing me too?', continuing the way in which she has made comic statements about herself throughout the play.

These examples show that Shaw's statement is true in two ways. The play both contains separate elements of comedy and seriousness, and it also at times uses comic statements to make serious points and so approach 'high tragedy'.

... A good specific instance of the technique in practice.

Close link with the title here.

Be careful with 'contemporary': be clear whether it means the writer's time, or the present day.

Serious and comic are joined to the play's effect on stage here.

A valid further definition of the question's claim – don't be afraid to do this after a full discussion.

Think about the idea of 'tragedy' in the essay on Edward II. Does Saint Joan follow it?

EXAMINER COMMENT

This is a sound answer on the way that Shaw uses comic statements to make serious points. Notice that the complex tone of several speeches is well described, showing how apparently comic statements are also serious – some good awareness of how the audience responds here, which in turn shows a grasp of the play as it works in the theatre. The answer is less effective, however, in tackling the idea of 'high tragedy'. This could easily be remedied by expanding the references to the tragic movement of the play and the stature of Joan as a heroine.

STUDENT ANSWER TO QUESTION 5

> ❝ This reads rather like a laundry list – but it does get your main points across quickly right at the start. ❞

Act II of The Shadow of a Gunman is effective in a number of ways in furthering the main concerns of the play. Perhaps the single most important aspect of this is in showing ordinary people caught up in the Irish 'troubles', and the ways in which violent action has its effect on their lives. It also continues the mixture of comedy and very serious action seen in Act I, the mixture of unreal idealism, heroic ideals and physical cowardice in Davoren and the idea that it is the women who are the really courageous figures in the situation the play presents.

> ❝ Good analysis of how the comic and serious come together to show the lives of ordinary people here. ❞

From the beginning of the Act, O'Casey's use of comedy is clear. It is shown, for instance, in Shields' mockery of Davoren's efforts to write poetry and his speech impediment. This continues when Mrs Grigson appears, and the two men mock her constant chatter. Adolphus Grigson adds to the comedy by shouting and behaving in a ridiculous way. Yet this comedy has a serious side to it, since it is frequently interrupted by gunfire and is brought to a halt by the arrival of the troops to search the house. This shows that the simple, everyday lives of these people are under threat from the events that are going on outside, so that the comedy is used to make the violent events seem even more destructive. The comedy also serves to avoid any sentimentality which might arise in the description of the people's lives: we are never allowed to feel pity for them, despite the conditions in which they live.

> ❝ Solid treatment of a major concern of O'Casey's. ❞

It is also clear that the people who are really making life continue in the tenement are the women. Mrs Grigson is deeply concerned for her husband when he is out late, and tries gently to get him to be quiet and go downstairs when he returns; and it is Minnie Powell who takes the bombs away from Davoren, an act of devotion which might seem sentimental and unconvincing in another play but which, because of the comic elements of the scene, is far easier for the audience to accept. That Minnie is killed at the end shows this further; it is the women who have the courage, however much Davoren talks about revolution and making the life of the people more 'poetic'.

> ❝ Some strong stuff here – but the writer's feelings don't overwhelm the critical point being made. ❞

It is this final event which reveals the true tragic nature of the play. Despite all his speeches, Davoren is essentially a coward, and it is Minnie Powell's act of bravery which ends in her own death. That the army lorry is ambushed, and she may be killed by the IRA, places the whole action in another context by revealing both the depth of the effect of the occupation on the ordinary people of Dublin and the sheer, bloody waste of the fighting in which people are killed for no reason. This arbitrariness is shown also in the way the soldiers drink Grigson's whisky, and in the fear Davoren and Shields have of being beaten up by the soldiers.

The fact that the play ends with no resolution or clear message is the culmination of this theme. It is concerned with ordinary people who are not heroes, the men largely drunken layabouts and the women trying to hold their ordinary family lives together, in the middle of violence which is senseless and to which there is no solution. O'Casey's use of humour in this scene, and its very ordinariness before its violent conclusion, makes this a very effective part of the play which brings its main concerns to a shocking end.

EXAMINER COMMENT

> ❝ Feelings like this can't be learnt – either you have them or you don't ❞

This is a deeply-felt answer which shows a strong personal response to the play – something which examiners would take into account. It lists a small number of main concerns and shows well how the Act develops them, stressing the effectiveness in the mixture of comedy and violence. It could perhaps mention other themes, such as Minnie's love for Davoren and its incongruity in this situation, but overall it covers well the main importance of the Act and reveals clearly the feelings of the writer.

STUDENT ANSWER TO QUESTION 6

> ❝ Good limitation of the question at the start. ❞

The Chorus is crucial to the growth and development of Murder in the Cathedral, but whether it constitutes the 'main dramatic appeal' of the play is less easy to answer. The moral growth of Thomas himself, the dramatic tension of the story and the ritualistic action of the play are also important features.

At the beginning of the play, the women reveal their desolation and lack of control over their lives;

> For us, the poor, there is no action,
> But only to wait and to witness.

They want to continue their lives in peace, as their next statement makes clear:

> O Thomas our Lord, leave us and leave us be, in our
> humble and tarnished frame of existence,

which reveals the moral low point of the Chorus at the start of the play.

Yet the beginnings of compassion can be seen at the end of Part One when they ask Thomas to leave: 'Save us, save yourself that we may be saved'. Their main concern is for their own wellbeing, but at least there is the beginning of a moral awareness in their desire for Thomas to 'save' himself by flight.

In Part Two the moral growth is much greater. They realise that there is a close link between 'the councils of princes' and 'our veins, our brains'. The women then make an explicit appeal which shows their contrition for their earlier lack of compassion, a sure sign of moral growth which is powerfully moving in the theatre:

> O Lord Archbishop, O Thomas Archbishop, forgive
>   us, forgive us,
> Pray for us that we may pray for you, out of
>   our shame.

This movement is enhanced dramatically by the increased contact between Thomas and the Chorus. At the end of their first speech, he says they will know 'the sudden painful joy' of God's love and bids them 'be at peace with your thoughts and visions' — a human compassion to which they respond in their increased concern for him.

As Part Two progresses, the Chorus become more aware of their own weakness, but not in the selfish way of the opening: now, it is a genuine sense of humility before God:

> Dust I am, to dust am leading,
> From the final doom impending,
> Help me, Lord, for death is near.

The accompaniment of this speech by the chanting of the Dies Irae adds much to the dramatic force of what the women have to say.

The Chorus next speak while the murder is being committed. They feel 'united to supernatural vermin' as they do not stop the murder. The calls to 'clean the sky!' shows a desire to purge themselves of the guilt they feel so strongly — a long way from the rejection of Thomas through concern for their own safety in the opening scene, and in some ways the climax of their moral growth. The final scene shows the women asking God for forgiveness, with a humility that shows that their spiritual growth has kept pace with their moral change.

Overall, the chorus have moved from indifference and fear for their own safety to a sense of humility before God and a desire to help others. This is a powerful dramatic shift in the play; but it is not the only source of its dramatic appeal. Thomas himself undergoes very considerable moral turmoil in deciding whether or not he should submit to what he knows will happen, and wonders whether he is guilty of pride because he is deliberately seeking martyrdom. His Christmas Day sermon shows him wrestling with this issue, and his own moral stature provides another important movement in the play.

The nature of the play's action must also be considered. The elements of ritual which are present have considerable dramatic effect, especially the murder itself; the singing of the Dies Irae and Te Deum Laudamus balance and offset this ritual, almost as if good and evil are being symbolically expressed. All of these aspects contribute to the dramatic appeal of the play; the moral growth of the Chorus contributes a great deal to this, but it is by no means the only source of such appeal in the play.

66 This comes close to narrative, but avoids it at the end by referring to moral growth. **99**

66 Good link with the play's action. **99**

66 You could explain briefly what it adds – and convince the examiner you know what the *Dies Irae* is. **99**

66 Useful summary after more detailed account. **99**

66 Discussion of other sources of 'dramatic appeal' is left very late and done very sketchily here. **99**

EXAMINER COMMENT

> Getting the balance right may mean leaving out your favourite points – 'murder your darlings' as Arnold Bennett said.

This shows a very thorough knowledge of the play in the way it traces the moral growth of the Chorus. In one sense, it is too thorough in this, as it concentrates on this to the extent that other very good points – the moral growth of Thomas himself, and the ritualistic action of the murder and other events – are made rather briefly at the end. Be careful about this sort of balance. In a question which claims that one feature is the main concern of a text, or the main cause of its success, you should always leave time to consider others, and then argue towards a clear conclusion.

CHAPTER 12

SHAKESPEARE

READING SHAKESPEARE

SHAKESPEARE'S LANGUAGE

SOME SHAKESPEAREAN THEMES

SOME STAGE CONVENTIONS

TYPES OF QUESTION ON SHAKESPEARE

PRACTICE QUESTIONS

GETTING STARTED

Whatever the combination of texts and papers you are studying, Shakespeare will almost certainly be a part of your studies. Many people feel rather uncertain about this when starting to study: why, they ask, should the works of one man have so much importance in the study of literature? Isn't it all some gigantic confidence trick on the part of the critics? The answer, simply, is no, it isn't: the plays of Shakespeare have an immense richness and diversity which is found in the works of no other single writer or dramatist, and the importance given to them in syllabuses is totally justified.

Once that is said, it's important to realise several things about Shakespeare. In many ways his plays can be approached like any other plays; there are still new and exciting things for you to say about the texts; and, most important, the plays themselves are endlessly entertaining, exciting, and moving, whether you see them in the theatre, see them on film or read them to yourself with a vivid imagination. Despite all the efforts of critics and producers, the energy and depth of the plays still shine through.

How, then, should you approach studying Shakespeare? Much as you would approach any other dramatist, and certainly not with a kind of grovelling humility which talks about 'the immortal bard', or 'the swan of Avon' – leave that to the naturalists.

Like any writer of his time, Shakespeare presents certain difficulties to his modern-day readers. These concern:

- the language – both the meanings of individual words and some changes of grammar and syntax;
- contemporary references – mainly to systems of belief common then but unfamiliar now;
- the stage – conventions of action which, until mastered, can be confusing.

This chapter gives guidance on the process of studying Shakespeare, dealing with these aspects and with others of related importance. As usual, it ends with a selection of questions on Shakespeare's plays, which you should attempt to answer before going on to study the answers and comments which follow them.

" As with all plays, try to combine the study and the stage. "

ESSENTIAL PRINCIPLES

The process of reading and studying a play by Shakespeare is really the same as that of reading and studying a play by any other author. You should follow the process laid down in Chapter 10 for reading a play, and the suggestions made in Chapter 1 about the process of studying.

FIRST READING

Begin by reading through the play fairly quickly, if possible at a single sitting. As you read, try to visualise what's going on, seeing a stage peopled by actors presenting the speeches. You may find that it helps to read a brief summary of the action of the play before you start. This will put you in the position of an original Elizabethan or Jacobean playgoer, since most of Shakespeare's plays were based on stories that were well known to his audience. Whether or not you choose to do this, at the end of your first reading you'll have a very general idea of the main characters, the action, and perhaps some of the themes and issues the play raises for discussion.

Using the text

Before you begin the process of detailed study it's essential to get hold of a good, modern text of the play or plays that you're studying. Forget about large, expensively-bound single-volume collections of all the plays: these may look good, but they certainly don't contain what you need. Instead, use a modern, single-volume edition of the play that you're studying. The best edition currently available is the New Arden Shakespeare series, published by Methuen. All are available in paperback, and most libraries will have them, so they are easy to obtain.

The edition contains:

" What a good text should have. "

- a full introduction, covering themes of the play, stage history and other topics of interest and value;
- the text of the play in the most accurate version;
- notes *on each page* to explain passages, point out different versions of the text and make other related comments;
- in some plays, appendices containing stories which Shakespeare used as sources for his plays, longer notes on especially important parts of the text, and other relevant material.

Once you have obtained a good text, you need to *use* it.

DETAILED READING

" What to look for. "

This is the stage of going through the play scene by scene, thinking about:

- *the action* – you must get clear what happens before you can understand all its significance;
- *the language* – images, allusions and any other particular uses of language and their function in revealing character or theme;
- *stagecraft* – how Shakespeare uses the stage to present comic or serious action: in other words, how the scene *works* in the theatre and what effect this produces on the audience;
- *themes and ideas* – how the action or argument advances the treatment of themes and issues which are the play's concern.

You can gain an understanding of this by:

" Often talking about your ideas helps to make them clearer. "

- reading the play aloud, preferably in a group where each person can take a separate part. Don't worry if it doesn't sound too good at first – you'll soon get the hang of it, and there is no substitute for having your mouth full of Shakespeare;
- discussing what you think the passage means or how it is important in the growth of the play, either in a group with a teacher or with a fellow-student at home;

■ using your edition of the text. Look up difficult words and phrases in the notes; check the appendices or longer notes; refer to the stage history or other relevant parts of the introduction, to clarify your understanding of the scene.

> **Check the notes in Chapter 10.**

While you are doing this, take quick 'commentary' notes, writing down points of interest and importance in the scene (see Fig. 10.1, p. 108). Later on you can draw these together under different headings for various themes, kinds of language, use of the theatre and so on (see Fig. 10.2, p. 109): for the moment it's important just to get down points as they occur to you.

LATER APPRECIATION

The purpose here is to bring together the work you've done when reading the play in detail, and to see it once more as a whole. You can do this in various ways:

■ Read the whole text yourself, trying to 'hear' the speeches said by different actors and to see the action taking place on a stage.

> **Always be wary of special 'schools Shakespeare' productions: many are wonderful; some aren't.**

■ Go to see a production. This can be very useful – but it can also be disastrous. Since Shakespeare is so often set for exam study, his works are very often put on by companies to appeal to students. Some productions are excellent, resting on a thoughtful reading of the text which really brings together the study and the stage; others are inexcusably bad, and can well ruin your impression of the play. So take care. Even seeing a laughably bad production can be useful, though: you can argue with it, showing how and why it was so bad, and suggesting how the play *should* have been produced.

> **There's no 'Authorised Version' – the single, perfect way of staging the play. Always remember this.**

■ See a film version. Once again, some are good and some not. The BBC Television Shakespeare, easily available on video, is of variable quality. Once again, *use* the production by saying what you think is good and suggesting alternatives for the less effective parts.

■ Hear the play on radio or records. Here you need to use your imagination to see the action, but hearing professional actors speak Shakespeare's language is always valuable.

Don't assume, though, that seeing a film or video or hearing a record is automatically better than reading and speaking the text yourself. Literature is not best received through electronic boxes: reading and thinking is hard to beat as a critical approach.

SHAKESPEARE'S LANGUAGE

> **Try reading a speech to see how one image suggests another in the dramatist's mind.**

Shakespeare's use of language is both free and controlled. It is *free* because his imagery is often very spontaneous in feel, so that when we read it we can almost follow the mental processes of the dramatist, one image sparking off another in a rich process of association.

It is *controlled* because, in the great majority of his plays, he writes in unrhymed iambic pentameters, a form of verse which uses lines of regular patterns of stressed and unstressed syllables. Technicalities of this sort don't matter in themselves; but they matter immensely in terms of what Shakespeare does with them, and detailed study of passages of your set plays will reveal this very clearly. Look at the speech in which Hamlet addresses his father's ghost; Claudius' attempt at prayer; and Gertrude's speech about the death of Ophelia, for example. These show the immense range of meaning, pace and mood in *Hamlet*, and a similar range can be found in almost all the other plays.

> **Think about how language reveals character and mood in the play.**

Language is also used to show character: the dark, knotted utterances of Leontes at the start of *The Winter's Tale* reveal his mental suffering with great precision, and the lucid, simple structures he uses at the end of the play show the distance he has travelled towards a fuller understanding of Hermione and of himself.

Sometimes Shakespeare will move away from this poetic structure and use other forms. The chant-like rhymes of Puck in *A Midsummer Night's Dream*, the evil incantations of the witches in *Macbeth*, and the snatches of song in *King Lear* show him using other structures when they are needed to create particular effects in the theatre, demonstrating again the way in which his writing is intensely *dramatic* – suited for its purpose on the stage.

> **Prose in Shakespeare is just as flexible as poetry.**

Shakespeare does not always write in poetry. Many of the plays contain speeches in prose. Often the lower-class characters use prose, to set them apart from the aristocracy. Yet this does not mean that the prose is less vigorous, theatric or full of significance about characters and action than is the poetry. The exchanges between Prince Hal and Falstaff, the scenes of Bottom and the rustics rehearsing in *A Midsummer Night's Dream*, or the scenes with the plebeians in *Julius Caesar* all show a similar matching of language with dramatic effect.

All of these effects and techniques are things you should be closely aware of when reading, speaking or listening to Shakespeare. Study of the imagery, associations and movement of the language is fundamental to a grasp of the plays: but plays they are, and you should always remember that the language is theatric in effect, and try to show how it works on the stage when analysing or writing about your Shakespeare texts.

> **A grasp of the techniques discussed in Chapters 4, 5 and 10 is essential when studying Shakespeare.**

SOME SHAKESPEAREAN THEMES

Each of the plays has its own concerns, but it is possible to isolate some *themes* which occur frequently in many of Shakespeare's plays.

The growth towards love

> **Shakespeare often explores themes by having pairs of characters to make contrasts between each other.**

In a sense, all of Shakespeare's comedies have this as their central concern; the movement from confusion, uncertainty and a lack of self-knowledge towards a serene understanding of oneself and others through a deep, secure love of someone else. In *A Midsummer Night's Dream*, the confusions in the wood move towards the 'something of great constancy' shown in the wedding celebrations; in *Twelfth Night* the disguise of Viola as Cesario ends in her marriage to Orsino and her rediscovery of her brother whom she had feared drowned, with a parallel love plot at a lower social level between Maria and Sir Toby Belch.

This movement is never straightforward. The threat to the lovers in the wood is grave, and the duel between Viola and Sir Andrew is alarming as well as comic. And there is often an outsider: Malvolio in *Twelfth Night* and Antonio in *The Merchant of Venice* are both excluded from the circle of love with which the comedies conclude.

Appearance and reality

The disguise of Viola as a man in *Twelfth Night* is one aspect of the theme of the difference between *what seems* and *what is*, which comes very frequently in the plays. In *Hamlet* it is perhaps most pronounced: is the ghost a real ghost, or sent from the devil? The King seems to be a good king, yet gained his throne by murder; Hamlet seems mad, but is really affecting an 'antic disposition'. In *King Lear*, the King is unable to tell the difference between the genuine love of Cordelia and the false love of Goneril and Regan; later, near the body of Cordelia, he says 'I know when one lives and when one's dead', but doesn't.

Shakespeare's concern for appearance and reality is related to his fascination with the idea of play and theatre. The play-within-the-play in *Hamlet* shows this, as does Hamlet's refusal to 'play' the 'role' of revenger for his father's death. In *Henry V* there are references to 'this wooden O' – the Globe theatre – and *The Tempest* ends with great beauty and tenderness with the words: 'our revels now are ended'.

Kingship

> **Kingship is part of a general Elizabethan concern with rule and order.**

The ideal of kingship seems to have fascinated Shakespeare, since it is something that he discusses in many of his plays. *Richard II* shows a king who is compared to Christ in his suffering, being deposed because he is unable to rule the kingdom; *Richard III* shows a king of ruthless ambition who fails because he takes his desire for power too far. Lear fails to realise that the trappings of kingship must be relinquished with its title; Prince Hal, in the two parts of *Henry IV*, shows a king growing in stature by rebelling against kingship, to emerge in splendour and unify the kingdom in *Henry V*.

This theme is not only found in the so-called 'history' plays. Ironically, Claudius in *Hamlet* is far better suited to be king than is the prince himself: he knows how to control his subjects, employ spies (Polonius) and treat potentially dissident elements (Hamlet). The prince, by contrast, is much too concerned with metaphysical speculation to be a good practical monarch. The conflict between love and kingship is shown in *Antony and Cleopatra*, the nature of the ideal ruler discussed once again in *Julius Caesar*.

These are only three of the themes which Shakespeare returns to frequently. There are many others, and each individual play is concerned with issues which go beyond the surface significance of the plot or story. Yet you should not approach the plays – or any other text – as simply a coded statement of a set of ideas, a sort of message in a bottle, with the actual words and action the bottle, which can be thrown away once the 'message' has been extracted. Try always to relate themes and ideas to language and stage action: in this way you will arrive at a much fuller grasp and appreciation of the way that Shakespeare's plays work and the effect they have on the audience.

SOME STAGE CONVENTIONS

Reading a Shakespeare play is made easier if you understand some of the conventions of the time – ways of acting or behaving which were taken for granted by both actors and audience.

- **Disguise** In Elizabethan and Jacobean plays disguise is always inviolable. No matter how obvious it is that Cesario is really a woman, the characters will not penetrate the disguise until the dramatist wants this to happen. Don't fight it; that's just how it is.

- **Asides** Characters often speak in asides – statements directed straight at the audience. These are taken to be thoughts going on in the speaker's mind, and thus are not audible to the other characters on stage.

- **Settings** Shakespeare's theatre made minimal use of scenery and staging. The setting is thus conveyed by the action, or by clues in the speeches – 'This is Illyria, lady', for example. A modern setting may have very elaborate scenery, but in Shakespeare's day the actors and the words did almost everything to convey the scene – worth recalling in modern productions of *Lear* where wind machines and artificial rainstorms do their best to drown not only Lear's speeches but also the actor delivering them.

- **Music** Music is immensely important in Shakespeare's plays. Its most common uses are as fanfares to introduce kings and important characters, and in songs. The songs of Feste, the fool in *Twelfth Night*, set the mood of exquisite melancholy; those of the Fool in *Lear* make serious and ironic comments about the situation of the king. Don't imagine that they are there by accident or as some kind of light relief: they are central to the dramatic movement of the plays.

> Remember: always try to SEE what you read.

- **Action** There are often minimal stage directions in Shakespeare's plays. This doesn't mean that little action is taking place. Remember, while reading, that the opening entrance of Claudius, Gertrude and the courtiers in *Hamlet* would take several minutes, and reveal a great deal about the pomp of the court in stark contrast to the black robes of the prince.

    Remember, too, that in Act IV scene iv of *The Winter's Tale*, the stage is full of characters of all social ranks celebrating the sheep-shearing festivities. No sheep; but a full cast of people acting out this celebration of a country process successfully completed, showing the place of order in nature which is so important in the play as a whole.

TYPES OF QUESTION ON SHAKESPEARE

In the exam, questions on the plays will be of four main kinds.

1   Short questions on passages

Here you will be given a short passage and asked a number of separate questions on it. Answering questions of this kind is dealt with in detail in Chapter 3.

2   Questions based on passages

> Check your syllabus and some recent past papers to see what kinds of questions you'll get.

Some papers will reprint a passage of twenty or thirty lines and then ask you a question about it. Often this will involve commenting on qualities in the passage and relating them to issues in the play as a whole. Plain-text papers may ask you to do this with a longer passage, or to explain the importance of a whole scene in the dramatic movement or thematic development of the play as a whole.

3   Quotation questions

These are the familiar kind of question which give you a quotation and then ask you to comment on it in some way, with close reference to the text.

What you must remember to do here is:

- define the quotation – work out exactly what it means by looking closely at its key words and relating them to the text;

- define the task – you might be asked simply to discuss the quotation, or you might instead be asked to relate it to one aspect or part of the play. Make sure that you know what your task is before you start planning and writing the essay;

■ relate the task to the play. Think quickly and find points to make which relate the play to the question. Support each one with a quotation or close reference to the text in your plan – and then write the essay.

4 Questions on topics in the play

These work in the same way as quotation questions except that they ask you directly to comment on a particular aspect of the play. As before, work out your task, marshal your points, select supporting evidence, plan, and write.

PRACTICE QUESTIONS

This chapter ends with some sample questions on Shakespeare plays that are commonly set at A-level. Look closely at them and answer those which are on the plays that you are studying. Then compare your answers with those given, and read the examiner comments thoroughly. Even if you are *not* studying the plays on which the questions are set, you should still read the answers and comments on them: they will help you to gain a general understanding of writing about Shakespeare, and give you points which you can apply to studying and writing about the plays which *are* on your syllabus.

1 '*Othello* is a great tragedy but has too many inconsistencies to be wholly convincing'. Discuss.

2 What view of kingship and the divine right of kings does Shakespeare express in *Richard II*?

3 Read the following extract and then answer these questions:
   i) Discuss Hamlet's thoughts and feelings in this passage. (*10*)
   ii) How is the passage important in the play as a whole? (*15*)

HAMLET:
    O, what a rogue and peasant slave am I!
    Is it not monstrous that this player here,
    But in a fiction, in a dream of passion,
    Could force his soul so to his own conceit
    That from her working all his visage wanned,   5
    Tears in his eyes, distraction in his aspect,
    A broken voice, and his whole function suiting
    With forms to his conceit? And all for nothing!
    For Hecuba!
    What's Hecuba to him, or he to Hecuba,   10
    That he should weep for her? What would he do
    Had he the motive and the cue for passion
    That I have? He would drown the stage with tears
    And cleave the general ear with horrid speech,
    Make mad the guilty and appal the free,   15
    Confound the ignorant, and amaze indeed
    The very faculties of eyes and ears.
    Yet I,
    A dull and muddy-mettled rascal, peak
    Like John a-dreams, unpregnant of my cause,   20
    And can say nothing. No, not for a king,
    Upon whose property and most dear life
    A damned defeat was made. Am I a coward?
    Who calls me villain? Breaks my pate across?
    Plucks off my beard and blows it in my face?   25
    Tweaks me by the nose? Gives me the lie i' th' throat
    As deep as to the lungs? Who does me this?
    Ha, 'swounds, I should take it, for it cannot be
    But I am pigeon-livered and lack gall
    To make oppression bitter, or ere this   30
    I should ha' fatted all the region kites
    With this slave's offal. Bloody, bawdy villain!
    Remorseless, treacherous, lecherous, kindless villain!
    O, vengeance!

4   Read the passage given below and then answer the questions which follow it.

KING: This castle hath a pleasant seat; the air
   Nimbly and sweetly recommends itself
   Unto our gentle senses.
BANQUO: This guest of summer,
   The temple-haunting martlet, does approve   5
   By his loved mansionry that the heaven's breath
   Smells wooingly here. No jutty, frieze,
   Buttress, nor coign of vantage, but this bird
   Hath made his pendent bed and procreant cradle.
   Where they most breed and haunt, I have observed   10
   The air is delicate.
      Enter Lady [*Macbeth*].
KING: See, see, our honoured hostess!
   The love that follows us sometime is our trouble,
   Which still we thank as love. Herein I teach you   15
   How you shall bid God 'ield us for your pains
   And thank us for your trouble.
LADY MACBETH: All our service
   In every point twice done, and then done double,
   Were poor and single business to contend   20
   Against those honours deep and broad wherewith
   Your Majesty loads our house: for those of old,
   And the late dignities heaped up to them,
   We rest your hermits.

a) Explain 'those honours deep and broad' (line 21).   *(1½)*
b) What is the significance of 'The temple-haunting martlet' (line 5) and 'We rest
   your hermits' (line 24)?   *(3)*
c) What is revealing about Macbeth's absence from this scene?   *(3)*
d) Why is this passage important in the play?   *(5)*

STUDENT ANSWERS WITH EXAMINER COMMENTS

STUDENT ANSWER TO QUESTION 1

In *Othello* there are too many inconsistencies, unsolved questions and enigmatic characters to make it one of Shakespeare's best works.

To begin with, the plot is extremely improbable: if Iago had wanted revenge on Othello he could have achieved it more successfully than by conveying Desdemona's handkerchief to Cassio to confirm Othello's suspicions.

When he agrees to kill Cassio if Othello kills Desdemona, Iago must know that there are two possible results. First, that he will carry out the murder successfully, remain undiscovered, and live on, in which case his revenge will be unsuccessful; secondly, that he will be executed, in which case Iago could have killed him outright, evading the consequences by some devious trick. This all makes the elaborate plot unnecessary.

The scene in which Roderigo and Iago make Brabantio aware of the situation is rather hard to believe, too. Brabantio is of a social order higher than Iago and Roderigo and he would probably have sent his servants to get rid of what he considered a pair of drunkards. Even assuming that he did listen to them it is unlikely that he would have believed them. In fact not only does he listen but also believes them, when most Venetian noblemen would consider this the bawdy ranting of drunkards.

Roderigo seems an ineffectual character. On the one hand he is a perfect dupe for Iago, believing all he says, yet on the other he is Othello's ally later in the play. The real paradox is that Othello is very faithful to Cassio at first, making him his lieutenant, yet later is swayed by the evidence of Iago into believing that Cassio has stolen his wife.

Desdemona is no less perplexing. The well-educated daughter of a nobleman, she falls in love with a 'Blackamoor'. Not only does she marry him, but also appears to make advances to Cassio on their wedding night. Why does she risk so much by making Othello jealous while their marriage is still only a few hours old?

As to the general theme of the play it is hard to say what Shakespeare was concerned with. There is no large theme, such as the effect of love on a great general in *Antony and Cleopatra* or the nature of kingship as in *Richard II*. Instead there is a range of possible meanings which revolve around the nature of jealousy and misunderstanding based on misplaced trust.

The language of the play, however, removes our doubts about the inconsistencies and makes us fully aware of its greatness as a tragedy. It must be remembered that the uncertainties would have been less troublesome to a contemporary audience used to plots depending on coincidences, who had probably read the original story on which the play was based.

However, the fact remains that *Othello* contains some great poetry and a great deal of tragic feeling and is therefore still a great tragedy.

> ❝ Because questions like this can't be answered doesn't make the plot unconvincing. ❞

> ❝ Very vague – much more analysis is needed here. ❞

> ❝ Examples of the language are needed to support this point. ❞

EXAMINER COMMENT

This would probably just fail at A-level, because it doesn't really address the question in the right way. The inconsistencies of plot are all true of the play, but the essay says nothing about the ways in which it *is* convincing. People *do* act with very little motive and make foolish, rash decisions such as Othello's rejection of Cassio: Desdemona's attraction to Othello is something which we can explain as little as we can explain any attraction between two people. The tragic nature of the play hangs on a series of small elements and wrong decisions, and it is that which *makes* it tragic.

Instead of listing the apparently unconvincing elements of the play, this answer should have said more about what makes it genuinely tragic: Othello's speeches just before he kills Desdemona, in which his delusion is apparent but so is his greatness, and the way in which we are involved with his feelings. Perhaps most of all, the answer needs to show how the relationships work *on stage*, where we can see Desdemona magnetically drawn to Othello, and the diabolic workings of Iago in arousing Othello's jealousy. The language of the play, too, needs to be discussed in more detail instead of simply referred to in passing as one of the play's redeeming features.

This is an example of the kind of answer where much more thought is required, along with the ability to see a play as it works in performance, instead of considering only the details of the plot which might be thought unconvincing.

> ❝ What the answer should have said. ❞

STUDENT ANSWER TO QUESTION 2

> Heaven's is the quarrel; for heaven's substitute
> His deputy anointed in his sight,
> Hath caus'd his death; the which if wrongfully,
> Let heaven revenge, for I may never lift
> An angry arm against his minister

These words of John of Gaunt about Gloster's murder show how deeply the speaker believes in the divine right of the monarch as God's deputy on earth, and this belief is shared by almost all the characters in *Richard II*. Even though Richard has killed one of his closest friends, Gaunt finds himself powerless to confront the king, such is his respect for the monarch.

Small, apparently insignificant, remarks show how common this view is. The Lord Marshal's 'In God's name and the King's' shows the natural coupling of the two in the belief that the king is God's minister. Norfolk, before (as he thinks) fighting his duel, says 'defend my loyalty and truth/ To God, my King' and later talks of 'A traitor to my God, my King, and me' showing that God and King are almost the same in their significance. The monarch has absolute control and has no qualms about the

> ❝ A quotation is a strong way of starting an essay. ❞

> ❝ Good list of quotations here – perhaps a little long, endangering later points in exam conditions. ❞

different sentences he gives the two duellists, and they acknowledge this power, saying 'such is the breath of Kings'.

The rebellion against Richard begins because Bolingbroke and others believe that the King is abusing the divine right, not that it should not exist, so in a sense the usurpation shows a strong belief in kingship rather than the rejection of it. A similar, if not so extreme, view is taken by the Bishop of Carlisle when Richard hears of defeats:

> Fear not, my lord, that Power that made you King
> Hath power to keep you king, in spite of all.

> A useful sentence drawing together the points of the paragraph.

He goes on to say that the King is not taking full advantage of that power and not following heaven's will. In refusing to return Bolingbroke's land, Richard himself says that 'my master, God omnipotent' will refuse this, showing his own feeling of being God's deputy. All these examples show that Richard and the other characters have a strong belief in the power of kings, but that most of the court feel that Richard is not using that power properly.

> This needs far more development.

Another example of this comes in the scene in the Duke of York's garden, where Richard is compared to a gardener who does not cut back the overgrown plants in his failure to rid the land of the rebels. This states clearly the view that the king must rule strongly and forcefully reject any opposition.

Richard's failure to take control leads to his downfall, yet even here Carlisle feels that it is wrong for Bolingbroke to rule:

> What subject can give sentence to his king?
> And who sits here who is not Richard's subject?

He goes on to prophesy the collapse of the kingdom as a direct result of the usurpation of the throne. Even though he submits to Bolingbroke's will, Richard still sees himself as the king:

> God save the king! although I be not he,
> And yet, amen, if Heaven do think him me.

He also believes that to break the line of succession is a mortal sin and 'heinous article ... damned in the book of heaven'.

In his final speech Bolingbroke, now Henry IV, realises his guilt and acknowledges the supremacy of Richard. All of this shows a clear belief in the divine right of kings — yet it is not something which a king may take for granted, since the frequent references to the need to rule and order the kingdom make clear that the monarch must be firm in order to justify his place on the throne.

> Still only passing reference to a major theme which the answer largely ignores.

EXAMINER COMMENT

This covers the ground thoroughly and has lots of quotations. Yet it really only covers the idea of divine right and is a little thin on the predicament of kingship – the problem faced by Richard, an essentially weak character who has to maintain the realm by using methods to which he is temperamentally unsuited. A couple of paragraphs on this moral dimension, supported by suitable quotation, would have turned this into a very good answer.

STUDENT ANSWER TO QUESTION 3

i) Hamlet is here comparing his own behaviour to that of the player king. The actor is able to weep and present himself with 'distraction in his aspect' with no emotional reason at all. Hamlet asks what he would do if he had the cause for grief that the prince himself has. By contrast Hamlet, with all his reasons for grief at the death of his father, 'can say nothing'. He asks himself if he is a coward, calling himself 'pigeon-livered', ending by saying that he will avenge his father's death on the 'Bloody, bawdy villain' who has killed him and is now ruling Denmark.

> This avoids being a narrative as it shows how Hamlet's thoughts progress and develop . . .

This progression in Hamlet's thoughts is matched by a gradual increase in the depth of his feeling. He begins by calling himself a 'rogue and peasant slave', but calms slightly to describe the acting of the player king, becoming more passionate when talking of what the actor would do if he had Hamlet's cause for grief. When he talks of himself, he uses terms of contempt — 'dull and muddy-mettled rascal' — and is bitterly angry, shown in lines 21–23. In the lines that follow he seems to be working himself up into a fit of extreme anger and contempt for himself, almost as if willing himself to commit the deed of revenge he has so far rejected. The climax of this comes in the outpouring of abuse against Claudius at the very end: he says he should have 'fatted all the region's kites/ With this slave's offal' and ends by vowing vengeance after angrily spitting out a string of abusive words about Claudius.

ii) This passage is important in the play as it is a turning point in Hamlet's treatment of Claudius. Before he has seen the play, he is not certain about what has happened, even though his suspicions have been aroused by the ghost. Because he is afraid that the ghost comes from hell to tempt him to evil, he does not act upon his accusations, but once Claudius storms out of the play because its plot reminds him of his guilt Hamlet is certain of what he must do.

This is not, however, as straightforward as it might appear, since Hamlet still delays in his revenge. A short while later he sees Claudius at prayer and says 'Now might I kill him pat', but rejects this as he knows that Claudius' soul would go straight to heaven. His delay continues, and it is only when he has returned from England that he is able to consider revenge seriously — and even then only when the duel is arranged for him.

The extract is important in revealing much about Hamlet's nature. It is not only his apparent indecisiveness which is shown here, but also his anger at himself about it. Hamlet is angry that his sensitive, educated nature, which knows that murder is wrong even in revenge, cannot do what he feels instinctively he should do. This inner conflict is very important in the play, and shows Shakespeare developing the traditional revenge theme by adding to it elements of contemporary humanism to make the plot and Hamlet's situation all the more shocking.

> *... and this is matched by an analysis of the parallel development of his feelings to the climactic outburst.*

> *He decides to do it, but still doesn't – it's a change of attitude, not a change from thought to action.*

> *This relates the passage well to the rest of the play.*

EXAMINER COMMENT

A very good answer. Notice how each of the two sections is dealt with quite separately, and that the first deals first with thoughts and then with feelings – a sound and straightforward way of dealing with the topics.

More attention could have been given to the language in the first part, and something said about the dramatic effect of the lines in both parts – here, after all, Hamlet is alone after the departure of the actors, and his outburst has great power in the theatre as the 'reality' after the 'performance' they have given. This is asking a lot of an exam answer, though; overall this addresses the question directly and answers it very well.

> *Always remember the play's effect on stage.*

STUDENT ANSWER TO QUESTION 4

> *Clear, short answer, discussing nothing but the essential point of the question.*

a) 'Those honours deep and broad' are Duncan's making Macbeth Thane of Cawdor and his presence at Macbeth's home.

EXAMINER COMMENT

This is very good: note the repetition of the phrase in the question, which is not strictly necessary but helps to make the answer fluent and clear.

b) 'The temple-haunting martlet' is a martin or swallow, which is supposed to nest only in very safe buildings, suggesting ironically that Macbeth's castle is safe. In saying 'We rest your hermits' Lady Macbeth shows that she and her husband are willing to serve and pray for the king, as hermits pray for their patron.

EXAMINER COMMENT

Excellent again. Notice that not only the meaning but also the effect of the first phrase is given: a simple linking phrase like 'This irony continues in Lady Macbeth's saying . . .' at the start of the second part would have made clear the impact of this expression too.

> Expression could be clearer here; 'HIS indecisiveness' would be more precise.

c) The fact that Macbeth is not there when Banquo and Lady Macbeth greet the king suggests perhaps the indecisiveness which is later to make itself clear. Already it is hinted that Lady Macbeth is the dominant partner, since it is she who can pretend to welcome the king while all the time aware of her plan to kill him.

EXAMINER COMMENT

Be prepared for questions of this sort which ask you about characters who are not present or who do not speak in the excerpt. Here, the absence is very important: remember that the mere presence or absence on stage of a character can be significant, and that what they don't say can be as important as what they do say. The next words of Duncan are 'Where's the Thane of Cawdor?', so he has clearly noted the absence: but you would not be expected to know the text as closely as this to be able to make the point in the exam.

d) The extract is important because it contains dramatic irony. We know that Lady Macbeth has just decided to kill the king, and his references to the peace and safety of the castle show his ignorance of his fate. Duncan cannot understand this irony, showing his moral goodness — he would never dream that someone would plot to kill him. Lady Macbeth's hypocrisy is also shown here, in her ability to welcome the king while at the same time knowing that she will shortly kill him. It also shows Macbeth's comparative weakness in this respect, shown in his absence as the host.

EXAMINER COMMENT

This is a careful explanation making good use of the term 'dramatic irony'. Notice, too, that it does not just *say* where the passage comes, but incorporates the information into a more important point to show what we know and Duncan does not.

PROSE 1: CRITICAL APPRECIATION TECHNIQUES AND PRACTICE

THE NATURE OF PROSE WRITING

KINDS OF PROSE

READING A PROSE PASSAGE

COMPARING TWO PROSE PASSAGES

PRACTICE QUESTIONS

GETTING STARTED

As well as a poem and a passage from a play, the critical appreciation exam usually includes a piece of prose for you to analyse and comment on. You may have a choice between tackling the prose and tackling the dramatic passage. Even if, in the end, you choose not to write about the prose you need to be aware of the techniques of reading and analysing prose to give you a proper choice in the paper.

In addition, you need to know the basic techniques of reading and analysing prose so that you can study your set texts properly. You will almost certainly be studying one or more novels, and may also have a descriptive or analytical prose work to study. The techniques discussed in this chapter will give you help in working on these texts – and also, incidentally, help in reading critical works about your set texts should you do this as part of your study programme. For all these reasons, then, knowing how to read and appreciate prose should be an essential part of your critical skills.

This chapter discusses the nature of prose writing and shows you how to:

- identify the essential nature of the passage – whether it is descriptive, narrative, comic or has another main purpose;
- analyse the features of the passage by which it makes its main effects;
- read a passage with care and precision, looking at its various features and bringing them together to form your own coherent reading of the whole piece of writing.

The chapter ends by giving a series of passages with comments and analyses of the kind which you'll be expected to write in an exam.

ESSENTIAL PRINCIPLES

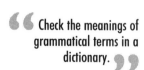

Defined simply, prose is any kind of writing which is not poetry – it is the ordinary, straightforward writing that we all read every day in letters, newspaper reports, novels and instructions for computer games. In itself, there's nothing special about prose – and, perhaps for that reason, many people find it hard to analyse prose, describe its features and say how it makes the effects it's aiming for.

There is, however, no reason why prose should be difficult to analyse. Although it is set out in a different way from poetry – not as separate lines but in continuous paragraphs – prose shares many of the devices and techniques of poetic writing. The problem often lies not in the prose itself, but in our attitude towards it – we're not used to looking analytically at a medium in which we read the football results or ask the milkman for two extra pints. So the first thing to do when confronted with a piece of prose is to make a slight, but significant, shift of attitude – think about it as a complex, subtle piece of expression, in which every word has a function to perform and nothing happens by accident. If you approach it in this way you will find that you will have no shortage of points to make about it.

IMPORTANT FEATURES

While you are reading a passage of prose, you need to look out for a number of features. Some will be familiar from poetry or dramatic writing; others are more specific to prose.

Meaning

Because of the nature of prose and the purposes for which it is most often used, we are more accustomed to look for its meaning first and its qualities of expression later, if at all. Indeed, many questions which ask you to look at prose passages in appreciation papers will actually mention the meaning or argument of the text as one of the main topics you should consider.

As a result, gaining a clear understanding of what the passage is *about* is a major priority when reading a prose text. It's not the *only* one; but it is one from which many of the others will follow since, once you *have* a grasp of the passage's purpose, you will be better able to analyse the features it uses to achieve that purpose. Looking for the meaning and significance of the passage, then, will be of much importance when you are reading a prose passage set for appreciation.

Grammar and syntax

In a poem, you may have to tease out the grammatical structure before you can grasp the significance of a line or longer passage. Although there will often be fewer complex structures – like inversions of syntax, for example – just the same is true in a prose passage. Understanding the grammar means finding the subject, main verb and object of each sentence, as we do automatically when reading (see Chapter 4, pp. 42–43).

In prose, you need also to consider various other questions about how the writer has constructed a particular passage:

- How are the various clauses and phrases related to each other? In other words, which is the *main clause* or phrase in a sentence? Unless you know this, you will find it very difficult to write coherently about the passage since you will not be in a position to grasp the basic points it is making.

- Does the writer use *balanced clauses* to show the relationship between the two points under discussion? Often a writer will deliberately put two points next to each other in two clauses of equal weight in a sentence, to show that they are of equal importance in the argument or description. You need to be able to recognise such features, and so show how the writer matches expression to content in the passage.

- Does the *position of a sentence* within a paragraph indicate its importance? Usually the first sentence in a paragraph will give the paragraph's main point, and those which come after will elaborate or clarify various aspects of it. Use this as a guide to the way the prose develops its points.

Diction

Just as the choice of words is important in poetry and drama, so it is in prose. The variety

Chapter 4 has more on diction

of possible kinds of diction is almost endless, as the chapters on poetry appreciation should have made clear. This is just as true of prose as it is of poetry. Try to focus on the diction of a piece of prose by concentrating on two related aspects:

- The special nature of the diction – whether, for example, it is composed of the technical terms of a particular job or profession; whether it is formal and impersonal, or colloquial and intimate;
- How this diction is appropriate to the purpose of the prose – to give importance to a public statement, for example, or to make a scene in a novel convincing by using words suitable to its main characters and historical and geographical setting.

In Elizabeth Gaskell's *Mary Barton*, for example, several characters speak in a north-country, working-class dialect. This is used to show the social divisions between rich and poor – the major theme of the novel.

Tone

The tone of a piece of prose will be rather different from that of a poem or dramatic passage, since both these will most likely be read aloud or performed by a speaking voice. The prose writer does *not* have this in mind, except when writing for the stage, and so the tone has to be conveyed just by the choice of words and the way they are put together.

Kinds of tone, and how they might change and grow.

The tone of a piece of writing may be tender, ironic, distant, formal; it may be playful, comic, offensive or provocative. Most often, it will be a combination of many of these – reflective and gently self-mocking, perhaps, or formal yet considerate. Be aware, too, that a passage may pass through several different tones of voice, especially if it is telling a story, or describing a series of characters or a situation unfolding between them. The death of Little Nell in Dickens' *Old Curiosity Shop*, for example, is gentle and tender in its tone – within the sentimental conventions of Victorian writing. Passages in William Golding's *The Spire* have a tone of ecstasy which matches the mood of Dean Jocelin's vision.

Don't assume, then, that the tone of a prose passage can be described in one word, which you can hang like a label around its neck. Good prose, like good poetry or dramatic writing, will change and develop, and convey a subtle mixture of different tones, which need care and thought if they are to be analysed fully and described clearly.

Rhythm, pace and sound

Try reading the passage aloud, or 'saying' the words silently to get an idea of these features.

Although the rhythm of a piece of poetry is more obvious than that of a piece of prose, this quality may nevertheless be just as important in conveying an essential element of the significance of a piece of prose. Rhythm might, for instance, be used in any of the following ways:

- to establish suspense by using long, slow-moving sentences;
- to clarify a complex argument by using sentences with a number of clauses and phrases of equal weight:
- to suggest a reflective mood by using long, slow words, often in conjunction with sounds which are long and slow too;
- to create fast action by the use of short, simple words and brief, efficient sentences.

None of these effects would be created by rhythm alone, of course. Sounds, meanings and associations of words would also have a great deal to contribute in many cases.

A sudden *change* of rhythm or pace can also be very effective in prose. A shift from long, slow words and sentences to short, brisk ones can suggest the switch from contemplation to action; a change from complicated diction and irregular rhythm to simple, clear words and straightforward, conversational rhythms can show the change in a character's mind as a result, say, of taking an important decision or hearing some reassuring news.

As with diction and tone, rhythm needs to be considered in conjunction with other aspects of a piece of writing, so make sure that you are aware of all of these features working in combination while you are reading a piece of prose for appreciation.

Figurative language

Look at Chapter 6 for more on these features of language.

Prose generally uses fewer metaphors, similes and images than poetry. But comparison and figurative language is an essential part of everyday conversation. We talk about being 'as dead as a doornail' or 'as deaf as a post', and stay at home 'snug as a bug in a rug' while outside it is 'raining stair-rods'. These are simple, conversational expressions – but they are also one kind of figurative language which you might well find in a piece of prose.

Alternatively, prose may make long, complex comparisons, every facet of which is explored separately, so that one metaphor may take up a whole paragraph. This is especially the case with many novels which use extended comparisons to present an object or relationship in a startling new guise: E. M. Foster uses figurative language, for example, to describe the strange nature of the Marabar Caves in *A Passage to India*.

Not every piece of prose which you are asked to comment on will do this – but you must be aware that a prose writer can use figurative language which is just as rich and various as that found in poetry, so keep alive to the metaphorical dimension while you are reading.

FEATURES WORKING TOGETHER

As with poetry and dramatic writing, it is not these features in isolation which create an effect in prose writing. It is the way in which they combine which gives the writing its special nature.

KINDS OF PROSE

> Prose usually has one or more clear purposes.

One major way in which prose differs from writing of the other kinds which you will be studying is in its *purpose*. When you are reading a piece of prose it is often useful to try to categorise it. This does not mean simply labelling it, as a Victorian butterfly collector would identify a butterfly and pin it lifeless onto a board for display. Instead it means trying to find the underlying purpose and intention of a piece of writing, so that this, and your awareness of those features described in the last section, will come together to give you a far greater sense of what the piece is concerned with and how it achieves its purpose.

The following list of categories is not exhaustive – and neither should you assume that every piece of prose can be slotted into one of the pigeonholes it represents. Instead, look on these categories as a series of possibilities to run through while reading, so that you will arrive at a closer awareness of the passage by seeing what kind of prose it might or might not resemble, or which features it might share.

Narrative prose

> Remember – who is telling the story can be as important as the story itself.

This is one of the most familiar kinds of prose. It simply tells a story, as in a novel or short story. Narrative prose can be written in different ways. There may, for example, be a single figure who tells the story. In the Victorian novel, this is usually an 'omniscient narrator' – the figure of the writer who tells the story but is not involved in the action in any way, and of whose nature and personality we directly learn nothing. Alternatively, the story may be told by someone who *is* involved with the action – a 'first person' narrative, so called because it is controlled by someone who writes as the 'I' of the story.

In addition there are various combinations of these two. The novels of Joseph Conrad, for example, are often narrated by a figure who is identified early in the book, so that we are given the effect of listening to a story-teller. Some novels will change the narrator at various stages in the story, so that we see things from various different viewpoints.

An awareness of the person who is doing the narrating is an important element in appreciating fiction – as Chapters 14 and 15 will make clear. When writing about a piece of narrative prose, you should try to be aware of the nature of the narrator, as it is revealed by the style of prose. Do this by studying closely the features described in the foregoing section.

Conversational prose

> Always make sure you know who is speaking in conversational prose.

Here the piece will record all or some of a conversation. Instead of just putting the name of each character at the left before he or she speaks, however, a piece of conversational prose will identify each speaker in more complex ways. Sometimes the words of the two speakers will be presented on alternate lines, so that the reader knows when a new person is speaking. Nevertheless, at times it can be quite difficult to work out *who* it is who has said something, making it necessary for you to work back to the last identified speech to be sure about the identity of the speaker.

The text may simply say 'George replied' or 'Alice spoke reflectively' before or after the actual words. More often, however, there will be sentences which will comment on what the characters are thinking while they are speaking. This makes the passage more complex, adding analysis of character and situation, as well as perhaps some further elements of narrative, to the passage. Be aware of this complex mixed purpose while you are reading, and always give special attention to short sentences between elements of conversation, as they may convey a lot of information in a very short space.

Descriptive prose

> Prose which describes often does other things too.

The main purpose here is to give an account of a geographical location, character or other phenomenon rather than to recount a series of events. It's unlikely that you'll have a piece of prose to comment on which does nothing other than describe, but description will often form a component of more complex writing. Writing about other countries or geographical exploration, for example, may well have a strong descriptive content; so, too, may writing about personal experiences such as learning to fly or feeling strong emotions.

Learning to tell when the descriptive shades off into the analytical or emotional is something which will come with experience. So, too, will the skill of knowing to what *use* apparently simple description is being put. Often, for example, a description of weather conditions will be in part a metaphor for a mood or feeling, or a preparation for an event or series of events to follow shortly in the piece of writing. In this way, descriptive writing is often more complex than it seems. Whenever you read a passage which appears to be largely descriptive, ask yourself whether the description could also have another, larger meaning as well as its surface one.

Atmospheric

> Work out what it is that the subject's being compared with, and think about the effect of the comparison.

This sort of writing is closely related to the descriptive. Very often, novelists wish to create a mood or atmosphere to prepare for or enhance the effect of a particular event; often, too, a travel writer will wish to convey not only the appearance of, say, a remote valley, but also to give an idea of the peculiar nature of being there.

Atmospheric writing may well make use of figurative language to make its effect, but not always; moods and feelings can be conveyed just as well by hard, apparently factual writing as by chains of imaginative images, so be aware that the style of writing such as this is not always ornate and flowery.

Explanatory prose

This is writing which seeks to explain. The subject might be a particular principle or concept, or the operation of a process.

Since writing of this kind is often found in the sciences or social sciences, or in writing which tries to give reasons for historical events and processes, it often occurs in combination with other kinds of writing. A passage might, for example, begin with a narrative of a sequence of events – perhaps with some atmospheric writing to create a sense of immediacy in the reader – and then move on to some explicative writing to attempt to explain the process just described.

As previous sections have stressed, you need to be aware of the changing tone of the passage to show how it may shift from descriptive to atmospheric and then to explicative, all with the aim of discussing fully a particular sequence of events.

Discursive prose

The aim of discursive writing is to present a logical argument. Each stage is presented with clarity and precision, and the overall intention is to clarify the logical sequence by stating firmly:

- the individual points;
- the relationship they bear to each other;
- the larger truths which evolve when the separate points are combined;
- the final conclusion of this logical process.

> List each separate stage by putting a number on the text.

Occasionally you may be asked to explain the stages of a logical development of this sort. To do so demands careful reading in order to separate each strand, and careful planning: take plenty of notes, listing the stages and clarifying the progression. Do not begin your final version until you are sure that you have a clear idea of each stage, the way it is related to the others and the overall logical progress.

Other kinds of writing

You may also come across writing of other sorts – comic, analytic, critical, meditative or instructional, for example. The main aim, remember, is not simply to *identify* a passage by hanging one of these labels round its neck, but to *use* your awareness of its purpose to clarify your knowledge of its aim and techniques.

Above all, remember that a passage may change in nature and aim during its course – just as the situation may change in a piece of dramatic writing.

READING A PROSE PASSAGE

See Chapters 4, 5 and 9.

Approaching a prose passage in an exam is very similar to the process of reading a poem or dramatic excerpt which has been discussed previously. While reading, be aware of any specific demands made by the question – does it ask, for example, for an account of the argument of the passage, or an outline of the techniques and features which make it suitable as the opening of a novel?

With this firmly – but not exclusively – in mind, read through the passage in detail. Look out for the features discussed in the first part of this chapter – diction, tone, rhythm and so on – and also for the various kinds and purposes of prose listed above. Develop an awareness of the individual 'moment' and its relation to the whole, and the way in which the expression of the writing matches its content. Ask yourself, too, how the passage changes in nature or intent as it progresses.

While you are reading, you need to take notes in the way discussed in Chapters 4 and 5:

- Jot down points as they occur to you.
- Make pattern notes or lists – whichever technique you find best.
- Underline or highlight key words on the passage.
- Number your points.

While you are doing this, after you have read the passage several times, finalise your own interpretation, based on the hypothesis you will have been developing and modifying in your earlier readings. If the questions asks for your response, make sure that you are clear about your own feelings and attitudes to the passage. Then write your appreciation, using the techniques and approaches laid out in Chapter 5.

COMPARING TWO PROSE PASSAGES

Check the passages of drama that are compared in Chapter 9 too.

Some examining boards may set a question which asks you to *compare* two passages of prose. To do this fully, you need to read both with equal care, and to use the techniques of critical comparison discussed with reference to poetry in Chapter 5.

Throughout the process of reading and writing remember to bring the two passages together, showing similarities and differences between them in a clear and quite explicit fashion. Only if you do this will you fulfil the demands of the question. Don't approach one passage and then the other one separately.

PRACTICE QUESTIONS

1 Read the following passage and then write a critical appreciation of it. Pay particular attention to the writer's attitude to the people he is describing.

The women of this island are before conventionality, and share some of the liberal features that are thought peculiar to the women of Paris and New York.

Many of them are too contented and too sturdy to have more than a decorative interest, but there are others full of curious individuality.

This year I have got to know a wonderfully humorous girl, who has been spinning in the kitchen for the last few days with the old woman's spinning wheel. The morning she began I heard her exquisite intonation almost before I awoke, brooding and cooing over every syllable she uttered.

I have heard something similar in the voices of German and Polish women, but I do not think men – at least European men – who are always further than women from the simple animal emotions, or any speakers who use languages with weak gutturals, like French or English, can produce this inarticulate chant in their ordinary talk.

She plays continual tricks with her Gaelic in the way girls are fond of, piling up diminutives and repeating adjectives with a humorous scorn of syntax. While she is here the talk never stops in the kitchen. To-day she has been asking me many questions about Germany, for it seems one of her sisters married a German husband in America some years ago, who kept her in great comfort, with a fine 'capull glas' (grey horse) to ride on, and this girl has decided to escape in the same way from the drudgery of the island.

This was my last evening on my stool in the chimney corner, and I had a long talk with some neighbours who came in to bid me prosperity, and lay about on the floor with their heads on low stools and their feet stretched out to the embers of the turf. The old woman was at the other side of the fire, and the girl I have spoken of was standing at her spinning wheel, talking and joking with every one. She says when I go away now I am to marry a rich wife with plenty of money, and if she dies on me I am to come back here and marry herself for my second wife.

I have never heard talk so simple and so attractive as the talk of these people. This evening they began disputing about their wives, and it appeared that the greatest merit they see in a woman is that she should be fruitful and bring them many children. As no money can be earned by children on the island this one attitude shows the immense difference between these people and the people of Paris.

The direct sexual instincts are not weak on the island, but they are so subordinated to the instincts of the family that they rarely lead to irregularity. The life here is still at an almost patriarchal stage, and the people are nearly as far from the romantic moods of love as they are from the impulsive life of the savage.

2   The following extract comes from a novel which is a parody of books which present life in the country as ideal. Show how the passage achieves the writer's aim.

Dawn crept over the Downs like a sinister white animal, followed by the snarling cries of a wind eating its way between the black boughs of the thorns. The wind was the furious voice of this sluggish animal light that was baring the dormers and mullions and scullions of Cold Comfort Farm.

The farm was crouched on a bleak hill-side, whence its fields, fanged with flints, dropped steeply to the village of Howling a mile away. Its stables and out-houses were built in the shape of a rough octangle surrounding the farmhouse itself, which was built in the shape of a rough triangle. The left point of the triangle abutted on the farthest point of the octangle, which was formed by the cowsheds, which lay parallel with the big barn. The out-houses were built of rough-cast stone, with thatched roofs, while the farm itself was partly built of local flint, set in cement, and partly of some stone brought at great trouble and enormous expense from Perthshire.

The farmhouse was a long, low building, two-storeyed in parts. Other parts of it were three-storeyed. Edward the Sixth had originally owned it in the form of a shed in which he housed his swineherds, but he had grown tired of it, and had it rebuilt in Sussex clay. Then he pulled it down. Elizabeth had rebuilt it, with a good many chimneys in one way and another. The Charleses had let it alone; but William and Mary had pulled it down again, and George the First had rebuilt it. George the Second, however, burned it down. George the Third added another wing. George the Fourth pulled it down again.

By the time England began to develop that magnificent blossoming of trade and imperial expansion which fell to her lot under Victoria, there was not much of the original building left, save the tradition that it had always been there. It crouched, like a beast about to spring, under the bulk of Mock-uncle Hill. Like ghosts embedded in brick and stone, the architectural variations of each period through which it had passed were mute history. It was known locally as 'The King's Whim'.

The front door of the farm faced a perfectly inaccessible ploughed field at the back of the house; it had been the whim of Red Raleigh Starkadder, in 1835, to have it so; and so the family always used to come in by the back door, which abutted on the general yard facing the cowsheds. A long corridor ran half-way through the house on the second storey and then stopped. One could not get into the attics at all. It was all very awkward.

. . . Growing with the viscous light that was invading the sky, there came the solemn, tortured-snake voice of the sea, two miles away, falling in sharp folds upon the mirror-expanses of the beach.

Under the ominous bowl of the sky a man was ploughing the sloping field immediately below the farm, where the flints shone bone-sharp and white in the growing light. The ice-cascade of the wind leaped over him, as he guided the plough over the flinty runnels. Now and again he called roughly to his team:

'Upidee, Travail! Ho, there, Arsenic! Jug-jug!' But for the most part he worked in silence, and silent were his team. The light showed no more of his face than a grey expanse of flesh, expressionless as the land he ploughed, from which looked out two sluggish eyes.

Every now and again, when he came to the corner of the field and was forced to tilt the scranlet of his plough almost on to its axle to make the turn, he glanced up at the farm where it squatted on the gaunt shoulder of the hill, and something like a possessive gleam shone in his dull eyes. But he only turned his team again, watching the crooked passage of the scranlet through the yeasty earth, and muttered: 'Hola, Arsenic! Belay there, Travail!' while the bitter light waned into full day.

Because of the peculiar formation of the out-houses surrounding the farm, the light was always longer in reaching the yard than the rest of the house. Long after the sunlight was shining through the cobwebs on the uppermost windows of the old house the yard was in damp blue shadow.

3   Write a critical comparison of the two passages of prose.

A

Thirty or forty factories rise on the tops of the hills . . . Their six storeys tower up; their huge enclosures give notice from afar of the centralisation of industry. The wretched dwellings of the poor are scattered haphazard around them. Round them stretches land uncultivated but without the charm of rustic nature, and still without the amenities of a town. The soil has been taken away, scratched and torn up in a thousand places, but it is not yet covered with the habitations of men. The land is given over to industry's use. The roads which connect the still-disjointed limbs of the great city, show, like the rest, every sign of hurried and unfinished work; the incidental activity of a population bent on gain, which seeks to amass gold so as to have everything else all at once, and, in the interval, mistrusts all the niceties of life. Some of these roads are paved, but most of them are full of ruts and puddles into which foot or carriage wheel sinks deep. Heaps of dung, rubble from buildings, putrid, stagnant pools are found here and there among the houses and over the bumpy, pitted surfaces of the public places. No trace of surveyor's rod or spirit level. Amid this noisome labyrinth, this great sombre stretch of brickwork, from time to time one is astonished at the sight of fine stone buildings with Corinthian columns. It might be a medieval town with the marvels of the nineteenth century in the middle of it. But who could describe the interiors of these quarters set apart, home of vice and poverty, which surround the huge palaces of industry and clasp them in their hideous folds. On ground below the level of the river and overshadowed on every side by immense workshops, stretches marshy land which widely spaced ditches can neither drain nor cleanse. Narrow, twisting roads lead down to it. They are lined with one-storey houses whose ill-fitting planks and broken windows show them up, even from a distance, as the last refuge a man might find between poverty and death. None-the-less the wretched people living in them can still inspire jealousy of their fellow-beings. Below some of their miserable dwellings is a row of cellars to which a sunken corridor leads. Twelve to fifteen human beings are crowded pell-mell into each of these damp, repulsive holes.

The fetid, muddy waters, stained with a thousand colours by the factories they pass . . . wander slowly round this refuge of poverty. They are nowhere kept in place by quays: houses are built haphazard on their banks. Often from the top of one of their steep banks one sees an attempt at a road opening out through the debris of earth, and the foundations of some houses or the debris of others. It is the Styx of this new Hades. Look up and all around this place and you will see the huge palaces of industry. You will hear the noise of furnaces, the whistle of steam. These vast structures keep air and light out of the human habitations which they dominate; they envelope them in perpetual fog; here is the slave, there the master; there is the wealth of some, here the poverty of most; there the organised efforts of thousands produce, to the profit of one man, what society has not yet learnt to give. Here the weakness of the individual seems more feeble and helpless even than in the middle of a wilderness.

A sort of black smoke covers the city. The sun seen through it is a disc without rays. Under this half-daylight 300,000 human beings are ceaselessly at work.

from *Journeys to England and Ireland*, 1835, by Alexis de Tocqueville

B

A long suburb of red brick houses – some with patches of garden-ground, where coal-dust and factory smoke darkened the shrinking leaves, and coarse rank flowers; and where the struggling vegetation sickened and sank under the hot breath of kiln and furnace, making them by its presence seem yet more blighting and unwholesome than in the town itself – a long, flat, straggling suburb passed, they came by slow degrees upon a cheerless region, where not a blade of grass was seen to grow; where not a bud put forth its promise in the spring; where nothing green could live but on the surface of the stagnant pools, which here and there lay idly sweltering by the black roadside.

Advancing more and more into the shadow of this mournful place, its dark depressing influence stole upon their spirits, and filled them with a dismal gloom. On every side, and far as the eye could see into the heavy distance, tall chimneys, crowding on each other, and presenting that endless repetition of the same dull, ugly form, which is the horror of oppressive dreams, poured out their plague of smoke, obscured the light, and made foul the melancholy air. On mounds of ashes by the wayside, sheltered only by a few rough boards, or rotten pent-house roofs, strange engines spun and writhed like tortured creatures; clanking their iron chains, shrieking in their rapid whirl from time to time as though in torment unendurable, and making the ground tremble with their agonies. Dismantled houses here and there appeared, tottering to the earth, propped up by fragments of others that had fallen down, unroofed, windowless, blackened, desolate, but yet inhabited. Men, women, children, wan in their looks and ragged in attire, tended the engines, fed their tributary fires, begged upon the road, or scowled half-naked from the doorless houses. Then came more of the wrathful monsters, whose like they almost seemed to be in their wildness and their untamed air, screeching and turning round and round again; and still, before, behind, and to the right and left was the same interminable perspective of brick towers, never ceasing in their black vomit, blasting all things living or inanimate, shutting out the face of day, and closing in on all these horrors with a dense dark cloud.

from *The Old Curiosity Shop*, 1841, by Charles Dickens

STUDENT ANSWERS WITH EXAMINER COMMENTS

STUDENT ANSWER TO QUESTION 1

❝ Good opening statement of the writer's dual attitude. You can only do this if you know all your points when you start writing. ❞

In this passage the writer is describing the women inhabitants of what appears to be a remote community. His attitude is one of considerable interest and almost of scientific detachment and enquiry, yet at times there is a strong suggestion that he is patronising towards the women of whom he is writing.

The writer begins by saying that the women are 'before conventionality' which means that they share some of the 'liberal' features of women from Paris and New York. This presumably means that the nature of their life has not allowed them to develop the conventional manners and inhibitions of some societies, so that they behave in a way which is thought free and uninhibited, similar to the standards of 'liberal' women of the two fashionable capitals he mentions.

❝ Notice how quotations are smoothly incorporated into the essay. ❞

Nevertheless in the next paragraph he rather haughtily dismisses many of the women as being of no more than 'a decorative interest' because they are contented, singling out a few as being 'full of curious individuality'. His attitude here seems to be a mixture of scientific detachment, writing as an anthropologist studying the ways of the subjects of his study, and of a surprised fascination, with a hint that he finds it odd that such women should possess individuality – a tone which seems to continue when he talks of the woman who is 'wonderfully humorous'.

His account of her 'brooding and cooing' and 'exquisite intonation' continues this dual tone, but the next paragraph, where he says that such 'inarticulate chant' is not present among men or those who speak French or German, moves back to the detachedness of an anthropologist or linguist. He also voices the view that men are further than women from 'the simple animal emotions', suggesting a traditional and rather sentimental view of the nature and role of women. This dual attitude continues at the start of the next paragraph, beginning with detailed references to 'diminutives' and 'syntax' but moving on to an account of the girl's fascination with Germany and the 'capull glas' of her sister which present her as naively fascinated with unfamiliar aspects of the natural and material world.

The next paragraph reveals that he has been staying with the people of this region for some time, as well as showing something of their living conditions: they burn turf for warmth, sit on stools and spin their own yarn, showing the simple nature of their lives. There is an air of detached and perhaps rather haughty amusement at the woman's suggestion about whom the writer shall marry.

In the penultimate paragraph the writer expresses what appears to be admiration of the people's language, and their view that the 'greatest merit' in a woman is to have children is presented without direct comment – although the comparison to Paris where, it is implied, children can earn money, perhaps suggests respect for the people in not wanting children simply as a source of income and instead valuing children as people in themselves. The final paragraph discusses the sexual morality of the people, the writer making the point that sexual instincts are centred on the family, so that 'irregularity' – presumably promiscuity and illegitimacy – are rare. The final sentence, however, is revealing: the life is still 'patriarchal' or governed by the men, so that there is neither 'romantic love' nor the 'impulsive life of the savage', so that, at the end, it seems that the speaker gives his approval to the people.

In many ways, the writer's attitude is ambiguous. He seems to observe the woman as an anthropologist and linguist, but also makes comments which are either patronising or approving. The passage may be interpreted in different ways, but I find the writer's attitude rather patronising to the women whom he is describing.

> A fair comment – it's clear that this is your own feeling about his attitude.

> Good clear point, which might be clearer in two sentences as the reader might get lost in the middle.

> Open statements of your feelings are fine, especially when they are well supported by argument and reference – as here.

EXAMINER COMMENT

This passage is an interesting example of something which may well come up in the exam: a passage which may awake strong feelings in some candidates. You might well have read this with a sense of anger at the way the writer talks of 'the women' almost as a separate species; some feminists would be outraged at the tone.

The answer above makes clear that the tone is patronising, but stops short of expressing anger. This is probably the best course to adopt if you find youself driven to strong feelings by a passage: try to control your anger and express it by making clear statements which are fully and clearly supported by close reading of the text. Simple accusations of blatant sexism are unlikely to do well if they are not supported by analysis of the text – where, why and how is the passage so offensive? You must make this clear. Alternatively, of course, if you find the passage reasonable, scientific and detached in tone, you should say so with equal support: it is always a matter of reading carefully and basing your opinions on the text.

STUDENT ANSWER TO QUESTION 2

This piece of writing sets out to reject the comfortable and rather sentimental view of life in the country presented in many rural novels. It does this by emphasising the bleakness of the setting in a way that is largely comic, and also making comic play of the idea of an ancient farmhouse that has been passed down through generations of one family.

The passage begins with a metaphor which compares the mist and wind to a large animal 'eating its way' through the thorn. This is the first of many images which compare natural features to wild animals, which continues in the fields being 'fanged with flints' in the second paragraph. These images do not, however, stress the benevolent side of nature; instead they emphasise its wildness and desolation.

Parody of architectural terms is introduced in the reference to the 'dormers and mullions and scullions' of the farmhouse. The first two terms are architectural ones, but the last is an invented word. The tone is continued in the second paragraph, which parodies the idea of the ancestral farmhouse which is at the heart of many stories of country life. The description of the building is simply absurd, with its references to rough triangles and rough octangles; this continues in the next

> You could say HOW it is comic, even right at the start like this.

> If you don't know terms like this don't worry – there are plenty of other details to focus on.

66 Watch repetition
– 'absurd' appears
very often here 99

66 What's the effect of
'viscous' here? A note on this
would help. 99

66 Notice how 'scranlet' is
explained in sound, meaning
and effect. 99

66 Is it really 'desolation'?
Does this take it a bit too
seriously? 99

paragraph, which parodies the history of buildings encountered in guide-books, with the number of collapses and re-buildings reaching absurd proportions.

The description of the access to the house, the front door facing 'a perfectly inaccessible ploughed field', and the lack of access to the attics, continues the description of a house which carries rural charm to absurd lengths, so that the final statement, 'It was all very awkward', is comic because of its understatement.

The picture of the man ploughing under the 'viscous light' continues the idea of the farm as a place of desolation. The light itself is accompanied by the 'tortured-snake voice of the sea', continuing the wild animal images applied to the wind in the first paragraph. The names of the horses called out by the man, and the 'grey', 'sluggish' and 'expressionless' nature of the ploughman continue the desolate atmosphere, which is the exact opposite of the rural paradise created by many writers setting novels in the countryside.

The desolation continues in the final two paragraphs, the farm being described as 'gaunt', the light as 'bitter', the shadow continuing to fall on the farmyard and the 'cobwebs' in the windows all confirming this. The use of the word 'scranlet' to refer to part of the plough is thin and weak in its sound and is perhaps intended to parody the use of technical terms for farm implements in country writing.

Overall the passage makes its effect by rejecting the sense of warmth and richness which most people feel in connection with farming and the countryside, and replacing it with a sense of desolation. At times this is comic, as in the account of the history of the farmhouse, but at others it is a more serious rejection of a falsely romantic view of country life. I find this passage quite funny in places, but in parts I found it depressing because it rejected a more positive view of life in the country.

EXAMINER COMMENT

This is a difficult passage to write about, as it is quite lengthy, and needs to be read carefully if the tone of parody is to be fully grasped. The above answer covers most of the main points but does not go into the kind of detail that earlier answers have. This is largely because of limitations of time and space. Ideally, it would be valuable to include more on the reasons *why* the description of the farmhouse is comic, and more on the diction. The names of the horses – 'Travail' and 'Arsenic' – could be discussed at greater length, to show the way the writer rejects the usual flowery names for animals in farm stories, with their cows called 'Buttercup' and 'Daisy'.

The amount of detail to include is one of the more important problems you will have to solve when writing on passages of this sort; it is a matter of balancing the demands of covering the whole passage with discussing parts of it in the right depth.

STUDENT ANSWER TO QUESTION 3

66 Involvement is the key
difference between the two – it
needs to be more prominent in
the answer. 99

These two passages both discuss areas of industrialisation and their effects upon the people who live in them, especially the poor. Both are written in a style of great power and express sympathy for the suffering people. Yet they differ in several respects. The first is written as a piece of scientific observation, the second as part of a novel, so that the second involves the reader more in the scene. This is achieved mainly by having two characters walk through the scene of industrial squalor, in contrast to the first passage which makes its effect by more general description.

One of the biggest differences is that in the first passage we are shown the whole scene, almost from a distance, where in the second we are taken on a journey through it. The first talks in general terms of 'Thirty or forty factories' in contrast to the second's singling out of 'a cheerless region' with, in the distance, 'tall chimneys'. The first has the force of numbers, wheras the second has the immediacy of personal involvement.

This difference continues in the account of the roads through the scene. The first talks generally of 'Heaps of dung, rubble from buildings, putrid, stagnant pools' whereas the second takes us through its region where 'nothing green could live but on the surface of the stagnant pools'. Instead of the first passage's general reference to the houses as 'the last refuge … between poverty and death' the second talks of individual people: the 'men, women, children' who tend the machines. This passage also links the people explicitly with the machines, a link not made so clearly in the first passage.

The machines themselves are also described in different ways. The first talks about 'palaces of industry' which cover the houses in 'perpetual fog'; the second of machines which 'spun and writhed like tortured creatures' which 'poured out their plague of smoke'. This animal imagery makes the forces of industry seem alive, as 'wrathful monsters' which devour the scene, covering it with 'black vomit', in contrast to the more distant, though no less passionate, statements of the first passage.

The first passage makes use of an allusion to the Styx, the river of hell, and to Hades, hell itself, in describing the scene. No such parallel is drawn by the second, which instead concentrates on the earthly reality of the experience of walking through such a district. The first passage talks generally of 'slave' and 'master' and 'the wealth of some, the poverty of most', whereas the second makes no explicit political or social comment about exploitation: it is enough for the writer simply to describe the conditions of the people who live in this place for the injustice of the situation to become clear.

A further difference is that the first passage ends with a reference to the number of people who live and work in the area, whereas the second finishes with the image of individual angry people and the 'wrathful monsters' polluting their living area. The first then returns to its general view seen at the opening, the second to its more personal, individual involvement of the reader with the action of the novel.

Of the two, I prefer the second, since it allows the reader to become involved with the scene by making it comprehensible. I also find that the rather general statements made in the first passage, with their political rhetoric – as, for example, in the penultimate sentence of the penultimate paragraph – are less effective in exposing the ills of the situation than the more specific references of the second, such as the last sentence of the second paragraph.

> " It's worth saying here that the second passage always has a human scale, making it more real to us . . . "

> " . . . in the way that it does here. "

> " A perfectly valid expression of preference. "

EXAMINER COMMENT

This is an answer which succeeds in drawing together two lengthy passages to make several genuine comparisons of style, approach and content. As with the second passage, a major problem is knowing what to say and what to leave out. This answer concentrates on the major area of difference in the two passages. Notice the use made of quotation to support the points made, and the references to specific parts of the passages where quotation would be too lengthy.

In this kind of exercise, there is no need to voice a preference, although a personal response, if founded on close reading, will usually be rewarded. Here, you might well have found the first passage the more effective, with its attempt at sociological description, its supporting of political statements with statistics and the passion of its political rhetoric. Whatever your views, make sure that they rest on a close reading of the text and that they come *after* an analytical discussion of the passages and the ways in which they make their effects.

GETTING STARTED

Studying works of prose involves many of the techniques and approaches familiar from studying poetry or drama, but there are also some different problems which need to be overcome. In almost all cases, the prose works which are set are novels, and most people read novels in a rather different way from poems or plays. We tend to read them for the story, getting involved with the characters and action, and reading on to see what happens next. Sorting out how much of this usual, everyday approach we can use when studying is the first and perhaps the biggest problem to overcome.

Then there is the problem of knowing what to look for. You can't examine the language of an 800-page novel in as much detail as you can study the text of a poem, so what *do* you look for? How important is the story, i.e. the sequence of events, which is why most people read novels when they are first published? What about the characters? Should we think of them as real people, or just vehicles used by the writer to get across a point? And what *is* the point, or points – the themes or ideas – of a novel?

Along with all these questions, there is the problem of working out who is writing the story – is it the novelist, or is it one of the characters, and how does this alter the nature of what we're told? On top of this, there's the question of making sense of a book which may have been written two hundred years ago or more: how can we understand all the topical details and references in a Victorian novel, or even one written as recently as the 1920s or 30s? When we have understood all these things, how can we write about it convincingly and support our points by close reference to the text?

These are some of the insistent and important questions which occur when we begin the process of studying a novel. In addition there are the more familiar ones: sorting out the language in the manner familiar from critical appreciation exercises, taking notes that will be clear and legible for revision, and making sure we can *bring together* the text and the question and write with precision and relevance in the actual exam.

This chapter sets out some answers to these questions, to help you at each stage of reading and studying novels for your examination. How these principles work in practice is shown in the next chapter. This gives you the chance to answer some exam questions on prose works, to compare your ideas with student essays and to study the comments an examiner might have made on them.

ESSENTIAL PRINCIPLES

When most of us read a novel for recreation, we try hard to become closely involved in the world it creates. People talk of 'really getting into a good book', and the most popular novels are those which allow people to escape into the alternative reality they offer. When you're reading a novel for study purposes, however, you need to read it in rather a different way.

Never forget that it's written by a novelist, who is inventing the world that is being written about and controlling the characters who inhabit it. This enables him or her to use the framework of the novel in a lot of ways – to discuss ideas, explore human relationships, make historical or philosophical points, or be satirical, for example.

First reading

When you begin to study a novel, you should read it through fairly quickly to get a general idea of what it's about. This can be a little difficult if you're not used to reading long novels – and a Victorian novel can be easily 800 pages in length. But don't be daunted.

- Try to timetable your reading – so many chapters each day, for example. Many eighteenth and nineteenth century novels are divided into separate 'books' or parts: try to read each one of these as a single unit in a fairly concentrated time-span, so that you can hold larger bits of the novel in your mind.

- By all means get involved with the plot to the extent of wondering what happens next, but don't get *too* engrossed. Always remember the directing consciousness of the writer who planned it – this isn't 'real life' but a work of art that you're reading.

- Think about the way the novel is written. This doesn't only mean style and language, although these are important – but also the themes and ideas which you think the novelist might be discussing. Don't, as yet, spend too long on this, but have these areas of thought always there at the back of your mind when reading.

Detailed reading

Now you should go through all the processes mentioned in Chapter 1, looking closely at the way that the expression and themes are developed in each stage of the novel.

While you are doing this, take notes in the manner suggested in Chapter 10, recording points of interest as they come up in your exploration of the text. Just what you might find here is explored in more detail in the section 'What to Look For'.

You may find it easier to take notes by writing on the text itself, perhaps using the approach suggested in Fig. 1.1 in Chapter 1. Be careful, though: you'll have at some stage to draw together the points you make about individual chapters, and it might be easier to start taking separate notes right from the start – a sheaf of papers is much easier to work through than a large, bulky novel when you're looking for one specific point. What these notes might contain is discussed in the section 'Taking Notes'.

A detailed reading of a novel is bound to take time. Even the shortest novel will probably take three weeks to work through in the necessary depth – perhaps by working through it in classes and then consolidating your work in the evenings and writing essays on important aspects and themes. A full-length Victorian or eighteenth-century novel will take longer; so don't be too impatient when studying a novel. Take it gently, and give yourself plenty of time for the ideas and their treatment to sink in.

Reading to revise

Once you've read the book through, first to grasp what happens, and then to undertake detailed reading and study, it's a good idea to draw together your work by again reading through the whole novel quickly. A good approach is to set aside a whole weekend and to just read the novel. You'll find that this will bring together the work very effectively, and help you to grasp its themes and development more completely than if you spread the third reading over a longer period.

This is something that you should do when you've just finished the detailed reading stage. When you come to revise the work, perhaps after not having read it for a few months, you should try the same approach: shut yourself away and just read through the novel rapidly, using your notes to refresh your memory of the ideas and themes you noted when studying it in detail.

Try other approaches too – a cartoon strip of *Tristram Shandy*!

At this stage, too, you might like to make a 'map' of the novel – an outline which tells you very briefly what happens in each chapter and lists any other important features so that you know where they come from and can find them quickly when you need to. More advice is given on this in Chapter 1. It's a useful technique when you're revising, as it helps you to get an overall grasp of the novel.

USING ADAPTATIONS

Adaptations are treatments of the novel – they can never replace it.

Many novels have been adapted into different forms. Stage plays, films and radio performances have frequently been made of well known (and some less well known) novels, and properly used these can be of value to you when revising.

Be careful, however, when watching films or stage adaptations. *Stage plays* will inevitably have to leave out certain parts of the action, especially in novels which are very long or which contain action that takes place in complex or frequently-changing settings. Very often, too, they will omit sub-plots or other aspects of the action, simply for reasons of time. Overall, they may present a version of the novel that is shorter in length and thinner in texture.

Much the same is true of *films*. They may deliberately extend the range of a novel, using locations or exteriors where the novel is concerned with the inner life of the characters. Some may concentrate on setting and visual effect to the detriment of deeper themes and ideas: some recent British films of E. M. Forster's novels, for example, have tended to do this. Beware of something visually stunning and intellectually thin.

Radio adaptations are often the most successful treatments of novels. They frequently combine the use of a narrator with dramatised action, thus keeping the narrative voice and nature of the original and adding to it further dimensions of the characters. They are often far closer to the spirit of the original, too. Make a point, then, of checking to see if an adaptation of a novel you're studying is due to be broadcast. Radio 4 is the best place to look for the more popular serious novels, but Radio 3 sometimes has adaptations as well, so a close scrutiny of *Radio Times* or its equivalent may be a fruitful exercise.

Here are a number of things to look for.

NARRATIVE VOICE

Find out who is telling the story as soon as you can.

Who is telling a story has a considerable effect on what the story is like. If you see a traffic accident, for example, your account of it will be very different from the account by the person driving the car, or the man on the bicycle who was knocked over.

The same is true of a novel. If the story is told by someone who is involved, you need to be aware of that, and to think about how his or her character influences the selection of incidents, the language used, and the general nature and movement of the story. If, on the other hand, the story is told by someone outside the action, the whole presentation will be different.

In a novel, the narrative voice may be:

1   An omniscient narrator

Here, the story is told by a figure who is not identified – the writer simply writes the story, deciding what to put in and what to leave out, and assuming complete knowledge of all the characters' thoughts and actions. This is the most common technique in the popular novel, where the reader never stops to think who is writing and what attitudes he or she brings to the events and characters.

2   An identified story-teller

Remember that the writer might be using the narrator to make an ironic point. The story teller's ideas aren't always the writer's.

Some novels are actually 'told' by a figure who is identified as the narrator, who tells the story in a clearly-defined situation. Conrad, for example, has most of his stories told by someone of this kind: *Heart of Darkness* begins with a group of characters gathered on the deck of a boat moored on the Thames, one of whom then tells the story. This changes the relationship between writer and reader, by putting in a clearly-identified 'character' between the two.

3   First-person narrative

This is named after the grammatical term 'first-person', meaning 'I'. It is used when the person tells the story as if events happened to him or her. Its advantages are that it allows

> While reading, keep asking yourself what the story reveals about the teller.

a direct involvement in the story; its disadvantages, perhaps, are that the narrative is coloured by this character's knowledge and attitudes to events. Sometimes it can be difficult to sort things out. The narrator in *The Great Gatsby*, for example, is involved with the action and tells the story to reveal his own feelings.

When you are reading, you should always make sure that you know *who* is telling the story, and what effect this has on the novel as a whole in terms of the view we are given of events, the tone of voice that is used, and the attitudes that are presented.

NARRATIVE STANCE

As well as who is speaking or writing the narrative, you need to know his or her attitude towards it.

1   'Realist' fiction

This term means something rather different in the novel from what it means in drama. It simply means the attempt to present the events as if they are really happening, with no presence or comment from the narrator – rather like the presentation of events in a traditional thriller or romance novel, where there is never any question of the role of the narrator but instead we are just told what happened next.

2   Self-conscious narrator

> Make sure you know when the writer is directly addressing the reader.

Here, the narrator will often speak directly to the reader, either in separate parts of the novel or while the action is actually taking place. Henry Fielding, for example, begins each book of *Tom Jones* with a chapter in which he addresses the reader directly, and often makes similarly direct comments in the course of the novel's events.

More recently, John Fowles, in *The French Lieutenant's Woman*, has used similarly direct address to ask questions of the reader, and break through the pretence of realism of the traditional popular novel. Such direct statements can be very effective, as they force the reader to think about the nature of the novel, and focus his or her mind on issues or themes being discussed.

3   Involved narrator

> First Person narratives add involvement to a novel.

Often the narrator will be someone who is involved with the events going on. A well-known example of this would be the character of Jane in *Jane Eyre*, who knows only what she herself sees and learns about other characters, or Pip in *Great Expectations*.

This narrative stance has a considerable influence on the nature of the book. As the story is told by someone who *doesn't* know all that is going on, it makes things more exciting for the reader, and an element of suspense is introduced. It also means that we come close to experiencing things directly ourselves when we read the novel. The 'I' of the narrator becomes the 'I' of each reader, and so we are drawn closely into what is happening.

Sometimes a writer will split the narration between a number of characters. In *Bleak House*, for example, Dickens uses both an omniscient narrator and one of the main characters in chapters headed 'Esther's Narrative'; in *The Moonstone*, Wilkie Collins changes the narration from one character to another as the novel progresses. These are exceptions, however: generally the narrator remains constant, and involved with the action throughout.

4   Ironic detachment

> Look out for irony – saying one thing and meaning the opposite.

If a book is being narrated by an omniscient narrator, very often a tone of ironic detachment may be used. Perhaps the most celebrated example of this is found in the works of Jane Austen, whose style is one of considerable irony in terms of her approach to the characters and the action. Read carefully to be aware of such an approach: if you fail to notice the ironic voice, your grasp of the novel will be severely limited and you will reach misleading conclusions about the writer's attitude and also even about the sequence of events and the characters' feelings being presented.

Narrative stances like these have a very considerable impact on the nature of the novel. As a result, one of the first things you need to do when reading one is work out both the narrative voice and the narrative stance. Until you do this, you will not appreciate the full meaning and resonance of the writing.

OTHER FEATURES OF THE NOVEL

THEMES

Novels discuss themes and ideas just as poems or plays do. They may not always be present in quite such an explicit way, but very often they will be of major philosophical or human significance. Read the text closely to try to work out what issues, if any, the novelist is attempting to address. Discuss your ideas with fellow-students, or with your teacher; when you are familiar with the novel, you might like to supplement your ideas by reading a critical study of the novel, being careful *not* to accept all the views it gives without reservation.

As you go through the book, make notes on the changing ways in which the theme or idea is treated, so that you can then assemble your notes on the topic in preparation for the exam.

Attitudes

Look, too, at the attitudes to particular topics presented in the novel. Be aware, of course, that the attitudes of the narrator may not be those of the writer, or that the novelist's ideas may emerge only when you compare the views of *several* of the characters. You may well have a question on this topic, so it's worth thinking carefully about it while you are reading the novel in detail and taking notes on any passages which seem to suggest a particular attitude.

HUMAN NATURE AND RELATIONSHIPS

Don't get too involved in details – go for the larger themes of human nature and relationships.

Many novels are concerned not so much with individual people from a particular historical period but with aspects of people which are common at all times. Jane Austen, for example, is concerned with human characteristics such as pride and humility; Dickens is often concerned with the nature of love, greed or evil among humankind.

Other novelists are more concerned with the interaction between people. D.H. Lawrence explores the range and extent of relationships between men and women in his novels, as well as that between humankind and the natural world – a topic which he shares with Thomas Hardy, although the two approach it in very different ways.

Once again, you need to think carefully not only to see the importance of such topics, but also to work out what you think the writer's attitude towards them might be.

CONTEMPORARY REFERENCES

Many novelists are concerned to make points about topics and events which they see as being of major significance to the time about which they are writing. George Orwell's *Animal Farm* is an extended allegory in which every event of the story is a precise parallel to an event in the Russian revolution, and is used to make a critical comment about Communism. Elizabeth Gaskell's *North and South* is a sustained criticism of attitudes and material conditions in industrial towns in the 1830s and 40s.

Beware of too much background.

These topics are often of major importance, so that you need to understand the contemporary references the novel makes. Usually this can be done by reading the notes in your edition, or perhaps by consulting a historical dictionary or history text book. Be careful, though, that you don't get so interested in the period that the novel becomes less important than the history. You need to know only enough about the times being written about to allow you to understand the novel and its themes fully: you will not be asked questions which will demand a detailed historical knowledge, and the text itself must always be your main concern.

USE OF THE SETTING

In many novels the physical circumstances in which the action takes place will be almost as important as one of the characters. Hardy, for example, uses the bleak setting of Egdon Heath in *The Return of the Native* to create an atmosphere of desolation; E.M. Forster makes India itself a major force in *A Passage to India*. Other novelists will use a setting for symbolic purposes; in *Bleak House*, for example, Dickens uses the foggy streets of London as a symbol of the obscurity and lack of direction of the lawsuit which is a major aspect of the plot.

Always think carefully about the setting of a novel and make sure that you are aware of what it contributes to the work as a whole on both a literal and a symbolic level.

PLOT

> Never just tell the story in an exam answer.

You will need to know what happens in the novel, of course, but the plot or story is not the major focus of your attention at this level. Always be aware of the other features mentioned in this section as well as of the simple sequence of events: in many novels, the story is simply a framework to support the discussion of elements of human nature or other political or social themes or philosophical concerns.

CHARACTERS

> Characters are part of the writer's larger pattern of themes and ideas – not real people.

Characters in novels are rather similar to characters in plays: they are an essential element of the structure of the whole, but they must not be seen as people in their own right. When making detailed notes about a novel, think about what the characters contribute to the development of the plot and the discussion of themes and ideas which are the novel's concern. You will not be asked to write a simple study of a character from a novel or play in the exam: you may very well be asked what techniques the novelist uses to make him or her real, or what he or she contributes to the discussion of various themes or ideas, and this should be the main focus of your attention when reading in detail.

TAKING NOTES

> Follow the examples shown in Chapters 8 and 11.

At the detailed reading stage, you'll need to take notes on all of the aspects mentioned above which the novelist uses in the text. Do this at first by *listing points* as you come across them in a chapter or part of a book. Then draw them together in a series of single sheets, each of which lists points about a *particular topic or aspect* of the novel, with carefully selected examples to support them. In a lengthy novel, you will have a large number of examples of a key topic, so think carefully and select only those which are of the most fundamental importance.

You need also to make notes on the *techniques* of writing familiar from analysing poetry. Symbolism, figurative use of language, diction, tone, and the use of irony are all used in some degree by many novelists. So make sure that you have a set of notes on the *ways* in which they are used, and on any other important techniques which a novelist employs.

Make a list of suitable *quotations* which you can learn for use in the exam. As with poetry and plays, you should try to learn short phrases which can be used to demonstrate several points – a technique as well as a theme or attitude, for example. Selecting such phrases will generally be a process of choosing those which appear on several of your sheets of notes on different topics or aspects of the book. This will help you to make sure that you can support all the points you are likely to make in the exam essay.

Remember, too, that you do not always need to quote – close reference to the text may be enough. Often a reference to a particular scene or passage will be sufficient, so be prepared to support your points in this way when you need to refer to a longer part of the novel and there is no suitable quotation for you to use.

WRITING ABOUT NOVELS

When you're writing about a novel, you need to plan and structure your essay in exactly the same way as when writing about a play or a collection of poems. There are, however, some other points to remember.

1   Don't tell the story

> Remember: the examiner has read the novel.

It's easy to get bogged down in narrative when you're trying to answer a question, simply because you want to explain where a theme is covered or how an attitude is shown and need to refer closely to the text. Remember, though, that the examiner will know the story well and will need only the shortest suggestion of the passage you mean.

Avoid narrative by always making your point *first*, and then citing evidence from the text to support it. Make sure, too, that the idea or concept is the main clause of the sentence, and the evidence is a subordinate clause like this:

Greene's use of symbolic detail, shown for example in Scobie's rusty handcuffs, is a major technique in the novel.

This will ensure that you get the balance right and do not write long accounts of the story of the novel, for which you'll get no reward in the exam.

2   Don't write about characters as people

As the last section made clear, you won't be asked to write about characters as real people. You may be asked *how* a novelist creates a character, or what the character adds to the discussion of a theme or idea in the novel, in which case you need to treat the characters very much within this context and not spend any time on unnecessary description.

3   Avoid 'background'

As with any other kind of text, you should not spend time in writing accounts of the novelist's circumstances when the novel was produced, or the historical setting in which it is placed, or any other element of its 'background'. As always, go straight to the text.

4   Use the present tense

When writing about a novel, always write in the *present tense*. Don't, for example, say:

> Pip's first meeting with Magwitch on the marshes showed the impact the convict was to have on him.

but instead:

> Pip's first meeting with Magwitch on the marshes *shows* the impact the convict *is* to have on him.

This will make the writing much clearer and also show that you understand the existence of the novel as a work of literature, not just a 'story' or sequence of events from real life.

Reading and studying a novel is not easy. For all of the reasons made clear in this chapter, it demands close attention and careful thought, in order to understand the main themes and ideas being covered as well as the writer's attitude to them. It also demands the ability to select passages which are representative of important ideas, and to write clearly and briefly to establish the key points in the narrative, so freeing you to discuss these ideas in your essay.

As always, the basis of success is close textual reading. Follow the advice given here about careful, detailed reading, and you should find that your knowledge of the prescribed novels will deepen considerably.

> " Writing in the present keeps your discussion alive. "

15

PROSE 3: WRITING ABOUT PROSE

GETTING STARTED

This chapter is concerned with putting into practice the advice given on writing essays – this time, about prose works. Like the equivalent chapters on poetry and drama it has a series of exam questions covering works often set at A-level, with student answers and examiner comments. As before, you should try to answer the questions on the text or texts you are studying to help you master the art of writing in the strictly measured time of the exam. Only then should you go on to look at the answers provided.

You should also read the questions and answers on texts which you are *not* studying. This will help you to get to know the kinds of question that might appear on your paper, and also give you some ideas about how to answer them. In many cases, the answers and the comments on them deal with problems of balance and expression which often occur when writing about novels – so they have advice to offer even though you may not be able to understand the specific points they make about the texts which you haven't read.

ESSENTIAL PRINCIPLES

Questions on prose works will be of three main types.

1 Questions which give you *a passage* from a text, with an accompanying question

> ❝ Check your syllabus and past papers to see what kind of questions may be set. ❞

In most cases, the aim of these is to get you to read a passage closely, to write about it in detail and to *relate* it to the text as a whole. You may, for example, be asked to show what it contributes to the discussion of a particular theme, how it is typical of the writer's use of humour, or how it demonstrates the tone or approach of the whole work.

Tackle these questions by reading the whole text and by identifying the specific features it demonstrates. Then find examples of these in the rest of the work, plan your answer under concepts or techniques, and write the essay.

> ❝ If there are two questions on a passage, spend longer on the one which has more marks. ❞

Sometimes, you will be asked two questions about a passage and its relation to the work. Generally, the first will be longer and more complex, the second shorter and more straightforward. You can always tell the relative importance of such questions by looking at the number of marks allotted to each section. If the first has, say, fifteen and the second five, you will know the the first part should be three times as long as the second – a very rough guide which should help you to plan the time you spend on each. Remember, too, that you will probably be able to answer the second in two or three sentences – so don't spend too long searching out hidden significances in the question: there usually aren't any.

In plain text papers, the questions will generally be of this sort, except that you will be given the page or chapter numbers for the passage involved instead of having it printed on the exam paper.

2 Questions with a quotation

Like similar questions on poetry or plays, these will make a statement about the work and then give you instructions about how to treat it – either to discuss it in general, or to relate it to a more specific theme or part of the text.

> ❝ Chapter 2 gives advice on this kind of question. ❞

As before, you must *read* the quotation carefully and make sure that you understand it before thinking about the task that you're asked to perform in response to it. Once you have done this, you need to work out exactly what you're asked to do. This will usually be one of the two alternatives given above. Then, think about the work as a whole, make a list of points each with supporting evidence from the text, and write your essay.

3 Questions on a particular aspect or theme of the book

These are usually fairly straightforward – if you know the text you should have no difficulty in using this knowledge by bringing it to bear on the topic given.

Once again, read the question carefully to define the topic; think about the book and make a list of points which *relate* it to the given subject; support each one with textual reference or quotation; and then write the essay.

1 'Colour, emphasis and colloquial vigour: these were the characteristic qualities of Elizabethan prose'. Discuss in relation to *The Unfortunate Traveller*.

2 'In Book IV of *Gulliver's Travels* Swift's attitude is one of total despair'. How far do you agree?

3 Show how Defoe draws together elements of the novel and elements of a historical narrative in *A Journal of the Plague Year*.

4 a) Compare and contrast these two letters, by Elizabeth and her father. You should in particular discuss what they show about their writers' characters and their attitudes to others.   *(14)*

   b) Suggest in a few lines how Darcy's letter to Lady Catherine might differ in tone and style from these two.   *(6)*

> From an unwillingness to confess how much her intimacy with Mr Darcy had been over-rated, Elizabeth had never yet answered Mrs Gardiner's long letter, but now, having *that* to communicate which she knew would be most welcome, she was almost ashamed to find, that her uncle and aunt had already lost three days of happiness, and immediately wrote as follows:
> 'I would have thanked you before, my dear aunt, as I ought to have done,

for your long, kind, satisfactory, detail of particulars; but to say the truth, I
was too cross to write. You supposed more than really existed. But *now*
suppose as much as you chuse; give a loose to your fancy, indulge your
imagination in every possible flight which the subject will afford, and unless   10
you believe me actually married, you cannot greatly err. You must write
again very soon, and praise him a great deal more than you did in your last. I
thank you, again and again, for not going to the Lakes. How could I be so silly
as to wish it! Your idea of the ponies is delightful. We will go round the Park
every day. I am the happiest creature in the world. Perhaps other people   15
have said so before, but not one with such justice. I am happier even than
Jane; she only smiles, I laugh. Mr Darcy sends you all the love in the world,
that he can spare from me. You are all to come to Pemberley at Christmas.
Yours, &c.'

Mr Darcy's letter to Lady Catherine, was in a different style; and still   20
different from either, was what Mr Bennet sent to Mr Collins, in reply to his
last.

'DEAR SIR,
'I must trouble you once more for congratulations. Elizabeth will soon be
the wife of Mr Darcy. Console Lady Catherine as well as you can. But, if I   25
were you, I would stand by the nephew. He has more to give.
'Your's sincerely, &c.'

5 Write an appreciation of this passage from *Great Expectations*, showing how far it is
representative of Dickens' themes and methods in the novel.

Next day the clothes I had ordered all came home, and he put them on. Whatever
he put on, became him less (it dismally seemed to me) than what he had worn
before. To my thinking there was something in him that made it hopeless to attempt
to disguise him. The more I dressed him and the better I dressed him, the more he
looked like the slouching fugitive on the marshes. This effect on my anxious fancy
was partly referable, no doubt, to his old face and manner growing more familiar to
me: but I believed too that he dragged one of his legs as if there were still a weight of
iron on it and that from head to foot there was Convict in the very grain of the man.

The influences of his solitary hut-life were upon him besides, and gave him a
savage air that no dress could tame: added to these were the influences of his
subsequent branded life among men, and crowning all, his consciousness that he was
dodging and hiding now. In all his ways of sitting and standing, and eating and
drinking – of brooding about, in a high-shouldered reluctant style – of taking out his
great horn-handled jack-knife and wiping it on his legs and cutting his food – of lifting
light glasses and cups to his lips, as if they were clumsy pannikins – of chopping a
wedge off his bread, and soaking up with it the last fragments of gravy round and
round his plate, as if to make the most of any allowance, and then drying his fingers
on it, and then swallowing it – in these ways and a thousand other small nameless
instances arising every minute in the day, there was Prisoner, Felon, Bondsman,
plain as plain could be.

It had been his own idea to wear that touch of powder and I conceded the powder
after overcoming the shorts. But I can compare the effect of it, when on, to nothing
but the probable effect of rouge upon the dead; so awful was the manner in which
everything in him, that it was most desirable to repress, started through that thin
layer of pretence, and seemed to come blazing out at the crown of his head. It was
abandoned as soon as tried, and he wore his grizzled hair cut short.

6 Show what use Graham Greene makes of the African setting in *The Heart of the Matter*.

STUDENT ANSWERS WITH EXAMINER COMMENTS

STUDENT ANSWER TO QUESTION 1

> 66 Using 'picaresque' sounds good, but will only get marks if you know what it means – see the examiner comment at the end. 99

> 66 Notice the close reference to parts of the text, which is as good as quotation in many cases. 99

> 66 This uses a technical term – 'Euphuistic' – and also makes clear you know what it means. 99

> 66 You may find this sexist, repulsive and politically unacceptable, but an exam essay isn't the place to say so. 99

> 66 Good, relevant short quotations incorporated into the text to support a point – if possible, do this more often. 99

> 66 Rather a weak ending – why not quote some of this splendid colloquial bawdy writing to finish with? 99

The Unfortunate Traveller is a good example of the Elizabethan picaresque novel, and as such it complies with all the conditions outlined in the question. The book certainly contains colour, both in the actual events and the enthusiastic narrative which describes them. Jack Wilton, the hero, undergoes a series of adventures which are certainly 'colourful', from the beginning where he is a member of the court of Henry VIII to the end, where the more ordered plot of the second half is concluded by a very lurid and detailed description of a public execution.

In the passage describing the massacre of the Anabaptists the scene is well set by descriptions of the sect's behaviour and ideas, and the reader is left in no doubt whatsoever as to the sympathies of the narrator – there is plenty of 'emphasis' here. The description of a palace belonging to the Italian merchant, whose mechanical beauties and marvels hold Wilton spellbound, is one of the highlights of the book, and the language used to describe the fantastic building conveys the great enthusiasm of the writer and is extremely colourful and effective.

The Euphuistic language used in the first half of the book, with its flowery metaphors and very elaborate, balanced sentences, also contributes greatly to the colour of the work, but in the second half the technique is not used nearly so much, as the 'plot' becomes more concentrated.

Emphasis is not lacking in the book, some of the best examples occurring in the second part. The rape scene, which takes place in a plague-ridden city, is described in detail, as is the final execution. This is described in full, with all the brutal, sadistic rites narrated for the enjoyment of the reader, and the contemporary reader would have felt the book incomplete without such passages.

Satire is used with much emphasis in the book, and Jack Wilton presents an almost xenophobic character, describing all the failings of other nations and all the virtues of the English. Satire is heaped upon the falsely-learned men of the age, and the over-indulgence in very extravagant idioms of speech, dress and behaviour: the best example of this is the account of the speeches at the University, and the general dress and behaviour of the members of that institution. Wilton talks of 'a miserable rabblement of Junior Graduates' and 'A bursten belly inkhorne orator', and in general derides the affair with a great deal of vigour and colloquial language.

Wilton's arguments against the Anabaptists are more reasoned but just as enthusiastic and emphatic. In general he has no qualms about expressing his own opinions on any issue of the day, and he does so in a very open, conversational style. The colloquial emphasis is also shown by the vigorous language he uses, as shown in the examples above and in phrases he uses to describe his actions: 'I was at Pontius Pilate's house, and pissed against it'.

It is this quality of conversational style which gives The Unfortunate Traveller its sense of enthusiasm, vigour and vitality which runs throughout the work. In the first part, where Wilton is a courtier, the elaborate and flamboyant Euphuistic style is used, whereas in the second part the language suits the bawdy, Rabelaisian nature of the plot. There are frequent digressions, which give the book an unusual appearance of spontaneity, to make it appear as if we are actually listening to a vigorous, forceful person telling us a story.

Colloquialisms are used to a great extent, especially when Wilton describes the actions and characteristics of foreigners. The book's plot, especially the more ordered sequences of events towards the end, adds to the liveliness of the language, so that the book does indeed contain all the characteristic features of Elizabethan prose fiction listed by the question.

EXAMINER COMMENT

This addresses the question directly, taking each of the three features in turn and giving examples for them. It would clearly pass, but would be better with more specific examples and some more quotations to support and supplement the textual points made. To make an excellent answer, some indication of the meanings of the technical terms used – 'picaresque' and 'Euphuistic' – would help; 'a series of loosely-connected adventures of a central roguish character' and 'a complex, ornate style with long sentences composed of balanced clauses and phrases and very ingenious comparisons' respectively, perhaps. This would convince the examiner that you know what you're saying, and are not just word-dropping. Another way of improving the essay would be to combine the three elements, to show how they work together to produce the vigour and effect of the novel.

STUDENT ANSWER TO QUESTION 2

The fourth book of Gulliver's Travels begins in a manner similar to the first three, with the introduction of the Yahoos as a race with some of man's skills but clearly far beneath his intellect and sensitivity, and the Houyhnhnms who are gentle and civilised. Yet it also contains elements which are much more serious and which can be taken to suggest a mood of total despair with humanity in the writer.

> You start off well by spelling Houyhnhnms correctly.

The first shock to the reader comes when the Houyhnhnms show their belief that Gulliver is a Yahoo with some powers of reason, presumably by a freak of nature. At first Gulliver argues with them, but then realises with shock that, if he differs from the Yahoos it is because he is worse, not better, suggesting a despairing view of humanity. We may at first assume that this is a satirical attack on eighteenth-century England, to suggest that the Houyhnhnms are the perfect race, but Swift is far less optimistic. They are gradually shown to be the soulless embodiment of an ill-conceived ideal. They have no word for 'love', live perfectly ordered lives, have no courage as they have no fear to overcome, and have no compassion towards each other. In their efforts to overcome the limitations of a balanced life, they have created a society in which the weakest do not survive, and most forms of self-expression are stifled. There is, for example, no need for poetry or music, as the Houyhnhnms see no need for originality or expression. The number of offspring per couple is limited, and sex only tolerated because it re-stocks the race with young. Overall, in their effort to rid society of suffering, the Houyhnhnms have also rid it of sensitivity and joy: the lack of perfection here would seem to suggest that Swift can find no ideal and sees humanity with despair.

> Here the writing moves away from narrative into analysis just in time.

> Examples of all these aspects would strengthen the point here.

It is, however, possible that Swift intended to show that there was a perfect state of humanity somewhere between the two extreme states presented in Book IV. Yet it seems unlikely that the ideal 'middle society' can be found if the Houyhnhnms are flawed when they were originally seen as the ideal.

> Good example of a writer's ideas emerging between the extremes of different characters in a novel.

The evidence that Swift is approaching despair here is considerable. He describes Gulliver's complete disgust with humanity on his return home, when even his wife and family repel him. He identifies his previous life with the squalor of the Yahoos, and overall there is the feeling that the position of the narrator is much more extreme than in the earlier books to reveal the depth of feeling of the writer.

Another argument in favour of this view is the fact that the final book contains far fewer incidents of narrative importance than the earlier ones; it seems, in fact, that Swift ends the book as a philosopher rather than as a novelist. If man does not change, he seems to be saying, he becomes a despicable beast; if he does, he leads a hollow life dominated by ideals and lacking compassion. Swift shows that there is no hope for man and his attitude in the final book is indeed one of total despair.

> The writing gets rather general at the end.

EXAMINER COMMENT

This is fundamentally sound in that it makes a secure argument in favour of the question's claim, but it rather lacks depth. This is mainly because the ideas are not supported by close reference to the text. Except for some details in the early paragraphs, the essay lacks any close textual reference and has no quotation. This is a pity because it argues along the right lines and will still get a good grade.

With a little work to extend its range, though, it would do much better and be a very good pass indeed.

STUDENT ANSWER TO QUESTION 3

Defoe uses elements from both historical writing and the novel in A Journal of the Plague Year, and indeed the success of the book is largely the result of this combination.

> Specific examples of how we become involved in the book as a novel . . .

Defoe uses HF as a narrator, a technique familiar from novels, so that we are drawn into what happens and sympathise with his feelings and experiences. When HF walks through the city we go with him; when he meets robbers at his brother's house, we share his anger, and we are also angry, with him, at the 'railers' who make jokes about the people suffering from the plague. His concern for the man who is trying to keep his family alive is something else which makes the book like a novel in which the narrator's feelings are the main factor in drawing us in to the events.

> . . . balanced by references to how it works as history . . .

These events are supplemented by hard facts taken from bills of the plague and tables of statistics issued during and shortly after the epidemic, which Defoe would have been able to consult, so that the book has elements of an historical account based on careful research. Shortly after the beginning of the book, for example, Defoe quotes the official orders controlling the plague. He joins together history and novel by having HF tell us the latest statistics as if he has just read them, so linking the two aspects.

> . . . and an example of how the two come together in a specific incident.

Further elements of the novel are added by the anecdotes and stories which HF tells us. The most extensive of these is the story of the three men of Wapping. Even here, though, there are elements which convey a real feeling of the events, as might an historical account: the men are given 'a porker' by people in Woodford, and find a purse containing 'about thirteen shillings'. These details suggest accurate historical records but at the same time help us to become part of the story, in a joining of the historical and the fictional which we find in the best historical novels.

> Paradoxically, it's often the gaps in a novel that make it more convincing.

One of the features which strangely makes the book more convincing is that it does not attempt to give a full account of the plague. True, it does cover a wide range of places and people in London, from the people marooned on ships in the docks to the mayor and city livery companies. Overall, though, we learn what is happening through the eyes of HF. This is a technique used in many novels which use a 'first person' narrator, but at the same time it makes the history appear more real because we see things as a person living through the times would see them – a technique used a lot in writing and teaching about history.

Even when HF says that he cannot be sure of the truth of what he is recording, saying that 'it was not confirmed' or merely that 'they told us', we believe in him as an honest witness, and this paradoxically makes things seem historically real.

> The conclusion unites the two elements and says why they come together so successfully in the book.

For all of these reasons, the book is effective in combining history with the novel. The most striking reason for this is not so much the use of accurate historical research but the presentation of what it has revealed by a single character with whom we can sympathise and become involved, the character of HF. In using this technique, Defoe does indeed succeed in drawing together the two kinds of writing mentioned by the question.

EXAMINER COMMENT

This answer illustrates well some specific difficulties encountered when writing about a text of this type, which is often encountered in papers on a single historical period. The main problem is to get the right balance between discussing the text as a piece of writing and analysing its historical context. Here, the question asks you to compare the book's success in combining two different kinds of writing. The danger is that you can easily get carried away in writing a long description of either the book or of the historical circumstances, when the aim is to discuss the *technique* the writer uses.

Notice that the answer tries to *combine* the two elements, rather than discuss first one and then the other. As with critical appreciation questions which call for comparisons, the aim must be to draw the two together. This question attempts this and in general succeeds. Notice that there is much more reference to the text than in the preceding answer; quotations do not have to be lengthy, and close reference will do just as well if it is specific.

STUDENT ANSWER TO QUESTION 4

> **❝❞ Don't be afraid of stating the obvious – that one letter is much longer than the other – if you say why it's important. ❞❞**

a) The greatest difference between the two letters may be seen in their length, tone and content. Elizabeth's letter is expansive, revealing the depth of her confidence and happiness, whereas Mr Bennet's is much briefer and rather terse, suggesting that his own outlook is markedly different from his daughter's.

> **❝❞ Good relation of the tone of the letter to the tone of other passages in the novel. ❞❞**

Elizabeth's openness about her feelings is shown when she confesses that she 'was too cross' to write. Here references to her own silliness (line 13), to being 'the happiest creature in the world' and being happier than Jane because 'she only smiles, I laugh' also show this. By contrast, her father's expressions of feeling are far more by implication than open statement. There is no statement of his reaction to Elizabeth's engagement, except the rather weary tone that is apparent right from the start of the novel in his dealings with his wife and family and which is seen here in the claim that he 'must trouble' Mr Collins for congratulations.

Both are very confident letters, however. Elizabeth's confidence is shown by her very full expression – in lines 11 and 12, for example – and in the witty reference to Mr Darcy's love in line 17. Her father's confidence shows itself rather differently, in its concluding reference to Darcy in comparison to Lady Catherine, which reveals an ability to sum up a person's character quickly and briefly.

> **❝❞ A clearly-indicated switch to the other main topic of the question. ❞❞**

The attitudes to others shown in the letters are also different. Elizabeth is outgoing, referring to 'my dear aunt' and asking her to indulge her imagination (lines 9–10) in a very free way. Overall, the letter reads as if it is written by someone who is very secure and confident in herself and her new relationship, and who allows this to colour her outlook on other people. By contrast, Mr Bennet is ironic. His request 'Console Lady Catherine as well as you can' reveals an awareness of Collins'

> **❝❞ Always be on the lookout for irony – especially when reading Austen. ❞❞**

obsequious devotion to Lady Catherine. His suggestion to 'stand by the nephew' shows a shrewd grasp of the character of Darcy, as well as an ironic allusion to Mr Collins' personality: 'He has more to give' is both a statement that Darcy is morally a better person than his aunt, and that Collins would do better to pursue *him* for help and patronage than Lady Catherine. Perhaps its very brevity also shows his lack of real concern for Collins, as someone not worth a longer letter.

Overall, then, the tone and approach of the letters reveal the two as very different characters.

> **❝❞ This part can be answered much more briefly, as it will gain only a few marks. ❞❞**

b) I think that Darcy's letter would be somewhere between the two in terms of tone and style. It would lack the rather gushing expression of feeling of Elizabeth's but also the ironic terseness of her father's, and would probably be couched in very well-mannered and polite language in keeping with the personality of Mr Darcy as it is revealed at the end of the novel.

EXAMINER COMMENT

This is a good example of the kind of passage-based question which occurs frequently in exams. Notice first the division of space between the two parts of the question: the first part is given a far fuller answer, as is appropriate because of its nature and the number of marks available for it. The second part is answered in just a few sentences to convey the main point: there is no need for a lengthy account of the changes in Darcy's character or his relationship with his aunt.

Notice that this answer concentrates on the elements suggested by the question as they are revealed in the passage but, when necessary, makes reference to the rest of the novel to clarify a point. Read the questions carefully to see the degree to which such reference is needed: here, the primary focus is definitely on the passage, whereas elsewhere you will be asked to relate the excerpt to the larger ideas of the novel.

STUDENT ANSWER TO QUESTION 5

> **This is true – but is it the best place to start?**

This passage is representative in several ways of Dickens' concerns and methods in the novel. Strikingly apparent is the closeness of observation of other people's dress and habits of behaviour which is clear in Pip from the very start of the novel, and which we see in his accounts of Estella, Miss Havisham and, perhaps most completely, in the behaviour of Joe when he comes to visit Pip in London. Dickens shows this by having Pip single out details, here for example in Magwitch's habit of wiping his knife on his legs, and of the effect of his wearing powder.

> **Good shift from Pip's nature to Dickens' technique.**

Another aspect which is of importance here as elsewhere in the novel is the relationship between outward appearance and inner nature. Miss Havisham's withered spirit is symbolised in the ancient, shrivelled wedding dress; Joe's coarseness in his heavy dress and incongruity when in the more refined rooms of Pip and Herbert Pocket. Here, Magwitch's nature as a convict is very clear despite the apparent sophistication given him by his clothes.

> **This point shows that the essay is well constructed, as it brings together the previous two points.**

This is related to what is perhaps the novel's major theme – the way in which social respectability and success are related to corruption and crime. Pip's 'expectations', after all, come from Magwitch himself, and although this is used by Dickens to undercut Pip's pomposity and sense of superiority, it is a social theme of much importance which he develops elsewhere, for example in Our Mutual Friend, and is a measure of his concern with social issues of the day.

Pip's character is also apparent here. Throughout the novel he is apart from the people who are around him – Mrs Joe inspires fear and mistrust, and his early closeness to Joe soon disappears with his new-found property. He is also afraid of Miss Havisham, and his feelings for Estella, however deep, are tempered by a sense of social distance which begins when she mocks him for calling jacks knaves and knowing only simple card-games. This distance is shown in this passage in the way that Pip does not feel compassion or sorrow for Magwitch's plight, but instead seems to feel only fear and apprehension.

> **It now returns to Pip, seeing him as a creation of Dickens, not as the storyteller.**

One further aspect should be mentioned. The passage is presented from Pip's viewpoint in his own words, and this is the major technique used by Dickens to give the novel unity and immediacy. Its achievement lies in the fact that, although Pip is 'writing' the novel with hindsight, we nevertheless experience its events as they occur, seeing them as he saw them at the time, first as a child and then in the succeeding stages of his personal growth. This passage is typical of the novel in capturing that immediacy, so that in theme and approach it is representative of how the novel as a whole functions.

EXAMINER COMMENT

The important thing to realise here is that the question is asking you to relate this passage to the rest of the novel by showing how it represents features of importance in the work as a whole. This answer does this clearly and directly, by seizing upon a group of points and dealing with each one separately, showing how the passage is typical of the text in its use of this device or theme.

If you have studied the text carefully in the manner suggested in Chapter 14, you should have no difficulty in drawing the two elements together in this way. Remember that such questions are not critical appreciation exercises, nor are they more conventional general essays: start with a detailed reading of the passage, work outwards from this to the text as a whole, and you should have no difficulty in producing answers like this one, which covers the major themes and concerns briefly and clearly.

STUDENT ANSWER TO QUESTION 6

Straightforward listing of examples here.

A problem of separating the 'functions' is that the same events have to be covered twice – but this is better than a narrative approach.

The most complex function, rightly left to last – but make sure you have enough time to do this in the exam.

Greene uses the African setting in three main ways in The Heart of the Matter. There are the physical effects it has on the characters; the way it helps to develop the action; and the way in which it reflects symbolically the moods of the characters.

The main physical effect is caused by the climate. The fact that Louise has malaria is a direct result of the climate and setting. This creates much of the distance between her and Scobie and finally makes her go to South Africa; thus the climate is also a major force in the novel's plot. Further importance of the climate is shown in the way that it contributes to Father Rank's depression, causes wounds to fester and prevents post-mortems from being held. Overall, the climate adds to the discomfort and pressures of life for all the characters.

> Straightforward listing of examples here.

Further effects are caused by the isolation of the setting. This makes Louise feel isolated and insecure, and increases the feeling of lust to which Wilson is prey, since there is so little companionship for him. The fact that there is a small group of Europeans in the country makes them herd together, encouraging gossip and mistrust, like that of Wilson at the club. It also encourages strange behaviour, such as the cockroach hunts which Harris goes in for. The state of war is also important, in creating shortages which affect everyone and add tension to their lives, for example in Louise's shortage of books. It is also used in the novel to create uncertainty and suspense, for example in the threat and reality of submarine attack, and in this it adds to the 'thriller' aspects of the novel.

> A problem of separating the 'functions' is that the same events have to be covered twice – but this is better than a narrative approach.

The setting's effect on the action has already been shown in its importance in making Louise leave for South Africa, something dependent not only on the climate but also on her loneliness and dislike of other aspects of the location, such as the rats and the general atmosphere at the club. The loneliness of the situation also throws people closer to each other so that, with few friends, the strains between Louise and Scobie become much more apparent. The climate causes Scobie's fever after Pemberton's suicide, and it is in this weakened state that he agrees to borrow money from Yusef, thus allowing himself to be drawn, however innocently, into the corruption of the country, so that once again the climate and setting are responsible in part for events important in the action of the book. Finally, just as the isolation of the colony reveals the distance between Scobie and Louise because they have to rely on each other's company, so it reveals the closeness between him and Helen, again furthering the action.

> The most complex function, rightly left to last – but make sure you have enough time to do this in the exam.

The use of the setting to reflect symbolically the characters' feelings is another major function. Whenever Scobie and Louise touch each other they begin to sweat, and this is both a literal and symbolic statement of the difficulties caused by the climate in moving them further apart. The festering wound which Scobie tries to dress while Louise and Wilson are talking downstairs is again the result of the climate, but symbolically represents the way that Scobie's despair festers inside him. Finally, the confusion and violence of the scene at the wharf – a very physical element of the setting – not only contributes to the action but also reveals Scobie's inner turmoil and the violence which will reveal itself finally in his suicide.

In all these ways, the setting is of major importance in the novel.

EXAMINER COMMENT

This is an answer which is solid and secure in the way that it covers the necessary ground. In many ways it is little more than a list, but it serves the purpose well and answers the question fully, with copious examples. Notice that, although there is no quotation, there is frequent specific reference, which is just as valid in this kind of answer.

The answer could have been better if it had avoided the rather rigid framework that it adopts. Instead of dealing with each of the three 'uses' of the setting which it finds, it could have looked at the ways in which setting performs a range of functions simultaneously. There is some reference to this early on when Louise's malaria is discussed, but in general the essay approaches the topics separately when, for an A grade, it would have been better to try to draw them together, perhaps by selecting key episodes for analysis on a deeper level.

The answer does, however, avoid the trap of going through the novel from beginning to end pointing out references to the setting. This you need to do, mentally, as a stage in the preparation of the essay; but it is far better to structure the essay around ideas or 'uses' even if, as here, they are a little on the rigid side.

LANGUAGE QUESTIONS

GETTING STARTED

Most examining boards offer only English Literature at A-level. Some syllabuses, including the Scottish Higher Certificate, include questions on language as well as those on literature. Others – such as London, JMB and AEB – offer whole exam syllabuses which concentrate on the language. Examinations at AS level may cover a similar range of language elements, too – either in addition to literary texts or as a completely separate subject.

The first priority when you're studying a syllabus which includes some language elements is to get hold of the syllabus and some past papers and to see exactly what you're expected to do.

Studying language is similar in some ways to studying literature, in that you spend a lot of time reading, thinking and talking about what you've read. But there are also differences (see Fig. 16.1). For most language syllabuses you need to know far more about the nature and structure of language, so there's much more factual information to be learnt.

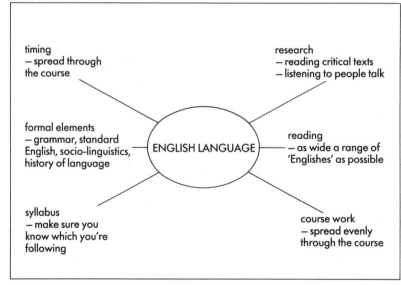

Fig. 16.1 'Spidergram' of English language course

ESSENTIAL PRINCIPLES

Language examinations may include several of the following elements:

- Questions testing your comprehension of passages.
- Questions asking you to summarise a passage in prose or note form.
- Analyses of passages of dialogue.
- Exercises in rewriting passages in a different style.
- Questions on the use of language for advertising, publicity or other specialist purposes.
- Questions on dialects or older forms of the language, sometimes involving paraphrase exercises.
- Essays on topics of general interest.
- Essays on the history and nature of the language.

Most also include a coursework element, which is dealt with in Chapter 17.

All of this represents quite a demanding range, so you need to know exactly what you'll be called on to know about and the tasks you'll be asked to perform in the exam. Make sure that you check with the current syllabus, too: English Language exams are constantly changing and developing, and so you need to be sure that you are studying the right things.

This chapter gives advice on how to study the language and prepare for your exam, giving advice on approaches to the topic and some sample questions with student answers and examiner comments.

Language questions can be divided into two main kinds: those which ask you to perform straightforward exercises to show your understanding or ability to write in shortened form; and those which test your understanding of the nature of language and the way it is used. These often ask you to write about some aspect of language, or to write in a particular style or format.

Comprehension questions

These are rather like the comprehension tests which may have formed part of your GCSE studies. You are given a passage of 200–300 words, and then asked questions about it.

Go about them like this:

"Don't rush."

1 Read the whole passage quickly, to take in its general meaning.
2 Read the passage again slowly, asking yourself questions about the meaning and language, to take in what's being said more fully.
3 Read through *all* the questions. This will stop you from answering two at once – giving a very full answer to one which also covers another.
4 Answer the questions:
   – go back to check the passage to make sure that you have the right answer
   – use your own words, not those of the question (unless you're asked to quote from it)
   – write in full sentences
   – make sure you number your answers exactly as they are in the question – use (a), (i), 1 or whatever form the question uses to avoid any chance of mistakes when the paper is marked
   – don't say too much. If you're asked for an alternative to a word, give *one* only – if you give more than one, you'll only be marked on the first, otherwise it's as if you've had several shots at getting it right.

Prepare for questions of this kind by reading suitable articles in newspapers and magazines and inventing appropriate questions to ask yourself. Try, too, to get hold of past exam papers and complete the questions they ask, doing this in measured time and exam conditions. You'll find that practice will greatly increase your speed and accuracy.

Summary questions

"First get your summary technique developed, and then practise summarising in measured time."

If you're asked to make a summary, the important thing to remember is that you need to read the passage several times before you write anything down. Then, make *notes* which record the main points, using your own words except for technical terms or proper names.

Only when you've done this, and checked your notes with the original to make sure you've included everything, should you start to write the final version. Write in a simple, straightforward prose style, relating the information directly. Don't refer to the original passage in phrases like 'The writer begins by saying . . .': instead, just make the point directly.

Prepare for the exam by summarising newspaper articles and similar passages in measured time. Give yourself half an hour to read the passage, take notes and produce a finished prose summary. When you've finished, show the original article and your summary to a friend, and ask him or her to say whether you've produced an accurate and complete version of the original.

PRINCIPLES OF THE LANGUAGE

" Knowing the terms used in grammar will help in all your language and literature studies. "

Studying grammar

Even if your syllabus does not include questions on grammatical structures, it's still a very good idea to be familiar with the basic principles of grammar, spelling and punctuation. You can do this by reading one of the many books which discuss the structure of the language and describe the functions of nouns, adjectives, phrases, clauses and the other components of the language (see Fig. 16.2).

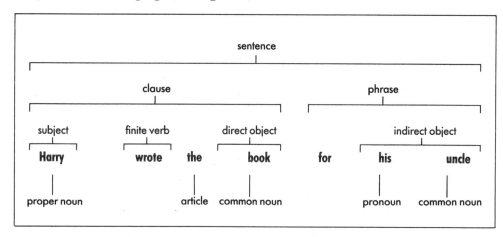

Fig. 16.2 A sentence divided into its component parts

Attitudes to grammar generally fall into one of two kinds. *Descriptive* grammar tells you about the grammar that people actually use when talking or writing; *prescriptive* grammar tells you what it *should* be to be 'correct'. Most old-fashioned text-books on grammar fall into the latter category; more modern works about semiotics and communication fall into the former. Consult your teacher or lecturer to see which kind of attitude towards grammar is appropriate for your course. In some courses you will be better off just studying language in order to be aware of the functions it performs in different situations.

Once you've built up your knowledge in this area, keep using it. Ask yourself questions about the structure of the language in anything that you read – whether it's a novel, an advertisement, a bus ticket or the label on a soft-drink can. This will prepare you for the exam – you might be asked about the structure of such pieces of writing, since the language to be studied will not be restricted to formal literary writing. It will also develop the habit of close analytical study of language, which you'll need in every part of the exam.

Standard English

Although everyone speaks in a different form of the language, according to where they live, where they were born, what they do for a living and – regrettably – their social class, linguists still have the concept of Standard English.

Standard English is usually analysed by linguists as a dialect of English. On purely linguistic grounds, it is not inherently superior to other non-standard dialects of English, but it clearly has social prestige and international use. Because Standard English has been used so much for academic and administrative purposes, the vocabulary and to some extent the sentence syntax have been greatly elaborated. Non-Standard dialects have the potential to be so developed, but for social and historical reasons they have not.

Standard English can be spoken with different regional accents, but one particular accent, 'Received Pronunciation', has special prestige in England. *Accent* refers to pronunciation whilst *dialect* refers to grammar and vocabulary, and for linguists no one dialect is superior to any other. This means that although some dialects are regarded as superior by some people, it is for social rather than intellectual reasons. This is particularly true in Britain where Standard English is a social dialect, used as a marker of social group membership in a society where the relationship between standard and non-standard dialects and social class is particularly strong.

Set against Standard English are dialects or different versions of English. There are so many of these that many linguists now talk of 'Englishes', to make it clear that there are a whole group of related languages including American English, English English, Singlish (English in Singapore), and any number of dialects from the regions of England itself.

A study of these may form an important part of your syllabus. You may be asked to write an essay on some aspects of dialects, or perhaps to re-write a passage from one dialect into another. Reading and listening widely are the best ways of acquiring a knowledge of dialects at first hand; there are also many books on the subject which your teacher or local librarian will be able to find for you.

Your knowledge of Standard English and the nature of the language's grammar can be the basis for questions of a wide range of types, the most important of which are discussed below.

> 66 Think about your own dialect and accent – we all have one. How would you describe it? 99

QUESTIONS ON THE USE OF LANGUAGE

> 66 Read the passage very carefully several times before you start on your answer. 99

Dialogue analyses

Questions of this sort will give you a transcript of a passage of dialogue. Generally you'll be told something about the people involved – two teenagers, a mother and daughter, or two middle-aged men, for example.

You will then be asked to perform various tasks. You might be asked to:

- rewrite the passage as it might appear in a book, adding proper punctuation marks to make clear who is speaking, removing any gaps or stammers and generally tidying it up so that it comes close to Standard English;

- rewrite the passage as if spoken by two people from another social or ethnic group, who would use different expressions to convey the same meaning;

- comment on the ways in which the language differs from Standard English;

- explain ways in which the speakers' knowledge of the language, or skill in using it, is limited;

- think about the context of the passage – who the people are, where they are speaking, why they are speaking, and other similar factors which form the overall setting of the exchange. These elements – known as 'socio-linguistics' – are very important in exercises of this sort, as they are in all parts of the English Language syllabus.

Answering such questions demands three abilities:

1 Understanding the notation – the series of symbols used to show pauses, emphases and moments when both people speak together.
2 A working knowledge of another dialect, so that you can 're-write' the passage in terms of that dialect.
3 The skill of writing clear and accurate descriptions of language and its function in the passage of dialogue (see Fig. 16.3).

> 66 Make sure you read the symbols correctly – getting them wrong can lose you marks. 99

Of these, the first can be acquired quickly, as the notation is generally explained in the paper. Read the question very carefully and make sure you know the symbols before de-coding the passage. The second can only be acquired by reading, listening , a study of grammatical forms and investigation into forms of language, perhaps as part of a project. The third can be developed by practice, not only in your English studies but in all other areas of your academic and private life.

Rewriting in a different style

> 66 Really study the passages – from every angle or viewpoint you can think of. 99

This is an exercise which combines many of the features of the different exercises already discussed. You may well be given a series of articles to study a short while before the exam. If so, spend the time reading them and gaining a thorough knowledge of how they use language. Don't waste time speculating on what the questions might be – a detailed

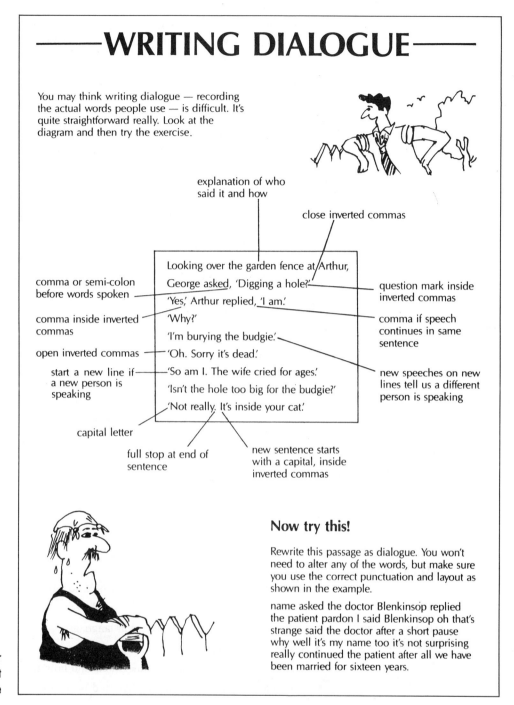

WRITING DIALOGUE

You may think writing dialogue — recording the actual words people use — is difficult. It's quite straightforward really. Look at the diagram and then try the exercise.

explanation of who said it and how

close inverted commas

comma or semi-colon before words spoken

comma inside inverted commas

open inverted commas

start a new line if a new person is speaking

capital letter

full stop at end of sentence

new sentence starts with a capital, inside inverted commas

question mark inside inverted commas

comma if speech continues in same sentence

new speeches on new lines tell us a different person is speaking

Looking over the garden fence at Arthur, George asked, 'Digging a hole?'
'Yes,' Arthur replied, 'I am.'
'Why?'
'I'm burying the budgie.'
'Oh. Sorry it's dead.'
'So am I. The wife cried for ages.'
'Isn't the hole too big for the budgie?'
'Not really. It's inside your cat.'

Now try this!

Rewrite this passage as dialogue. You won't need to alter any of the words, but make sure you use the correct punctuation and layout as shown in the example.

name asked the doctor Blenkinsop replied the patient pardon I said Blenkinsop oh that's strange said the doctor after a short pause why well it's my name too it's not surprising really continued the patient after all we have been married for sixteen years.

Fig. 16.3 A page from a grammar book showing how to set out dialogue

knowledge of the passages will be far more use, as it will enable you to answer any of the questions which you might be asked.

When tackling questions like this, you need to:

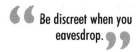
Think about how different people use the same word with different meanings.

- First of all, *read and understand* what is being said in the passage or passages to be rewritten. Unless you can do this, the final version is bound to be incorrect or incomplete. Look especially for particular meanings attached to key words – 'loaded' words, as they are known. These are words which reveal attitudes or prejudices in the writer, which in turn must be present in your rewritten version.

- *Understand the style in which you are writing.* It may help to think of yourself in the role of a particular person who you know speaks or writes in this way, and to act out the role while you write.

You can prepare for exercises of this sort by:

Be discreet when you eavesdrop.

- reading widely, from women's magazines to plumbing textbooks;

- listening to people talking. Queues are a good place to start – supermarkets for mothers with young children, post offices for older people collecting pensions, banks for working people in a hurry, shops for people buying consumer goods. Buses and trains are useful, as are launderettes, sports grounds and cafés. Be careful, though – don't look as if you're listening, otherwise you might get involved in exchanges which are far from verbal!

■ trying to re-write what people say in one dialect or style into another. Think of a builder talking like the Archbishop of Canterbury, or an Australian talking in a Dorset or other regional dialect.

These games will help you to develop your ear for language, and so allow you both to understand one register of speech and re-express it in another with far less difficulty.

Language in advertising and publicity

You may be asked to comment on the way that language is used in writing which has a clear commercial purpose – selling a product, advertising for new staff, or publicising a service, for example.

What you need always to remember here is that the language for such writing, usually known as 'copy', is chosen just as carefully as that for a poem or novel. It is designed not only to convey information, but also to:

■ influence the reader by fair or unfair persuasion;

■ appeal, in many cases, to a particular *kind* of reader, and use the sort of language he or she would use;

■ reflect an 'image' or collection of associations related to a product or service – a whole worldview which suggests, for example, that you are neglecting your children's welfare unless you use a certain washing powder, or that your failing virility can be restored by driving a 24-valve sports car (P.S. It can't). Once again, then, the overall context of the writing is vitally important.

Language of this kind often differs from Standard English, to achieve one of the aims noted here. Often, to make the statement more punchy, a sentence will be broken up, with phrases – groups of words without verbs – presented with full stops after them, as if they were complete. But there's no point in commenting on this feature unless you say *why* it's used, and what effect the copywriters were trying to achieve.

> ⁶⁶ Practise analysing advertisements by identifying the kind of people they're appealing to. ⁹⁹

> **ESSAY QUESTIONS**

These come in two main types.

1 Essays about the language

Depending on your syllabus, you may be asked to write essays on a range of topics which refer to the evolution and growth of the language. Here are some possible topics:

> ⁶⁶ Check your syllabus carefully about essays. ⁹⁹

■ Social snobbery as it is reflected in language

■ Sexism in language

■ Problems of spelling and pronunciation, and how to overcome them

■ The difference between descriptive and prescriptive grammar, and the value of the latter

2 Essays on topics of general interest

Essays of this sort are set not to test your general knowledge but to assess your skill in writing an essay which develops a logical argument about events or topics under general discussion. To prepare for such essays, the best approach is to keep well-informed: read the quality press, watch television news documentaries, and above all think and argue about what you read and see. Your treatment of the events is the main focus of the examiner's attention, remember – so logical structure and precise expression are the main priorities.

You should tackle questions of both types in this way:

> ⁶⁶ The advice on reading questions in Chapters 1 and 2 will help here, too. ⁹⁹

1 Define exactly what the question means, by looking at its key words.
2 Define your task – work out exactly what you have to write about. Once again, keywords will help here, in particular the verb – explore, explain, define, discuss, for example, all tell you fairly directly what approach is needed.
3 Make notes relating your ideas to the question.
4 Write your essay.
5 Check your essay for errors of meaning, grammar, punctuation and style.

You will find some more detailed advice on planning and writing an essay in Chapters 1 and 2. Although concerned with essays on literary subjects, the general points, especially on planning and structuring, are valid for essays on a wider range of subjects.

SOME GENERAL ADVICE

Whatever your language papers contain, you will do well in them only if you think very carefully about the language and how it is used. Read with care, asking questions about why the writer uses one word rather than another. Listen with care, asking what the speaker's style of speech reveals about his or her nature, outlook and upbringing. Don't jump at the first interpretation you think of: let the words sink into your mind, so that you gain a full understanding of every level of significance they contain. Write with care, weighing every word and mark of punctuation so that you avoid any chance of ambiguity and let your points emerge for themselves through the words, not in spite of them. Language is a precious way of bringing people together: don't make it a smokescreen.

PRACTICE QUESTIONS

This chapter ends with some questions of the kind you will find in language papers. Attempt those which are of the sort you will encounter on *your* syllabus and, when you've finished them, look at the student answers and examiner comments which follow. Look, too, at the answers to questions which are not likely to appear on your paper: they may still give you hints about how to use the language.

1 The following text is part of a transcription of a longer conversation between a woman and two men, all in their early 50s. The transcription marks the tone-units (or information units) of speech, with the words carrying stress in **bold** type. Intonation is not marked.
Places where speakers overlap are marked //.
Breaks in speech are marked (.) for very brief pauses (of one short syllable), and (–) for slightly longer pauses.
The sign (>) (as in > Charles) indicates that a speaker is continuing uninterrupted despite a simultaneous remark by another speaker.

i) Describe in some detail those features of the text which are evidence that this is a transcription of authentic spoken English conversation.
ii) Re-write the first part of the transcription as far as line 22 (Douglas' cough) in the form of a dialogue with connecting narrative suitable for a short story, and briefly describe the changes you have made.

Brenda	**yes** | that's **right** | . **but** er | I think that families are ever such hard – they're not **hard work** | – they're **hard** on your **nerves** |	
Charles	mm | –	
Brenda	and you c. you really could **do** with a **bit less wear** |	
Charles	well the sheer **numbers** // Brenda | you've got a particularly	5
Brenda	mm |	
> Charles	**big** family | –	
Brenda	**no** | that's the **point** | it didn't seem to **me** | when they were **little** | that there were a **lot** | .	
Charles	well there were rather a lot // by **objective** standards |	10
Brenda	there probably **were** | yes | . **by** | . sort of when // people **say** | . talk about families	
Charles	mm – **yes** |	
> Brenda	**nowadays** | and they talk about two and three // **children** |	
Charles	yes |	15
> Brenda	it seems a **lot** | – but it didn't seem a lot to **me** | – it never seemed to **me** | that they were hard	
Charles	**work** when they were **little** | // because they were all . in a **bunch** and |	
	mm |	
> Brenda	you **organized** them | // but as soon as they start organizing	20
Charles	yeah | .	

> Brenda **themselves** | . they're // **terribly wearing** |
Douglas presumably – // [coughs]
Charles ah yeah | . mm |
> Douglas yes an . and it becomes **centrifugal** | **yes** |
Brenda // **yes** | .
Charles mm | yeah | .
> Brenda **yes** | they really **are** – wearing | and **then** it isn't that er – they're
a comfort | for your old **age** | or anything | . // because you're not
Charles you haven't **had** your old age yet you don't **know** |
Douglas // **no** |
Brenda no but **I** can't see it **happening** | because **I reckoned** | that as
soon as you're **old** | – and it's no **longer** – sort of **necessary** | for them to use the **house** | .
as it **were** | – **I** don't think they'd be **particularly interested** in | coming to **see** us . or | – –
anything of that **sort** | . **I** don't **think** | that they **feel** – **terribly devoted** |.
Charles but you want to produce // **independent** people |
Brenda but I wouldn't **want** it | . that's the **point** |

2 Reports in newspapers of the same event or incident are often very different in their selection and interpretation of what happened. The following texts are taken from two daily papers in August 1981. Discuss the differences between the two reports, and comment on the attitudes towards the participants and the events which the choice of vocabulary and sentence structure implies.

A

Seven month sit-in ends as company is sold to ex-director

LEE JEANS WORKERS' HISTORIC VICTORY

THE SIT-IN heroines of Greenock yesterday drenched, themselves in their jeans' factory with foaming bottles of bubbly, and lifted their convener Helen Monaghan shoulder high.

This celebration of a famous victory was the first time that any of the 140 women, occupying the factory for nearly seven months since a cold night in February, has touched a drop.

Until yesterday, they relied on class spirit, good humour, and discipline to get by through the long shifts and weeks of waiting for something to happen.

Labour Party leader Michael Foot was among the first to dispatch a telegram describing the winning back of their jobs as 'a wonderful tribute to your courage and persistence.'

The whole of Greenock was saying 'they did well, they did well.' and there was quiet satisfaction for the thousands of shipyard workers on the Upper and Lower reaches of the Clyde who have levied themselves 50p a head every week for months in support of the sit-in.

Ms Monaghan said: 'We just wish we could tell everybody who has supported us personally "there is no way we could have done it without you".'

'I will be sending out circulars, and then we will have a victory dance.'

The former owners, the US-based Vanity Fair Corporation, sold the plant to its own former director of UK and Irish operations, Robert Charters, at a figure reported to be just over £600,000 after weeks of nerve-wracking haggling.

Nigel Wright, of the Dickie Dirt's London retail chain who was at one stage a potential purchaser, will guarantee the restart by buying 10,000 pairs of jeans a week.

So the women, who began the year as a small, totally unknown workforce in the Tailors and Garment Workers Union, on a remote industrial estate in the Firth of Clyde, have won and become the pride of the British labour movement.

But the sit-in is not quite over yet. Mr Charters will not be able to start production until the middle of September, and Ms Monaghan yesterday asked if the trade union movement could continue its magnificent support for just a little while longer.

Two of the older women, Mary Macleod and Jean Cracknell, praised the younger lasses who had been so considerate to them, and so determined when they might have lost heart.

Joked Mary: 'They say Scotsmen are tough, but they reckon without Scotswomen. Herr Hitler called our boys the ladies from hell, but I wonder what he would have made of a few battalions of us.'

Among the workforce are dozens of mothers and daughters, and sisters who will soon be the main breadwinners again for their families.

B

Women sit in and save factory

The Government is to make substantial discretionary grants to the Lee Jeans factory, in Greenock, where a seven-month sit-in by 140 women workers has ended in victory.

The closure of the factory was announced last January by the VF Corporation. It will be in production next month under a consortium led by Mr Robert Charters, formerly the VF Corporation director of operations.

The price paid for the factory has not been disclosed. It is thought to lie between the consortium's offer of £600,000 and the company's asking price of £800,000.

A financial institution, management associates and the Scottish Economic Planning Department helped to secure the future for the factory which will be supported by an order from a London retailer for 10,000 pairs of jeans a week.

3 The following texts are taken from a sequence of letters which were written to the editor of a national daily newspaper in August 1986. The subject of the correspondence began as an argument over the use of the word *cripple* in the headline to a news report. [The names of the writers have been changed]

Continue the correspondence by writing a further letter of about 250 words to the editor, which briefly sums up the argument so far over the use of the word 'cripple', and expresses your own views, with other examples of the controversial use of 'loaded' words.

Original headline:

Cripple beaten to death at home

1st letter

Sir – I wonder how a sensitive newspaper such as yours can permit the 'disabled person' or 'person with a disability' of your features page to become a 'cripple' when he/she is dead.

Jane Oldfield
The Association of Carers

2nd letter

Sir – I am puzzled and disturbed by the objection of the Association of Carers to your use of the word 'cripple' in a headline. There is nothing demeaning here in the word 'cripple', which succinctly identifies the particular and relevant disability from which the victim suffered.

A cumbersome expression such as the Association's 'person with a disability' is so wide that it is almost meaningless; it would include a person who lacked only a sense of smell and could perhaps be understood to extend to a person whose only distinguishing characteristic lay in dyslexia.

Campaigners with an excessive readiness to find offence in neutral words do their cause no good.

W. B. Carter
St. Albans, Herts

3rd letter

Sir – As one crippled for life in late childhood I could not agree more with W. B. Carter, who mocks the current mealy-mouthed banning of the one word in the English language which clearly and crisply defines my physical limitations.

Can we doubt that if Helen Keller were alive today she would not be listed, matter-of-factly, as deaf, dumb and blind, but rather fed into a computer as one suffering from aural,

oral, orthodontal and visual handicap?

Rather than this deadspeak let's have the guts to call a spade a spade!

Yours
Pauline Jackson
Carlisle

4th letter

Sir – W. B. Carter's wish for a term which defined people with disabilities within a precise and exclusive grouping is a poor and illusory justification for using unpleasant terms.

Many methods of labelling minority groups begin with a 'neutral' description. Such descriptions only acquire a cutting edge if they are frequently used in a disparaging way. The term 'cripple' has such demeaning implications which derive from longstanding use, and which suggest that alms and charity are the appropriate response.

The term 'disabled person' is unhelpful since it suggests that we are disabled through and through. Our acceptance in society should be on the basis of what we have to offer and not on those parts of ourselves which do not function properly.

James Morell
Forum of People with Disabilities
Sheffield

5th letter

Sir – Language is indeed a handicap and there's no end to semantic hair-splitting. For many years now, like all our 'with-it' colleagues, we have used 'people with special needs' as a more positive term.

Evolution lies in moving from the general to the particular: from the nonsensical 'cripple' to 'a person whose special need can be met by a wheelchair'. Most people are affected by demeaning labels.

Yours sincerely,
John Williamson
Handicapped Persons Research Unit
Newcastle

6th letter

Sir – I am astounded by John Williamson's letter suggesting the use of 'a person whose special needs can be met by wheel-chairs' in preference to 'cripple'. The fact is that words like 'cripple' and 'spastic' are being lost from polite conversation because some thoughtless people choose to use them as sneering insults.

I'm fed up with losing words from the language for this reason. We should use 'cripple' and 'spastic' as honest descriptions of people, and, where possible, correct those who use them as insults.

Or am I to call my diabetic father 'a person whose special need can be met by insulin'?

Yours sincerely
Jim Cooper
London NW5

7th letter

Sir – Speaking as someone who has cerebral palsy I must take issue with Jim Cooper's letter. It simply is not true to suggest that words like 'spastic' and 'cripple' have been devalued because some thoughtless people have chosen to use them in the wrong context.

The words themselves are offensive, in the same way as 'lunatic asylum' and 'nigger' are extremely offensive. Sometimes, however, it is necessary to be on the receiving end before one realises the full impact of such words.

Yours faithfully
Harry Webster
Solihull

---

4 Discuss and evaluate the evidence for the claim that the English language is sexist.

STUDENT ANSWERS WITH EXAMINER COMMENTS

STUDENT ANSWER TO QUESTION 1

> "The usual approach here – make the point first and then support it with evidence. "

i) There is much evidence of the authenticity of this passage. To begin with, there is much hesitation and uncertainty in both the speakers, showing that they are deciding what to say on the spur of the moment. The very first line contains 'but er'. This is also shown in the incomplete statements. Once again, there is one of these in the first line, when Brenda begins 'I think that families are ever such hard' and then changes to 'they're not hard work – they're hard on your nerves', showing that both the idea and the expression is being reviewed as she thinks what to say. Brenda's statement in line 12 continues this.

Further evidence of authenticity is provided by the way the speakers overlap. There are seven occasions when both people are speaking at the same time. The various noises each make to encourage the other – 'mm' and 'yeah' in particular – again show a degree of interaction, where the two are encouraging each other to complete what they have to say. This suggests a discussion between two people who are sympathetic to each other's point of view, who are talking spontaneously and without preparation.

> "In Standard English there's no word for 'mm' – here 'a grunt of agreement' represents Charles' contribution. "

> "A story will include details of actions, so it's legitimate to add these, from a careful reading of the text. "

ii) 'Yes, that's right!' said Brenda. 'But I think families aren't hard work – they're hard on your nerves'. Charles made a grunt of agreement as Brenda continued '– and you really could do with a bit less wear'.

'It's a question of numbers, Brenda – you've got a particularly large family,' said Charles. Brenda looked at him with disagreement.

'No, Charles, that's the point. When they were little it didn't seem to me that there were a lot,' she explained.

'Well,' said Charles with a laugh, 'there were rather a lot by objective standards.'

'There probably were, yes,' agreed Brenda thoughtfully. 'When people talk about families these days they usually mean two or three children,' she went on, as Charles grunted his agreement and then said emphatically 'Yes!'

> "This interprets the initial uncertainty of B's words followed by a greater sense of direction. "

Now that Brenda had begun her explanation, it was as if she understood where the difference lay. She continued, 'It seems a lot, but it didn't seem a lot to me. When they were little it never seemed to me that they were hard work because they were all in a bunch and I organised them: but as soon as they start organising themselves they're terribly wearing!'

> "Don't forget Douglas – this gets him into the story more convincingly than just saying 'Douglas said...' "

Charles had been following her speech excitedly, nodding his agreement. Douglas had been silent up to this point, watching the other two rather warily. Now he cautiously began 'Presumably,' but got no further because he interrupted himself with a nervous cough.

> "The explanation isn't complete – the points made in the margins all need to be mentioned here. "

The changes I have made here mainly relate to the way in which people speak and the overlaps between what they say. I have added words to show how Brenda and Charles speak, and to explain Douglas' behaviour at the end, and left out the 'mm' sounds from Charles because conventional writing makes it difficult to insert them while Brenda is speaking. I have also made clearer the actual words spoken by Brenda, removing the repetitions and uncertainties to make the whole exchange clearer to the reader in the manner usually adopted in a short story.

EXAMINER COMMENT

This answer covers the necessary data well. The first part lists the main features revealing that this is a real conversation – its hesitancy and uncertainty, and the overlaps between speakers. The second part adds various features as the commentary makes clear, although it rather lacks style – I can't imagine this being a very gripping short story. The main point, though, is that it shows a grasp of the standard conventions of presenting dialogue in literary writing, and so achieves the aim of changing a piece of actual speech into the accepted idiom of Standard English. The commentary at the end shows a sound grasp of the changes that are needed for this.

STUDENT ANSWER TO QUESTION 2

❝❝ Quotation supports points well here. ❞❞

The first passage is much more concerned with the 'human interest' aspects of the industrial dispute than the second passage. This is clear right from the start where the first talks of the 'sit-in heroines' who 'drenched themselves with foaming bubbly', whereas the second begins by a factual reference to the Government and the grant that is to be made. There is much more detail in the first one about this side of things, with references to 'class spirit, good humour and discipline', whereas the second one talks only of 'a seven-month sit-in' and makes no mention of the conditions or nature of the process. The first one also quotes one of the women speaking in a very colloquial style in the last but one paragraph.

❝❝ Good explanation of difference by bringing the two together here – see Chapter 5 for more suggestions on this. ❞❞

The vocabulary of the first one is concerned with individual achievements and is very positive, praising the women in words such as 'famous victory', 'winning back of their jobs', 'quiet satisfaction' and so on. The vocabulary is mainly simple and colloquial, as the references to 'foaming bubbly', 'a cold night in February', 'weeks of nerve-wracking haggling'. In contrast the vocabulary of the second piece is more formal, talking of 'substantial discretionary grants', a 'consortium', the cautious 'it is thought to lie' and the language of a business newspaper in 'financial institution', 'management associates' and 'director of operations'.

The sentence structures of the two show a similar difference, between popular speech and financial journalism. The first uses sentences which are freely constructed, linking clauses in a way which is common in speech. The second paragraph, for example, is a single sentence with one participle phrase, ending with the colloquial 'has touched a drop', so that the structure is used to throw the emphasis onto a point of human interest. By contrast the second passage uses a more clipped businesslike structure with much shorter sentences. The first sentence, for example, gets across the essential facts of the government grant, the sit-in, its successful ending, and the name of the factory in a careful piece of controlled structure. The second and third paragraphs of the second piece use four sentences, only one of which contains a subordinate defining clause.

❝❝ Notice that the answer deals with vocabulary and sentence structure first and then shows what they reveal about attitudes. ❞❞

All of these features reveal the different attitudes towards the participants in the events described. The first piece is far more concerned with individuals, mentioning them by name and quoting their speech in a way which stresses their everyday, human nature and the fact that the women have won a victory. The second piece, on the other hand, is more concerned with the economics of the story. There is no mention of Helen Monaghan, Mary Macleod and Jean Cracknell, and instead of the reference to 'Nigel Wright, of Dickie Dirt's' there is an anonymous reference to 'a London retailer'. In all, the first regards the story as a victory for people who work at the factory, whereas the second considers it from the viewpoint of a financial commentator, and this difference is reflected in the vocabulary and sentence structure that each uses.

EXAMINER COMMENT

This covers the major points, citing examples to support each of them. It deals with the three main areas in turn, and at the end brings them together to show how sentence structure and vocabulary reflect attitude. It shows clearly that detailed reading and analysis is the only basis for questions of this kind, and also reveals the importance of a working knowledge of the descriptive terms of grammar, so that you can apply these to the passage and explain the way in which they affect and reveal attitudes in the writer.

STUDENT ANSWER TO QUESTION 3

Dear Sir,
    I have followed with interest your recent correspondence about the use of the word 'cripple'. First Jane Oldfield takes you to task for using the term; then W B Carter expresses preference for the word over 'person with a disability', which he finds 'almost meaningless', a view shared by Pauline Jackson who wants to 'call a spade a

spade'. James Morell argues that 'cripple', once neutral in intention, has now become demeaning, and says we should avoid all such terms, instead judging people by what they can do, not what they can't.

'People with special needs' is suggested by John Williamson, to the anger of Jim Cooper who says that the fault is not the word's but its users': 'cripple' has become a term of abuse. Harry Webster finds 'cripple' and 'spastic' in themselves offensive and, since he suffers himself from cerebral palsy, we must in fairness give his view more weight.

It seems to me that this long debate reveals a great deal about the correspondents, in that they are far more concerned with the words than with the problems they label. If we were willing to take people on their own terms as individuals, and not as cripples, gays, lesbians – or even compulsive letter-writers – the world would be a better place.

Yours faithfully

> 66 This gives only the essence of each letter – there's no need for more. 99

> 66 Brief and forceful expression of your own views here. 99

EXAMINER COMMENT

A punchy and effective letter. Notice that all of the earlier letters are summed up very briefly, in the order in which they appear, grouped so that their similarities and differences are quite clear. Notice, too, that words and short phrases are quoted from letters to convey the essence of their points – a quite valid technique in such questions.

The final paragraph gives the writer's own view, makes a witty point about people who write letters – thus perhaps taking some of the intensity out of the exchange – and also by implication makes a striking point about language: is it separate from the issues it discusses, or is it an integral part of them?

STUDENT ANSWER TO QUESTION 4

> 66 Tackles straightaway a major point. 99

On the face of it, there is considerable evidence that the English language is sexist in nature, because of the assumptions it makes about gender and also because of the common use of the suffix '–man' in a large number of words describing occupations.

One of the largest problems with the language is the assumption that every noun is assumed to be masculine in gender. It is standard practice, for example, to write 'the poet develops his argument' or 'the designer has forgotten his instructions'. Purists would say that this is the old linguistic principle that if no gender is stated, then the male is automatically assumed, and use this to argue that the point is one of language and has nothing to do with sexism or any other kind of prejudice. Their opponents would argue that language reflects society, and that the automatic assumption in language that 'someone' is male is a reflection of social prejudices.

> 66 Both views expressed here, with neither dominating. 99

> 66 Knowledge of the history of the language is used here in the service of the argument. 99

It is interesting to note that this assumption has not always been the case. In Middle English the word 'hir' is a general purpose pronoun which can be used to mean his, hers, its or theirs, thus avoiding the gender-specific pronouns that many find offensive today and suggesting that the sexism of assuming automatic maleness is a much more recent development. It is certainly a more elegant usage than the present-day equivalents 's/he' or the clumsy repetition of 'his or her' every time a pronoun is needed.

> 66 Would this be better without the jokes, or do they have a serious point to make about people's attitudes to language? 99

Another evidence of sexism is the use of the suffix '–man' in many words naming occupations. 'Workman', 'businessman' and 'postman' all do this, reflecting the assumption that only men can perform such roles. The replacement of these by 'person' hardly seems the answer, although it is a step in the right direction – businessperson sounds awkward, and there is also the possibility of comic constructions like Personchester, and the well-known canine hermaphrodite, the Doberperson. Leaving out the 'man' can be successful in some cases, with 'chair' now accepted instead of 'chairman/woman/person'; but 'spoke' instead of 'spokesman' is unlikely to be taken into current usage.

Some of the charges against English are clearly unfounded. Using 'Midperson' instead of 'midwife' rests on a confused reading of the word's origin: 'mid' means 'with', and the word thus means someone who is 'with' the wife during childbirth, so

A good blend of history and socio-linguistics.

that 'midperson' is unnecessary as well as awkward. The abbreviation 'Ms' has a slightly different history. Up until the eighteenth or even the nineteenth century in some places, the word 'Mistress' was used of all women over the age of about twenty-five, whether married or single, so that marital status was, quite rightly, not specified by title. Only more recently has it been abbreviated to 'Mrs' and come to mean 'a married woman' – perhaps as a result of the dominance of the other meaning of 'mistress', in itself showing the effect of male dominance on the language.

Some of these points are serious and disconcerting, whereas others are of more limited importance. The greatest problem is in the use of pronouns: until the English language adopts a new genderless pronoun, it will remain either sexist or confusingly unclear. Perhaps we should return to Middle English: 'hir' has a lot to recommend it as a twenty-first century, truly egalitarian word.

A stylish ending.

EXAMINER COMMENT

This is an essay which contains several fundamental points in answer to the question. Yet it seems more concerned in places with making witty comments than in analysing the claim of the title in any real depth. Certainly its material is sound: the points about 'midwife', 'mistress' and 'hir' are all quite valid. But it seems to be more of a contribution to an after-dinner discussion than a serious piece of analysis of the degree to which complaints of sexism are justified. Be wary of this happening: it is very easy to write about language in a detached way which fails fully to realise the social issues it involves.

As before, remember that the context of language is very important; it's not always what you say, but when, where and how you say it, that matters.

COURSEWORK

CHOOSING COURSEWORK

LANGUAGE COURSEWORK

GETTING STARTED

An increasing number of boards offer coursework as a part of the final assessment. Instead of one of the exam papers, you produce a folder of work during the course of your studies. This is then marked by your teacher or lecturer, and the marks are 'moderated' by an examiner from the board, who makes sure that the marks are in line with the standards of the board as a whole.

THE TYPE OF WORK REQUIRED

What does coursework consist of? Generally it's any or all of the following elements:

1 A group of essays of between 800 and 1200 words – about the length of a regular piece of work done as part of your studies.
2 Longer essays, of about 2000 words.
3 An 'extended essay', usually of 3500 words but sometimes longer.
4 In some cases, the option to produce 'creative writing' such as poems, short stories and similar writing.
5 For Oxford and Cambridge Board only, a short test of oral proficiency – taking part in a play, debate, poetry reading or similar exercise with a literary subject.

English Language A-level and AS-level syllabuses also contain a coursework element, which may consist of:

1 A long essay about some aspect of language use.
2 A dissertation or extended essay about a passage of conversation recorded and transcribed by the candidate.
3 A collection of pieces including a summary, discussion, study of language, a piece of reflective or descriptive writing and an essay on a book or topic of relevance to the subject.
4 Pieces of writing aimed at different audiences, purposes and contexts, with a commentary, with the possibility of making a taped presentation instead of one piece of writing.
5 A collection of 'creative' writing with a critical commentary on it.

This chapter gives you advice on how to prepare for and write the more common of these pieces of work, and ends with an example of the kind of work you would be expected to produce for an extended essay.

ESSENTIAL PRINCIPLES

**CHOOSING
COURSEWORK**

You need to think carefully before opting to do coursework – assuming, of course, that it is optional and that your school or college offers it as part of the system of assessment. The first thing to do is to find out whether this is the case. If so, you can then talk to your teacher or lecturer and study the syllabus to see what is involved.

Coursework offers several advantages for some students:

❝ The good things about
coursework . . . ❞

- If you get nervous in exams, it allows you to show what you can do in a more acceptable working situation.

- It allows you to pursue your own interests with regard to texts or other kinds of writing – something which may be particularly attractive to mature students or those of an independent approach.

- It can extend and enlarge the range of texts usually studied at A-level.

- It lets you produce work which is often longer than the usual essays you'd write while studying, and so prepares you for the depth of study you'll need to do at university – so it's a way of finding out how you'd get on with work of that sort.

- In some cases, it allows you to write in more imaginative forms – poems or short stories – than the usual critical analysis.

As well as these advantages, there are disadvantages to taking the coursework option:

❝ . . . and the not so
good. ❞

- Unless you're careful you can attempt subjects too large for the time available.

- It demands constant application and hard work – you can't let things slide and catch up lost ground at the last minute.

- You have to be organised, with notes and other material kept carefully so that you can develop your ideas over a period into longer essays.

- If you find critical reading or hard analytical thought difficult, and aren't too keen on working on your own, then you might be better off not doing coursework.

❝ Think about how you
work, and how you get on with
your teacher, before choosing a
coursework option. ❞

All of these are things you need to consider before opting to submit coursework. The advantages are strong, and the disadvantages are not really peculiar to coursework – if you're not strong in these areas the chances are that you won't do too well in a more traditional course either. On the other hand, if you like working things out on your own, enjoy discussing ideas – both in person and in print – and can get on well with your teacher or lecturer in individual sessions to discuss the progress of your work, the coursework could well be a wise choice. (see Fig. 17.1).

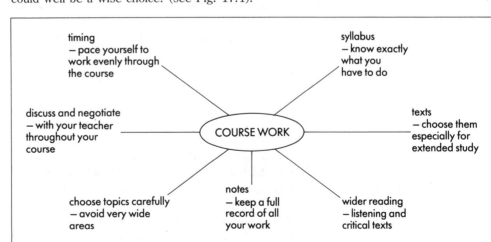

Fig. 17.1 A 'spidergram' of the
coursework option

If you do coursework which will contribute to your exam grade, you may be involved in some or all of the following projects:

1 SHORT ESSAYS

The collection of essays of between 800 and 1200 words which forms the basis of some coursework submissions is really the most straightforward of the options to produce.

Studying English always involves writing essays of this sort, so in effect what you are doing is letting the work you would produce anyway count towards the final result.

As with most things, though, there is a catch. With most of the work that you do in preparation for the exam, there is always the chance that you will make mistakes. This does not matter when you are using the essay as a way of learning. In the exam you can get things right, using both your essays and your teacher's comments on them to present an accurate and more complete answer to the questions. However, when you submit essays for moderation, there are no second chances of this sort – though of course you may have been able to discuss early drafts. But don't lose heart; there are ways round this:

How to make sure you submit only your best essays.

- Submit the *last* essay that you do on each text as part of the coursework. This will allow you to write from a more complete knowledge of the text, rather than from the more limited one you'll inevitably have while you're still working through it;

- Make sure that you work to a consistently high standard in *all* your essays, using the techniques and approaches suggested in Chapter 2.

- Discuss your work in draft form as much as you can with your teacher or lecturer. Course work is very labour-intensive for both of you, so be patient if there isn't as much time for discussion as you'd like – but, at the same time, do make sure that you get full comments and advice on what you're doing wrong and what you're getting right.

2   LONGER ESSAYS

Essays of an *intermediate length* – about 2000 words – are half-way between a normal course essay and an extended essay or small dissertation. Don't be put off by the length – most people write between 200 and 250 words to a page, so this kind of essay will only be about eight or ten sides long. You may well produce an essay of that length anyway if you're writing about a topic that you're very interested in. So this isn't very much out of the ordinary.

Time is essential here – give yourself plenty, to go through all the stages listed in Chapter 2.

Essays of this length are best done when you've completed your study of the text involved so that you can approach it from a full working knowledge of all the aspects you've covered already. Use all the techniques mentioned in Chapter 2 and *meet* your teacher *regularly* to discuss how things are going. The advice given on working for extended essays is also relevant here; read the next section carefully, even if you're not involved in a dissertation of this sort, as it will still help you to write an essay of intermediate length.

3   EXTENDED ESSAYS

When you are approaching an *extended essay*, the most important single thing is to pace yourself. Allow plenty of time for the process of thinking and writing, and above all keep on top of your work so that you never lose sight of points or have to cram everything in to the last available few days.

Approaching an extended essay.

All of the advice given in Chapter 2 becomes even more important when writing a long essay. There are also other points to consider.

1 Begin by *discussing the whole area with your teacher*. You need to know whether he or she thinks you can do it – and, if there are doubts, it's probably best to take your teacher's advice.

2 *Think very carefully and widely about the subject.* You need to choose something that is fairly restricted in scope – a study of 'Poetry in the First World War' is much too large. Something which depends too much on original research will also be unlikely to succeed as you'll need to look at a lot of original material and to use research libraries. Make up for this by having original *ideas* of your own. Ideally, your subject should allow you to:

Choose a manageable subject.

- use published material as your main source (the text of a collection of poems or a novel, say);
- incorporate other similar texts for purposes of comparison (the work of other poets contemporary with the one you're studying, for example);
- bring in wide critical reading (essays and books about the poet's or novelist's work);
- give your own views as part of the dialogue and debate that is going on amongst critics (which interpretation you prefer out of those you've read, or how you'd modify a range of views to arrive at a final interpretation);
- reflect your personal enthusiasms.

3   Even when you've decided on your subject area, *don't fix your title and exact subject too soon.* Things often change *while* you're writing, and you may – with luck – come across new ideas which will change your view.

"" Be flexible. ""

4   *Allow plenty of time for ideas to sort themselves out* in your mind. Elsewhere I've used the term 'marinating' to describe this. Leave your thoughts to soak in the creative juices of the unconscious – you'll be surprised how effective this can be. But it only works if you give it time.

5   *Never lose sight of your ideas.* At regular intervals – perhaps once a week – have a brainstorming session in which you map out your current ideas and how you want them to develop. There's no need to start writing as yet, as long as the ideas are recorded somewhere.

6   If you think of a good sentence or a way of tackling a particular problem, *write it down straightaway.* It's easy to forget stray thoughts like these, so don't take any risks.

7   *Test out your ideas* – on fellow-students, on friends, on your teacher or lecturer. Think about their response, and be prepared to change; but don't follow every suggestion that you get. This is *your* work, so stick to your guns if you're convinced you're right.

8   When you take notes from critical sources, make sure that you *record full details of the source*, perhaps using record cards. This will help you to find it if you need it again (Fig. 17.2) and also form the basis of your *bibliography* – the list of books you have consulted which you should include at the end of your essay. It's a basic law of academic research that the book whose exact title and location you didn't record is the only one you need to find again in a hurry.

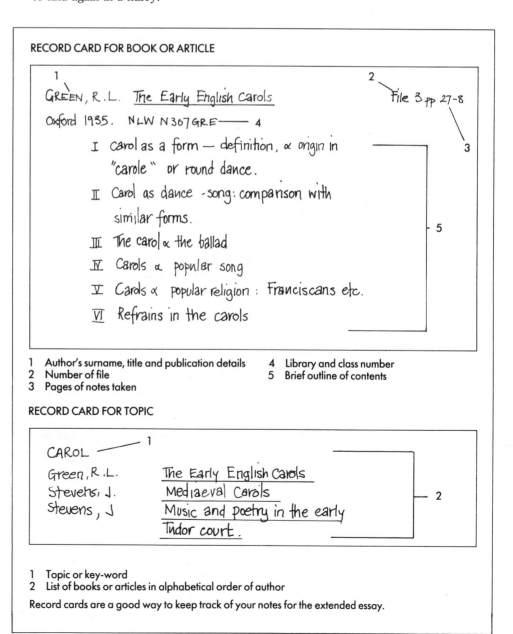

RECORD CARD FOR BOOK OR ARTICLE

GREEN, R.L. The Early English Carols   File 3 pp 27-8

Oxford 1935. NLW N367 GRE———— 4

   I   Carol as a form — definition, & origin in
        "carole" or round dance.

   II Carol as dance -song: comparison with
        similar forms.

   III The carol & the ballad

   IV Carols & popular song

   V   Carols & popular religion : Franciscans etc.

   VI Refrains in the carols

1   Author's surname, title and publication details   4   Library and class number
2   Number of file   5   Brief outline of contents
3   Pages of notes taken

RECORD CARD FOR TOPIC

CAROL ———— 1
   Green, R.L.   The Early English Carols
   Stevens, J.   Mediaeval Carols
   Stevens, J   Music and poetry in the early
                       Tudor court.   2

1   Topic or key-word
2   List of books or articles in alphabetical order of author

Record cards are a good way to keep track of your notes for the extended essay.

Fig. 17.2 Using record cards

It shouldn't be necessary to point out that you should never copy out whole passages from someone else's writing and pass it off as your own; instead, make brief quotations and give the source in a footnote, or summarise the points the writer makes and acknowledge their source in the text of your essay.

9 Try to *split the essay into sections*. Working on three sections of a thousand words or so each is less daunting than trying to tackle the whole thing at once, and it will also make the essay clearer to read. You might, for example, structure the essay according to the nature of the text you're writing about. If it is an extended *personal critical reading*, then talk about critical views from other readers, and finally draw the debate together by giving a view of your response in the light of other people's. The structure of the essay, along with all other aspects, should of course be discussed with your teacher at the regular meetings that will be arranged to discuss its progress.

Writing the essay

The important thing to remember here is that, if you start early enough, you'll have plenty of time to get it finished. This means that you'll have plenty of time to revise and change what you've written. Remember that most professional writers spend far longer planning and revising than they do in actually writing – and just knowing that you can change what you write can be immensely liberating, because you know that you're not finally committing yourself. A word - processor can help here – but the backs of envelopes can be just as good.

People go about writing in different ways. For some, planning is the essential stage, in which you sort out all the ideas so that all (all!) you have to do when writing is find the right words. For others, writing is a way of sorting out ideas as you go. By now, you'll probably have a good idea of how you work best yourself. Whatever method you use, allow plenty of time for writing and revising, by spreading the load across your working week and sticking to a timetable as far as you can.

When you've completed the essay, make sure that you include:

1 Footnotes

These can either be at the foot of each page, or at the end of the essay – in general it's easier to include these at the end. They will normally be concerned with giving the *source* of the passages which you have quoted.

2 Bibliography

The list of books you've consulted should also go at the end, and include the elements shown in Fig. 17.3. Arrange the books in alphabetical order of author or editor's surname, and include all the details given in the example. Generally speaking, the bibliography will include all the books you've consulted which have significantly aided your research, and of course all the books from which you've quoted.

When you're taking notes from any printed source, record its exact details for presentation in footnotes and your bibliography. There are various standard forms for doing this, but the following is reliable and clear. This is the order for a book:

Author (surname and initials): Title (underlined): Publisher: Place of publication: Date of publication.

An example would look like this:

Carter, D.N.G., Robert Graves: The lasting Poetic Achievement, Macmillan, London, 1989

For an article in a periodical, the order is as follows:

Author: Title of article (in quotation marks): Title of periodical (underlined): Volume and number of periodical: Date of periodical: Page numbers of article.

For example:

Johnson, W.S., 'Memory, Landscape, Love: John Ruskin's Poetry and Poetic Criticism', Victorian Poetry, vol 19 No 1, Spring 1981, pp. 19 —34

Fig. 17.3 Footnotes and bibliographies

Further advice on the writing process is given in Chapter 2 so look carefully through that while you are working on the extended essay.

4 CREATIVE WRITING

Creative writing doesn't just happen.

Contrary to popular belief, you *can* teach yourself how to write *creatively* – poems and short stories are not things which just happen by spontaneous combustion, but need to be worked on.

The best preparation for such writing is careful thought and discussion – with yourself, with fellow-students, and with your teacher. Think carefully about those *ideas* which would make a good story or poem, or *structures* which might be interesting to pursue. Consider unlikely situations or ideas, or try to put yourself inside someone else's mind to record his or her feelings. These approaches will help you to get the *basic idea* – which you then need to hone carefully over a sustained period.

Writing commentaries.

The only difference between creative writing for a language syllabus and that in a literature course is that, in the former, you are often asked to write a *commentary* on what you have written. This could:

- explain your aims;
- say how far you think you've achieved them;
- analyse the writing critically;
- suggest influences on the writing.

The commentary should *not* be a lengthy explanation of the circumstances under which you wrote the piece, as this does not discuss the writing itself. When writing this sort of exercise, try to be practical and specific. Avoid lengthy metaphysical speculations on how you were aiming to summarise 'the quintessential vacuity of the post-Freudian dilemma'; it may sound impressive, but it doesn't actually mean very much.

Make your comments specific – follow the advice in Chapters 4 and 5.

Comment instead on specific words, images or structures. A close look at some of the student answers in Chapter 7 will help you here – and a glance at the chapters on critical appreciation of poetry (4), drama (9) and prose (13) will help you to look at the work dispassionately. It's often a good idea to leave your work for a little while before writing a commentary about it – in this way, you'll see the whole thing much more clearly and be able to write about it with greater detachment and honesty.

5 ORAL WORK

This is something which is best prepared for by working closely with your teacher. Remember that you'll be assessed on:

1 *Clarity of speech* – including volume and audibility, and quality of diction (sounding ts and ds, for example).
2 *Quality of speech* – matching your intonation (the pitch of your speech) to what you are saying, and avoiding speaking always at one level, which is dull and fails to convey the nature of what you're saying.

Get people to hear you speak – but only ask people whose judgement you trust.

3 *Understanding* – the degree to which your expression shows that you understand what you're reading, in the sense of pausing in the right places, emphasising important words, and pronouncing unusual words correctly.

Apart from getting advice, the best way to prepare for this is to *practise*. If you can, do it before an audience, to get used to speaking in front of others. At first, or if you find talking in public difficult, do it in private – try a dramatised reading of Anthony Burgess in the bathroom!

LANGUAGE COURSEWORK

Chapter 16 discusses English Language exams.

The English Language exam at A- and AS-level is covered in more detail in Chapter 16. Almost all language syllabuses contain a coursework element, in which you are asked to produce work of a range of kinds. Going about this is similar in many ways to producing coursework for a literature syllabus. You still need, for example, to organise your work carefully and to spread it over the available time, and the research techniques for longer essays are fundamentally the same. But there is far more emphasis on collecting ideas and information *yourself*.

1 ESSAYS ON LANGUAGE USE

Allow plenty of time for this kind of work.

All of the techniques suggested with reference to the extended essay are important here. In addition, you will need to carry out individual research in the field, by listening to people talk and analysing their language.

Go about this as a scientist would go about organising an experiment:

- try as far as possible to keep an open mind about the topic you're covering – although you might need an initial hypothesis to test out in practice;
- observe very carefully what's going on in the exchange;
- think carefully about what you saw, analysing the language, gesture and other key elements;
- develop an interpretation or hypothesis about the exchange, which you think explains its main features;
- support this by reading accounts of similar exchanges in books on language or linguistics;
- bring all of these together in your final essay.

Taken step by step, the procedure is fairly straightforward – which does not mean that it will always be easy to reach a single, clear conclusion. Sometimes you may find that you have a hypothesis or interpretation of the particular kind of language before you observe it; if so, use your observations to test it carefully. Test your hypothesis still further by checking it against any existing research that's been done in that field.

Be prepared to change your ideas.

If your chosen topic does *not* call for an analysis of an actual exchange, you may need to work closely with text books, relating your own ideas and interpretations to those which they provide.

2 TRANSCRIPTION AND ANALYSIS

Use reliable recording equipment.

The whole basis of this exercise is a short piece of conversation of a particular kind, lasting between three and five minutes, or a piece of narrative or other speech from one person which lasts four or five minutes. You will need to *record* this – so the first thing to do is to make sure that you can use a cassette recorder which is capable of picking up dialogue and reproducing it clearly.

Choose your subject carefully. The speech needs to be something which can be discussed and analysed, so it's important to use something that you can really come to grips with. You might choose:

- a dialogue between two very young children, which shows a developing mastery of language;
- a radio advertisement, which shows language used for sales purposes;
- a sermon, using language to make a religious or moral point;
- a piece of casual conversation, to show how people communicate in how they speak as much as in what they say;
- an argument, to reveal the way people's emotions often obscure the clarity of an idea in their speech.

Be careful, too, when you make the recording: people are sometimes understandably reluctant to have their lives taken down in this way . . .

Be honest; describe the exchange as it was, not how you wanted it to be.

Although you will need to consult authorities on different kinds of language – your teacher or librarian will help here – you should still give your *own* response. You need to be honest and straightforward about the exchange, acknowledging the difficulties you encountered and accepting that your findings are inconclusive if that's the case. You'll get far more credit for this than for a project which fakes the evidence so that everything comes out perfectly: remember that you're discussing language in real life, where very little is perfect.

The exercise will consist of five sections:

What the transcription exercise contains.

Introduction; explaining the kind of language chosen and how you approached it;
Description; stating the circumstances of the recording, describing the speakers, and making any other points about this specific exchange;
Transcription of the whole passage;

Analysis of the exchange's significant or unusual features;
Evaluation, commenting on what the analysis has revealed, and drawing conclusions on what the study has discovered.

Once again, the exercise is straightforward if approached in a series of stages.

Approaching the transcription.

1   Make your recording.
2   Write a description of the exchange – the people, circumstances and anything else of interest. Do this immediately after you have made the recording, so that there's no chance of your forgetting anything.
3   Make your transcription, using *symbols* (which are clearly explained) to show pauses, overlaps and other features (see p. 171).
4   Make your analysis.
5   Write your evaluation.
6   Write the introduction.

This may seem to be in quite the wrong order, but there is a logic to it. If you save the introduction until last, you will know exactly what you are going to say throughout the rest of the piece. This means that you will make no mistakes in terms of referring to material which is not presented in the various sections. Further, because you know what your conclusions are, you'll be able to say much more clearly what is interesting about the piece of discussion.

Avoid padding.

Exercises of this sort are usually about 3000 words in length, excluding the transcription. Each section will not be of the same length, though: it's likely that the longest part will be the analysis, closely followed by the evaluation. The description can be fairly short, as long as it conveys all the necessary information; and the introduction will be most effective if it suggests ideas briefly, to prepare for their more detailed discussion in the last two sections.

3   SHORTER EXERCISES

Chapter 18 discusses shorter language exercises.

The writing of summaries and other kinds of writing will generally be done after discussion of techniques and approaches in class, or after looking at suitable material which shows the techniques in practice.

Wide reading and lots of practice are the best ways of preparing for these exercises, but further hints on summaries are given in Chapter 16.

4   WRITING FOR VARIOUS SPECIFIC PURPOSES

Make a chart, showing aim, audience and context for each piece you write.

Here the main aim is to identify the purpose and intended audience of your writing and to produce something which satisfies both. In particular, think about:

■ *Your aim*. Do you want to persuade, inform, encourage; more specifically, are you trying to sell something, get people to give money to charity, or just tell them about a fire at a tyre factory?

■ *Your audience*. How extensive is their vocabulary, both in general and specifically about the topic on which you're writing? How old are they? You can use 'streetwise' language for young people, but you need to use a more general vocabulary for older people or in any writing for the general public.

■ *The context*. Is this a newspaper article which people will read quickly, or an advertisement handout which people will glance at quickly and then throw in a bin? Or is it an article in a magazine which they'll take time over?

All of these aspects need careful thought, so that while you are writing you need to hold them firmly in mind. When you've written each piece, put it away for a day or two and then read it again in the role of your ideal target reader. Change anything that this person would not understand or would find offensive.

Along with these pieces you need to write a *commentary*. In this, you need to:

■ define your purpose, readership and context;
■ say how far you think you have matched the writing to these three.

Further advice on writing commentaries is given in the earlier section, with regard to so-called 'creative' writing. Language courses often make no distinction between writing that is 'creative' and that which has a more worldly purpose, and so many of the same techniques of reading and analysis can be applied. The important thing is that you stand back from your writing and look critically at it, checking whether it makes a clear statement of its aims and saying how far you think it achieves them.

STUDENT EXTENDED ESSAY WITH EXAMINER

COMMENTS

This chapter concludes with an example of a piece of extended course work produced by an A-level student, along with preparatory notes and comments. Look at it carefully to see the kind of work that is required, in terms of:

- length
- subject
- content
- approach
- the planning procedure

QUESTION

'A critical comparison of the thematic use and portrayal of nature as conveyed in the poetry of G.M. Hopkins, Ted Hughes, Seamus Heaney, Edward Thomas and Dylan Thomas'

> 66 This title could be improved – see overall comment at the end 99

NOTES AND PLANS

Notes and a plan are essential for the extended essay. You need to be especially careful to structure the essay clearly – and you should be confident that it will turn out the right length, too! (See Figs. 17.4 & 17.5.)

> a) A first plan or brainstorming session for a coursework extended essay. Don't worry about order or logical links at this stage – just get ideas down as quickly as you can
>
> Fig. 17.4 Notes for extended student essay plan

a) Structure of poems (in essay)
(5000 words ~ 15 sides)
 – one full analysis of a poem of each poet :-
ie WINDHOVER   PERSONAL HELICON
    OLD MAN   FERN HILL
    THOUGHT FOX
about 2 sides for each straight analysis (ie free of comparisons)
+ ½ side intro. ½ side conc. (1 ½ intro) = 11 sides
leaves 4 sides for integration of other poems,
                                     themes
                                     language (HOW!)

b) _Possible theme / language comparisons_

WINDHOVER : Thought Fox
            Hawk – in-rain (wind)
            Hawk roosting
            Sir John's Mill
OLD MAN :   Heaney's childhood poems
            The Barn
            Personal Helicon

THOUGHT FOX : (Windhover) Digging
PERSONAL HELICON : Inversnaid   The unknown Bird
                  Spring   Old Man
                  (digging)
FERN HILL : Barn   (Heaney's childhood poems)
           Blackberry picking

Themes: Man in relation to nature (the world)
        God / Religion
        childhood innocence ⇒ adulthood
        history / politics (roots)
        human nature & emotions
Language – How?   (which poets especially)
<u>Alliteration</u> : Hopkins Hughes
              E. Thomas

<u>Hyphens</u> : Hopkins
(ie linking and joining of words to make things of verbs / adjectives)
<u>Strong adjs</u> : Hughes Heaney Hopkins
     <u>Verbs</u> : Hughes Hopkins
<u>Compressed lang</u>. D. Thomas Hughes
<u>acute Observance</u> : Hopkins Heaney E. Thomas
<u>Colloquial spellings</u> : Heaney E. Thomas
<u>transferring word order</u> : D. Thomas Hughes
<u>Length of lines</u>   <u>Long, flowing</u>   <u>shorter, more precise</u>
                    Hopkins   Hughes
                    D. Thomas   Heaney
                                         E. Thomas

<u>Exclamations / abrupt endings</u> Hopkins
<u>Tone & special characteristics of each poet</u> :-
<u>Hughes</u> : Remoteness serious separateness mysterious
        Man / environment – where does he fit ?
                            how important is he ?
        Human nature / emotions
        Creativity from nature around him
<u>Heaney</u> : Political Historical – roots (tradition)
                       his own & Ireland
        (rural) skills Exploration of himself Richness /
                                        mystery of childhood
<u>Hopkins</u> : Beauty, vitality of nature (his own love of nature)
          INSCAPE (essence...) INSTRESS (energy...)
          God's presence in nature
<u>E. Thomas</u> : unpretentiousness, directness, love of countryside
                               sort of faith
          neglected / secret nature desire for perfection
          yearning nostalgia. Quest for SELF & search for
          happiness Coming to terms with less than perfect
          world Moral comment
<u>D. Thomas</u> : World of childhood – lost, birth of adulthood
          Associates God with creation of nature wonder of
          World & innocence of child – DIVINE

b) A second plan, developing each idea more fully. The points are presented here with greater clarity, but there's still plenty of space so that you can make changes later

SUBJECT MATTER :- MAN/NATURE - NOTES + HOW ACHIEVED? TONE? COMMENTS?

HUGHES	HEANEY	HOPKINS	E. THOMAS	D. THOMAS
Human nature + emotions, creativity from nature around him.	Ancestry/history/ tradition Present + past + their connections Political (Ireland)	Beauty/vitality of nature his love of nature expressed	Themes:- harmony man/ nature beauty and SECRET neglected nature	
Strong adjs, verbs Use of alliteration Compressed language Gd. structure	Strong adjs V. descriptive - acute observation Gd. Structure heavily crafted	Imagery V. accurate description essence/imageries -INSCAPE	Love of countryside - sort of faith.	transfers word order long lines
Tone:- remoteness Separateness Serious mysterious	Moral dimensions of behaviour etc. Serious	energy that creates this quality - INSTRESS Vivid	Direct. accuracy of observation unpretentiousness affection for the everyday colloquial speech.	lost wonder of childhood but not hanging on to it - death of childhood/birth of adulthood
Where is man in relation to his environment?	He's lost wonder of childhood (must capture it in poetry)	Life/vitality mid line exclamation (sudden halts for impact/ emphasis) strings of nouns, verbs, adjs, similes metaphorical expression alliteration	Moral comment longs for something better - desire for perfection - trying to grasp the ungraspable!! pessimism, longing yearning nostalgia/melancholy	Associates God with creation of nature
How important is man in relation to his environment?	Political outlook expressed in poems unavoidable	Gods/relationship Gods presence in nature (corruption/sin in God's world - spring)	Always trying to find right language but often can't find it Uses nature to explore and communicate what he sees as central human experience - what matters etc.	Holy joy human enjoyment
	Skills of rural people Not nostalgic (just) important			Man - inheritor of earth innocence of child } both wonder of world } divine
	Exploration of himself		Quest for SELF + search for happiness	
	Richness/mystery of childhood (Helicon)		Coming to terms with a less than perfect world	richness/mystery of world + childhood

Fig. 17.5 Notes for extended student essay: a chart showing the poems discussed and points made about them. It's often useful to produce charts like this — especially when you're trying to organise large blocks of material in longer pieces of writing. As well as organising your ideas before you start, they help you keep track of your progress as you get the writing done a little at a time

STUDENT ANSWER

The poetry subsequently analysed has been selected to give an insight into the individual ways in which five poets have portrayed nature and used it as a base for further theme development. Beginning with Hopkins, the poetry chosen ranges from the latter part of the nineteenth century to the present day. Although influence from other poets can be found in much of the work, each poet has successfully developed his own style to complement his personal interpretation of Nature; thus a brief focus on each author provides a necessary introduction to his work.

Hopkins, a Victorian, is renowned for his originality and ability to capture the beauty and vitality of nature. Although the only nineteenth century poet (E. Thomas didn't begin writing poetry until the early twentieth century) Hopkins can be compared alongside the twentieth century writers for, as we shall see, he had considerable influence over some of their earlier work. Essential distinctions of Hopkins are his power to demonstrate the essence and uniqueness or 'Inscape' of things and his exploration of the energy that creates this quality; the 'Instress'. These serve to complement the major theme of God's relationship with Nature and to convey his personal lore of the subject.

Edward Thomas, also born a Victorian, broke away from the traditional Georgian style of his contemporaries, offering a very individual approach; a personal poet incorporating his love of the countryside with a sense of dissatisfaction and yearning. His career as a poet ended after only five years by his death at Arras in 1917.

Born in 1914, Dylan Thomas wrote mainly in the thirties and forties. His poetic interest lay in the wonder of childhood and the association of God with Nature's creation. The poetry combines both an adult and child's view of the world.

The modern day poets, Ted Hughes and Seamus Heaney, have similarities in tone but contrast in subject matter. Hughes explores human nature and emotions, finding creativity from Nature around him. The underlying theme in his work is the importance and status of man in relation to his environment: Heaney, an Irish Catholic, focuses especially on human nature. His poetry examines roots, tradition and culture – both at a personal and national level – alongside the richness and mystery of childhood and Nature itself. He uses his poetry as a means by which he can explore himself.

Hopkins' poem 'The Windhover' concentrates on a single bird and the qualities it has which give it uniqueness and splendour. Also present is the theme of Christ; the poem is dedicated 'To Christ our Lord' and close links are made between the falcon and God.

The poem is personal, beginning 'I'. Thus Hopkins is writing down his own perception of this bird with such intensity of detail as can only be obtained by close, personal observation. Hence the 'Inscape' already mentioned. He begins with a lengthy phrase, incorporating word repetition and varied, relating adjectives to achieve the feeling of grandeur and dominance he associates with the falcon. The compound adjective 'dapple-dawn-drawn' expresses how the hawk seems to be drawn by the dappled morning, and achieves extra effect by alliteration continued from 'daylight's dauphin'. The line ends, 'in his riding', the simplicity of which gives a kind of release from the conjunction of adjectives. 'Riding' is positioned such that during the slight pause between lines, the bird seems quite free. The air is made 'steady' by the falcon, 'striding high' over the 'rolling' or undulating ground. The long syllables of 'high there' contain a kind of exultation and admiration, and, as well as the literal meaning of flying high up in the heavens, the phrase suggests the calling of the poet's heart to the bird. 'Rung upon the rein of a wimpling wing' gives the image of flight-control – relating to the reins used to restrain a horse – as though the bird is hovering under the control of his rippling wings.

The verse suddenly becomes stationary with the impact of 'in his ecstasy!' As well as describing the satisfaction of flight, the purpose is to allow the reader to feel in his mind the bird's hovering before it breaks 'off forth on wing' in continuation of its flight; flight depicted by curve imagery, a shiny skate cutting a perfect curve on ice. 'The hurl' suggests that the bird has been thrown through the air, and the next minute is 'gliding', all the while driving back the 'big wind' with its power of motion.

Then Hopkins returns to focus on himself with 'My heart in hiding'. Here he's drawing attention to his own mood and emotions, 'hiding' suggesting depression. He expresses great admiration for the creature: 'The mastery of the thing!' 'Thing' contains the notion

---

Examiner comments (margin):

" Might be clearer to say 'analysed below' or 'discussed here'. "

" This could be clearer – 'a starting point for their own themes and ideas', perhaps? "

" Be careful about influence – Hopkins wasn't published until 1918, when Thomas had been dead for a year. "

" 'Combining' "

" Good brief, introductory statements on the poets' work and stances towards nature – the points on Heaney are especially strong. "

" 'varied relating adjectives' is a little confused. "

" Yes – but the rhythm and pace are also essential here, as they create the movement of the bird. "

" – and the strong religious association of 'wimpling', referring to a nun's headdress. "

" Some good explanatory writing here. "

" Isn't it rather a sense of *awe* before the bird? "

of individuality; the 'thisness' or 'Inscape' here is evident.

The second stanza lists attributes of the falcon broken up by 'oh' an exclamation of wonder and amazement. The description is abruptly halted with the verb 'Buckle!' which could either refer to the combination of these attributes or to the collapse of them as they fade into insignificance beneath the splendour of the bird's sudden sharp flight. 'AND' is written in capitals for emphasis and hold, perhaps as the bird itself hesitates before plunging. Hopkins sees the falcon as more beautiful and dangerous than ever: 'O my Chevalier' relates back to the 'valour' and could also be Hopkins addressing Christ. Certainly this stanza expresses the essence of Christ in the Windhover.

The poem ends with other aspects of nature which could also reflect Christ's splendour. The simple ploughing of the earth, and the sillion strip between the furrows are made to shine, as do embers in a fire which spark out beautiful colours as they fall in the grate. 'Ah my dear' shows another side to the 'Chevalier' as Hopkins speaks intimately and affectionately with Christ. After the violence and ecstacy of the first part, the poem ends quietly, the falling of embers representing the beauty and sacrifice in death, just as Christ himself did.

In 'The Windhover' Hopkins uses the falcon to convey his own excitement in the God-Created world and the individual magnificence he finds in nature. A strong characteristic we have seen in 'The Windhover' is the use of exclamations. This technique is common in much of Hopkins' poetry, often in religious content. 'The Wreck of the Deutschland', for example, begins 'Thou mastering me/ God!' and contains similar phrases throughout: 'And seal of his seraph-arrival!'; 'The majesty!' A second characteristic — which we shall later discover to have influenced Hughes — is the use of hyphens in linking and joining words. Both in dual conjugations: "white-fiery and whirlwind-sunveiled snow" and longer links: "Miracle-in-Mary-of-flame".

Thirdly, attention must be drawn to the stringing of adjectives and nouns — The Windhover 'act oh, air, pride, plume ...' compares with 'swift, slow; sweet, sour; adazzle, dim' from 'Pied Beauty' and 'Pride, rose, prince, hero of us, high-priest, ...' (Wreck of the Deutschland).

Critics have closely compared 'The Windhover' with Ted Hughes' 'The Hawk in the Rain' — both poets convey the power and energy of the bird with similar rhythm and choice of 'violent' words, for example 'The hurl and gliding/ rebuffed the big wind' comes close to 'suffers the air, hurled upside down' and the endings of magnificence are paralleled 'Fall, gall themselves, and gash gold-vermillion' and Hughes; 'Smashed, mix his heart's blood with the mire of the land.' 'The Hawk in the Rain' also examples Hopkins' technical influence on Hughes: "last-moment-counting" needs no further explanation of origin.

However, there are obvious differences. Hopkins' falcon has close connections with Christ; 'Hawk in the Rain' is not specifically religious. Hughes' Hawk seems to have the power to choose when to die, and although its ending will be dramatic there is no suggestion of after-life as 'gash gold-vermillion' could well represent.

'Hawk Roosting' would appear to be a development of Hughes' first Hawk poem. The content is similiar; the hawk dominates man and thus man's insignificance in his environment is stressed. But the style is Hughes' own: violence, exaggerations, egoism are all common to his animal poetry and are often there for emphasis rather than of literal meaning. The Hawk claims to 'hold creation in (his) foot'; '(His) eye has permitted no change.' Similarly in 'Thrushes', the common garden bird is 'terrifying ... more coiled steel than living ...'

The opening line of 'The Thought-Fox' — "I imagine this midnight moment's forest" — gently imitates Hopkins but the poem differs considerably from those mentioned so far, the title itself seems an odd combination of words; however, close analysis produces links. Both hold the idea of mystery and sudden approach without warning. The development of an idea parallels the slow, wary approach of the fox. The fox is a rather solitary creature, like the poet, whose wildness of thought ties in with the wild creature.

Like 'Hawk Roosting' the poem is in the present tense, though this time is related specifically by the poet. The mysterious atmosphere of the poem is emphasised by the word 'forest', suggesting darkness and evil. It is also the poem's first connection with the fox, being the animal's natural habitat. 'Loneliness', besides being literal, suggests the poet is waiting for an idea to enter his head — all he is aware of is the clock ticking.

Margin notes:

66 Yes – the 'danger' element is one that you could usefully discuss more, I think. 99

66 The intimate relationship with the falcon is transferred to Christ here. 99

66 Both, perhaps, are related to the ecstatic immediacy of experience in his poems. 99

66 An original and striking expression. 99

66 'Exemplifies' 99

66 True – although Philip Sidney uses such expressions in the 1590s – for example, 'long-with-love acquainted eyes'. 99

66 Some taut points here, well supported by brief and relevant quotation. 99

66 A perceptive point – you could tighten it by mentioning the opening of 'Windhover'. 99

66 Some strong linkings of the two worlds of the poem. 99

He sees 'no star' – no inspiration or guidance for the poem he is trying to write. 'Something ... is entering the loneliness'; there is a sense of apprehension as the poet's thoughts are awakened. 'Cold, delicately' describe not only the fox, but also the furtive, uncertain gathering of his thoughts. The next three stanzas describe the fox's movement. Firstly hesitant, which Hughes emphasises by writing each footstep: "now, and now, and now ..." Then more boldly as the fox comes 'Across clearings'. The crossing movement is divided between two stanzas, hence the gap suggests the leap of the fox into the open, and brings confidence into the rather tentative movement so far described.

The fox's eye widens – he is alert, aware of his surroundings. Here Hughes strengthens the image in the reader's mind by the use of long, confident adverbs. In the final stanza the poem reaches its climax. A pause after the word 'Till' sets the subsequent phrase apart from the rest of the poem. The alliteration in 'a sudden sharp hot stink of fox' is used to lay stress on an already violently strong image – contrary to that previously produced. So far the fox has been depicted as a distant, beautiful creature. Now it is suddenly 'there', it has entered the consciousness of Hughes – has taken over his imagination and caused inspiration for the poem.

To round the poem off, Hughes refers back to the first stanza 'The window is starless still; the clock ticks.' The inspiration is over and no longer needed for, as Hughes simply states, 'The page is printed'.

'The Thought-Fox' describes the way a thought enters the mind and then develops. Hughes uses a movement in nature to parallel an intellectual process. By contrast, Seamus Heaney in 'Personal Helicon' is concerned with any immediate physical experience of part of the natural world. The water in wells seemed to hold a fascination for him, and exploring wells 'and old pumps' became a pleasurable pastime. He 'loved the dark drop, the trapped sky, the smells ...' The depth of the well allowed Heaney to make use of his imagination – for the darkness held a kind of mystery which he couldn't quite come at. The sky is captured as a water reflection, but the confined area of the water's surface allows the sky to be 'trapped' inside the stone boundary. His sense of smell is also important; the dampness 'of waterweed, fungus and dank moss' brings out a sense of lushness and also of time – for moss and fungus develop over the years.

In stanzas two, three and four, Heaney describe specific features of various wells, thus exploring their own uniqueness. This close description compares with that of Hopkins, closely imitating the poem 'Inversnaid' in which the colour, shape and feel of a mountain stream are acutely depicted. The intensity of richness and substance are also to be found in Hopkins' 'Spring' where the sky is 'all in a rush with richness' and weeds grow 'long and lovely and lush'.

The 'rotted board top' adds to the damp imagery and sense of time by its erosion. Heaney uses his sense of taste – 'I savoured the rich crash' – in place of hearing. This intensifies the experience, making it especially enjoyable. Here we see some of the seriousness to be found in 'Blackberry picking', 'Churning Day' and the title poem, 'Death of a Naturalist'. In the former of these Heaney describes the blackberries as having 'flesh ... sweet juice thickened wine .../ leaving stains upon the tongue and lust for picking.' And from 'Churning Day', '... the four crocks, spilled their heavy lip of cream, their white insides, into the sterile churn.'

This sensuous use of language again emphasises the delight Heaney finds in nature and the closeness of his association with it. This portrayal of pleasure compares with Dylan Thomas' 'Fern Hill'. As a child, Thomas was 'prince of the apple town ... green and carefree', 'And playing lovely and watery/ And fire green as grass.' Hence we can see a thematic link between the two poets: that of childhood innocence combined with the beauty of Nature in the world.

'Plummeted' is a very exact verb to describe the bucket's drop down to water 'so deep you saw no reflection in it'. This echoes the 'dark drop' imagery of the first stanza, and the mystery and use of Heaney's imagination connected with it: 'Fructified' is another strong verb, depicting the fruitful, fresh qualities of the water and weeds. Time has allowed 'long roots' to obscure Heaney's view of the water. 'A white face hovered' when the roots were cleared. Although obviously Heaney's own face, the poem avoids stating it as such, making it seem another of water's mysteries. The 'clean new music' added to his voice in the well's echo suggests an added richness, as if the sound has picked up another quality or 'tune' from the water. This relates to Heaney's adult exploration of

> Good – 'white space' often has important things to say in poems.

> A careful and well-structured account of the poem's two levels.

> True – you handle well the poem's use of direct sensory response.

> Is it an imitation or a resemblance? Worth thinking about.

> A carefully prepared shift from a discussion of one poem to a more general point – this is always difficult, but you do it well here.

Another point which grows and develops with both logic and sensitivity.

You write well on the use of poetry to perform this self-reflection and examination.

Remember to underline titles of collections.

Good comparative point here.

The point about ritual is far more important than the point about alliteration here – you could develop it at greater length.

Is there room for a comparison with Heaney's use of memory here, perhaps?

himself in the way that his childhood experiences have been added to by writing them down as poems. On reading back the poems, it's as though they give Heaney something back to hold on to – like the reflections and echoes of the wells. He is able to use language to restore what otherwise will be lost.

The final stanza expands on this idea. He is an adult now and these childish explanations are 'beneath all adult dignity'. A child's gaze into water and fascination at the 'white face' that stares back, is harmless. For an adult to do the same, it would be considered vanity – like Narcissus, in love with his own reflection. The last line relates back to the well imagery: 'I rhyme to see myself, to set the darkness echoing.' Darkness could be Heaney's past; he writes poetry to bring it back, though in a different form perhaps he is trying to understand things about himself that he didn't understand before, and take his explorations further than his easily accessible childhood experiences.

To delve deeper into his own psychology he must first purge himself of his childhood, just as he 'dragged out the long roots' to see his face. Hence the poem leads him from 'Death of a Naturalist' on to his next collection: 'Door into the Dark'.

In comparison with 'Digging' the poem is not idyllic, nor is it nostalgic. It is written just as it happened and used to explore Heaney's adulthood. Nature itself is examined in its qualities of beauty and secretiveness – all elements important to Edward Thomas' poetry, but without the inadequacy of memory that Thomas feels. Heaney needs to collect a picture of his past before he can go on to explore himself; Thomas sees existence as worthless without the ability to remember the accumulative pattern of events that make up life. The difference is that Heaney is satisfied with his poetic capture of childhood whereas Thomas is dissatisfied with the inadequacy of language and incompleteness of memory.

'Old Man' is a poem about a herb and its association with a young girl and Thomas himself. It is a poem about the things that last, that really matter, which introduces the themes of time, meaning, inadequacy and nostalgia.

The poem is split into three sections. The first part is a description of the herb itself, the second describes a child's connections with the herb and the last is an explanation of the herb's significance to Thomas. The herb is ordinary, the elaborate names serve to 'Half decorate half perplex the thing it is'. Already we have two paradoxes: that of the names, and also their ability to both 'decorate' and 'perplex' the herb. The second stanza contains more. Thomas, despite not liking the herb, loves it, 'as some day the child will love it.' Hence this love comes from the time element of the herb, locked away in his memory, rather than from its appearance or smell. Thomas uses alliteration to describe the child's action on the herb, 'Snipping the tips and shrivelling the shreds.' The way she 'plucks a feather from the door-side bush' is a kind of ritual, a habit she is probably hardly aware of. 'Perhaps thinking, perhaps of nothing' emphasises the lack of definiteness about the action, in association with the almost timeless quality of the herb and the vague and open tone of the last stanza.

He wonders whether the child will remember this experience, these surroundings, like he himself is struggling to do: 'where first I met the bitter scent is lost.' His action is like that of the child – 'I too, often shrivel the grey shreds, sniff them ...' – yet he takes his action one step further in trying to place the incident in terms of his life. But he cannot, his memory has grown dim with age. He's not even sure of what he's trying to remember.

The 'in love with pain' idea that is sometimes associated with Thomas is captured in the line 'I cannot like the scent, yet would rather give up others more sweet ...'. He enjoys the depth and meaning that this plant holds for him; they are important – he dislikes the actual herb and its bitter scent.

The theme of memory is central to the final stanza. He feels he has 'mislaid the key' and cannot fit in with life. He needs the past to reassure him, give him a greater sense of belonging. Thus, unable to remember, he feels his existence, or the meaning of his existence, is inadequate and unsatisfactory. The ending is negative and nostalgic.

'No garden appears, no path, no hoar-green bush .... only an avenue, dark, nameless, without end.'

The 'avenue' refers to his past. It is 'dark' in his memory, and its vagueness gives it no finality. The final line is almost depressing and lonely, an example of Thomas' dissatisfaction at being unable to place life's events in a sequential order.

The time pattern of the poem itself is complex: the man in middle age; the experience of the young child; the man thinking about the child not remembering; and he himself being unable to remember. He's using nature to express the importance of memory and his despair at losing this vital link to his life.

The tone is conversational; it changes direction, it is hesitant and thoughtful, doing justice to Thomas' re-enactment of his response to the herb and all it symbolises. As a result he takes the reader along with him and we share with him the finding of the final negative truth. The colloquial nature of the language has the same effect: 'not a word she says,' 'but for certain I love it.' In the same way that he finds his lack of memory an inadequacy to his life, so the language is inadequate in describing the herb, for it is impossible to prove it without seeing it, there are no words apt enough to capture it on paper.

> *Yes: you could perhaps compare the conversational style of this poem with the much more rhetorical style of Hopkins.*

The inability of Thomas' memory to pinpoint a distinct incident is especially apparent in 'The Unknown Bird'. A quote from the second stanza serves to express the unreachability of the bird:—

'La-la-la! he called, seeming far-off
As if a cock crowed past the edge of the world,
As if the bird or I were in a dream.'

It's almost as if the creature is part of a dream world, and is actually non-existent. Thomas can sense when the bird is near by the volume of his voice, though even then the bird is 'somehow distant still ...' This gives an example of the words R. S. Thomas uses to describe Edward's feelings of inadequacy at the gap between man and nature and his desire for perfection; 'a world he never could quite come at.'

The ending of this stanza is sad in tone, like that of 'Old Man'. The words 'sad only with joy too' perhaps parallel Thomas' own feelings: he is saddened by the world, his regret at the unreachable, but is happy to be amongst nature, to have the ability to hear what others cannot.

> *Good use of critical readings here, though it would be nice to know what you feel about the poems.*

From these two poems alone we see that 'Nature is the starting point from which he explores himself, and, by implication, mankind in general'[1] and have several examples of 'the sense of directionlessness'[2] and 'fine feeling for detail'[3] common to much of his poetry.

The former of these relates to Heaney's use of poetry — we have already seen how he draws on his childhood to explore himself. The latter compares with Heanay's precision of language. From 'The Barn' the simile 'like grit of ivory' admirably describes the texture and size of the 'threshed corn'; it is white, shredded and clean — also valuable like the ivory, for it is important to the farmer's living. Similarly accurate, the 'two narrow shafts of guided motes, crossing, from air-holes slit/ High in each gable.'

'Swallow thronged loft' and 'flies from the chimneys' from Dylan Thomas' 'Fern Hill' contain the same feeling of accuracy of detail but without the carefully related precision of language. Instead the quality is achieved by condensing the language and transferring word order. The style itself is lilting, relatively closely to that of Hopkins. The long lines give continuity to Dylan's childhood experiences and the feeling that he is savouring them.

> *You have a sure control of the essay's progress here.*

I have already compared Heaney and Dylan Thomas in terms of the thematic lyrics of childhood innocence and of the world's natural beauty, but also important as a parallel is their ability to capture the exact 'feel' of childhood by writing with a child's perspective on the world. In 'Blackberry Picking', Heaney 'always felt like crying. It wasn't fair that all the lovely casfuls smelt of rot.' 'It wasn't fair' especially captures the childish language and the disappointment and annoyance a child feels when things aren't as he would have liked in an idyllic world. 'Fern Hill' expresses Dylan's childish exhilaration and vivid imagination. 'I was huntsman and herdsman, the calves / sang to my horn ...'

1 Hewett (*A Choice of Poets*)
2 F.R. Leavis (*New Bearings on English Poetry*)
3 *Penguin Companion to Literature*

The poem begins 'Now as I was young and easy ... and happy as the grass was green.' The simile is unusual but serves its purpose well; it is not so much the literal meaning that is important to the poem – more the tone and mood captured by the language. Dylan uses 'honoured ... was prince of the apple towns'. Nature has made him feel important, in command and respected. He 'lordly had the trees and leaves trail with daisies and barley': a continuation of his feeling of power over nature. It's as if these plants are all part of his kingdom and thus shows us his closeness with the land. 'Time' has been personified; it is the one thing that appears to dominate Dylan. Yet in his childhood time was kind to him. Thomas here expresses the happily playing child's lack of awareness of time.

The second and third stanzas are very much a re-wording of the first 'And as I was green and carefree, farmers ...' He himself is now 'green' and the yard 'happy'. The transferal of adjectives could portray the flexibility of a child's mind; symbolising the way in which a child can be easily distracted and move onto something else. The calves 'sang', foxes 'barked clear and cold', the sabbath 'rang slowly'. Dylan has contrasted the warmth of the farmyard sound with the distant chilly call of foxes. The sabbath 'rung' with bells, but perhaps more significantly with happiness, for Sunday was a time to be free. 'All the sun long' gives an example of the effectiveness of word compression, followed by 'it was running, it was lovely' – flowing childish words expressing the on-goingness of a wonderful day. The echo of this – 'and playing, lovely and watery' perhaps symbolises the way in which a child repeats his own words due to happy excitement.

For Dylan, night-time too was an intensive experience. He 'rode to sleep' yet because of all the secrets he shared with the land he was conscious of Nature's presence 'all the moon long', – another effective compression of words.

On awakening the farm was 'like a wanderer white ... it was Adam and Maiden.' Here Dylan has used further religious imagery in depicting the Garden of Eden. This could serve two purposes: that of the sense of time, as if Dylan feels that time begins again for him with each new daybreak; and also the idea of childhood innocence and a hint of the inevitable comparison once childhood has passed. The stanza ends with the notion of man looking back on the Beginning of Time in the religious sense, with the Christian Birth. 'On to the fields of praise' completes the imagery, incorporating a thankfulness to God for the world's creation.

The penultimate stanza relates back to the carefree attitude of the opening stanzas, with similar transferal of word order: 'happy as the heart was long ... in the sun born over and over'. The ending of the stanza describes the move from childhood innocence to adulthood. Yet unlike Heaney, there is no nostagia nor exorcism in the the change. Dylan is saying that childhood is a short stage in life but a happy one, and that adulthood must be met and greeted in a new light. The final stanza expands on this. It is now 'the moon that is always rising'. Time is no longer kind. 'Time held (him) green and dying' holds obvious contrast to 'green and golden'. And the ending line expresses the 'chains' of adulthood. He feels captured by maturing – the childhood freedom which opened the poem is now lost. Yet the ending doesn't have the negativeness of Heaney or Edward Thomas. Instead, he 'sang ...', expressing the positive side to adulthood, the birth of a new era. The sea imagery contrasts with the 'holy streams' of the third stanza. He is no longer in freshwater but with added emotions, guilt, opportunities and new ground to explore, symbolised by the salt, size and power of the sea. The list preserves both the negative and positive sides of adulthood, and shows Dylan's readiness to take on his new role of adulthood.

Although the poem contains religious imagery, this appears to complement the child's connection of God with the Creation, rather than expressed as a theme in its own right. It helps to represent the divinity connected with both the child's universe and the wonder of the world – unlike E. Thomas, the tone is not a moral one. Neither is he grappling to hang onto childhood like Thomas and Heaney. In this sense the poem is more like Hughes, but without any feeling of man's insignificance in his environment.

Dylan Thomas' 'Over Sir John's Hill' relates back to 'The Windhover' and Hughes' two Hawk poems. 'Hawk on fire' could easily be a line from Hopkins and the idea of the hawk being an executioner who 'pulls to his claws' smaller birds, contains the action and violence of Hughes.

The poem depicts the hierarchy of birds — each one a killer. Rather than the theme of childhood into adulthood, the emphasis here seems to be on 'the burden of human consciousness, in a world which accepts mortality unconsciously'[1] — closer in tone and theme to Hughes or even Edward Thomas. However, the language is much the same as in 'Fern Hill': 'Through windows of dusk and water I see the tilting whispering Heron ...' And the religion present would seem to serve the same purpose as before; a device that comes easily to D. Thomas.

To compare five poets' 'use and portrayal' of nature involves an analysis of both the poetical themes and also the style, tone and format of the poetry. We have looked at four hawk poems, linked by content but made individual by the different use of language of each poet. Having closely studied work from each writer, a list of language characteristics begins to form, this enabling recognition of unseen poems and the ability to spot influences of one poet on another. In the preceding analyses I have tried to do justice to this, yet a brief comparative summary is perhaps a necessary addition to draw together the technical rather than thematic devices of each poet.

> " Influence is always a difficult area – perhaps 'resemblance' is a better concept. "

Vivid description is especially apparent in the work of Hopkins, Heaney and Edward Thomas, brought about by acute observation. For Thomas and Heaney this includes the use of colloquial speech; for Hopkins the unique use of mid/end line exclamations and abrupt endings. Hughes, Heaney and Hopkins make good use of strong adjectives and verbs: Hopkins and Hughes employ hyphens for linking and joining words — Hughes for exactness and precision, Hopkins to create strings of adjectives/verbs for emphasis, Hughes and Dylan Thomas both use compressed language and the transferal of word order to achieve this. Examples of alliteration can be found in the work of all five, though is especially notable in Hughes and Hopkins, to complement their powerful choice of verbs and adjectives.

> " A sound list – though I think that, in isolation, it doesn't add much to the deeper, more analytical parts of the essay: and I'm still doubtful about the value of alliteration! "

Form can only be loosely categorized, varying to fit the mood and subject of the individual poem, but in general Hopkins and Dylan Thomas express themselves in long, flowing lines, and Hughes, Heaney and E. Thomas with short precision.

In these analyses we have examined the main Nature themes introduced in one short summary of each poet. To briefly re-cap, these are: man in relation to his environment, God's presence in Nature, the richness, mystery and innocence of childhood, and human nature and emotions. However, it is important to recognise that the poetry analysed sets out to give a view of the poet only in terms of these themes: Hughes and Heaney especially have been examined in terms of their earlier work, and have since matured to include a broader range of aspects. Heaney, for example, goes on to focus more heavily on politics, using Nature to express national rather than personal views, and further on still explores mythology and pre-Christian ideas. Hughes also moves on to more difficult verse, likewise bringing in mythology in a late collection, 'Crow'. Nature, however, in whatever form, remains common to all five poets both as a theme in its own right, and as a base for each poet's personal expansion of style and content to achieve his full potential.

> " A valid and necessary qualification. "

1 Critic from Open University — UNIT GUIDE ON DYLAN THOMAS. 3RD Level 20 POETRY.

> " Overall comment
> This is a very strong piece of writing – close, detailed reading of a small number of poems with a few valid generalisations and some perceptive comparisons. It's always difficult to reach large-scale conclusions on the basis of only a few poems, but you avoid the temptation to do this. You might perhaps have included some of Dylan Thomas' poems from the war years – those in *Deaths and Entrances* for example ('A Refusal to Mourn' in particular) which suggest a very different relation between mankind, God and nature; but it's impossible to cover everything in an essay of this length. In all, you write with accuracy, logic and sensitivity; a very sound piece of writing which well justifies the effort you invested in it. "

INDEX

YORK NOTES

★ **The most comprehensive range of study guides to English Literature**

★ Over 7,000,000 copies sold since publication

York Notes give an ideal introduction to English Literature for A-Level and GCSE students, and also provide good background information for first-year university students. Each guide is written by an expert and will help the reader think independently about the text being studied.

	ISBN (PREFIX 0 582)	QUANTITY
CHINUA ACHEBE		
Things Fall Apart	02312 2	
EDWARD ALBEE		
Who's Afraid of Virginia Woolf?	02321 1	
MARGARET ATWOOD		
Cat's Eye	29350 2	
The Handmaid's Tale	21538 2	
JANE AUSTEN		
Emma	02263 0	
Mansfield Park	03967 3	
Northanger Abbey	78123 X	
Persuasion	03578 3	
Pride and Prejudice	02297 5	
Sense and Sensibility	78107 8	
SAMUEL BECKETT		
Waiting for Godot	023181 1	
ALAN BENNETT		
Talking Heads	29349 9	
JOHN BETJEMAN		
Selected Poems	09643 X	
WILLIAM BLAKE		
Songs of Innocence and Songs of Experience	03342 X	
ROBERT BOLT		
A Man for All Seasons	78181 7	
HAROLD BRIGHOUSE		
Hobson's Choice	31352 X	
CHARLOTTE BRONTË		
Jane Eyre	02273 8	
EMILY BRONTË		
Wuthering Heights	02324 6	
ROBERT BURNS		
Selected Poems	26252 6	
LORD BYRON		
Selected Poems	79250 9	
GEOFFREY CHAUCER		
The Franklin's Tale	78161 2	
The Merchant's Tale	03577 5	
The Miller's Tale	02286 X	
The Nun's Priest's Tale	02290 8	
Prologue to the Canterbury Tales	02298 3	
The Wife of Bath's Tale	03348 9	
SAMUEL TAYLOR COLERIDGE		
Selected Poems	03092 7	
JOSEPH CONRAD		
Heart of Darkness	02269 X	
DANIEL DEFOE		
Moll Flanders	03757 3	
Robinson Crusoe	78111 6	
SHELAGH DELANEY		
A Taste of Honey	09644 8	
CHARLES DICKENS		
Bleak House	03093 5	
David Copperfield	78131 0	
Great Expectations	31339 2	
Hard Times	31341 4	
Oliver Twist	78254 6	
EMILY DICKINSON		
Selected Poems	03746 8	
JOHN DONNE		
Selected Poems	02274 6	
DOUGLAS DUNN		
Selected Poems	21537 4	
GEORGE ELIOT		
Middlemarch	03087 0	
The Mill on the Floss	78103 5	
Silas Marner	31472 0	
T S ELIOT		
Selected Poems	02310 6	
The Waste Land	02319 X	
HENRY FIELDING		
Joseph Andrews	78174 4	

	ISBN (PREFIX 0 582)	QUANTITY
F SCOTT FITZGERALD		
The Great Gatsby	02266 5	
E M FORSTER		
Howards End	79243 6	
A Passage to India	03350 0	
JOHN FOWLES		
The French Lieutenant's Woman	02093 X	
BRIAN FRIEL		
Translations	29348 0	
ELIZABETH GASKELL		
North and South	78183 3	
WILLIAM GOLDING		
Lord of the Flies	31403 8	
OLIVER GOLDSMITH		
She Stoops to Conquer	78226 0	
GRAHAM GREENE		
Brighton Rock	02257 6	
THOMAS HARDY		
Far from the Madding Crowd	78296 1	
Jude the Obscure	78126 4	
The Mayor of Casterbridge	31426 7	
Selected Poems	78294 5	
The Return of the Native	02300 9	
Tess of the D'Urbervilles	02311 4	
L P HARTLEY		
The Go-Between	02264 9	
NATHANIEL HAWTHORNE		
The Scarlet Poems	02305 X	
SEAMUS HEANEY		
Selected Poems	02306 8	
ERNEST HEMINGWAY		
The Old Man and the Sea	78224 4	
SUSAN HILL		
I'm the King of the Castle	31381 3	
BARRY HINES		
A Kestrel for a Knave	31402 X	
HOMER		
The Iliad	79227 4	
The Odyssey	03353 5	
ALDOUS HUXLEY		
Brave New World	03355 1	
BEN JOHNSON		
The Alchemist	03361 6	
Volpone	02317 3	
JAMES JOYCE		
Dubliners	78215 5	
A Portrait of the Artist as a Young Man	03088 9	
JOHN KEATS		
Selected Poems	03362 4	
PHILIP LARKIN		
Selected Poems	06564 X	
D H LAWRENCE		
The Rainbow	03363 2	
Sons and Lovers	02308 4	
Women in Love	04034 5	
HARPER LEE		
To Kill a Mockingbird	31529 8	
LAURIE LEE		
Cider with Rosie	03365 9	
CHRISTOPHER MARLOWE		
Doctor Faustus	02262 2	
ARTHUR MILLER		
The Crucible	31528 X	
Death of a Salesman	02260 6	
A View from the Bridge	31324 4	

YORK HANDBOOKS

– A companion series of background study guides in English Literature and Language.

★ **Designed to meet the wider needs of students of English and related fields**

★ **Each volume is a compact study of a given subject area, written by an authority with experience in communicating the essential ideas to students at all levels.**

	ISBN (PREFIX 0 582)	QUANTITY
A DICTIONARY OF LITERARY TERMS (SECOND EDITION)		
Martin Gray	08037 1	
ENGLISH POETRY		
Clive Probyn	79271 1	
AN INTRODUCTION TO LINGUISTICS		
Loreto Todd	79293 2	
STUDYING SHAKESPEARE		
Martin Stephen and P A Franks	03572 4	